FINDING YOUR
BIPOLAR MUSE

"Creativity and bipolar disorder have long been linked, but only recently acknowledged. In this easy-to-read new book, Lana Castle explores the challenges faced by creative artists who *also* live with bipolar disorder. As a bipolar patient herself, Ms. Castle has come to terms with the illness while sharing personal wisdom and the perspectives of others—patients and researching psychologists."

—**Nancy Rosenfeld**, coauthor of *New Hope for People with Bipolar Disorder*

"A book brimming with hope and compassion, and framed with patience, grit, and discipline. Lana Castle offers not only a handhold along the precipices and comfort through the plummets of the wilderness of the psyche's extremes, but the tools to begin to carve a path of one's own, along with generous doses of inspiration and the courageous examples of others who have found their creative balance."

—**Tim Farrington**, author of the *New York Times* Notable Book
The Monk Downstairs and *Lizzie's War*

"Lana Castle's book focuses on effectively taking control of one's life, including the impediments that may be associated with a bipolar condition, for purposes of achieving a more gratifying and financially rewarding career. Castle offers many practical techniques aimed at directing one's particular creative interests in ways that will work in the workaday world. These aspects of the book will also be of interest to many persons with creative bents who are not bipolar."

—**Charles L. Bowden, MD**, Nancy U. Karren Professor of Psychiatry, University of Texas Health Science Center, San Antonio

"A unique approach that leads to healing."

—**Andy Behrman**, author of *Electroboy*

Praise for *Bipolar Disorder Demystified*:

"*Bipolar Disorder Demystified* is a very useful book written by a woman who has been there. Lana Castle has distilled her own experience with this illness into many drams of helpful advice. This book will tell you how to successfully live with bipolar disorder and avoid the many pitfalls that are inherent in mood swings."

—**E. Fuller Torrey, MD**, coauthor of *Surviving Manic Depression*

"Lana Castle has written from experience in providing an 'owner's manual' for bipolar disorder. And what a resource—not only has she presented helpful information, including an extensive glossary and index, but she has identified a number of Web and print resources for further understanding, treating, and living with manic depression. Indispensable!"

—**Pierce J. Howard, PhD**, Director of Research, Center for Applied Cognitive Studies, Charlotte, North Carolina; author of *The Owner's Manual for the Brain*

Lana R. Castle is a writer, speaker, and mental health advocate based in Austin, Texas. She is the author of *Bipolar Disorder Demystified: Mastering the Tightrope of Manic Depression* and a member of the national speakers' bureau for the Depression and Bipolar Support Alliance. Castle has a bachelor's degree in speech and theatre from Kansas State University and a master's in instructional design from The University of Texas at Austin. Her mission is to openly and honestly communicate her thoughts, feelings, and experiences with mood disorders, creativity, and recovery to help as many people as possible. Visit her online at www.castlecommunications.com

▪ LANA R. CASTLE ▪

FINDING
YOUR
Bipolar Muse

HOW TO MASTER
DEPRESSIVE DROUGHTS AND
MANIC FLOODS AND ACCESS
YOUR CREATIVE POWER

MARLOWE & COMPANY
NEW YORK

FINDING YOUR BIPOLAR MUSE:
*How to Master Depressive Droughts and Manic Floods
and Access Your Creative Power*

Copyright © 2006 by Lana R. Castle

Published by
Marlowe & Company
An Imprint of Avalon Publishing Group, Incorporated
245 West 17th Street • 11th Floor
New York, NY 10011-5300

AVALON
publishing group incorporated

Library of Congress Cataloging-in-Publication Data

Castle, Lana R.
Finding your bipolar muse : how to master depressive droughts and manic floods and
access your creative power / Lana R. Castle.
p. cm.
Includes bibliographical references and index.
1. Manic-depressive illness—Treatment. 2. Self-care, Health. I. Title.
RC516.C37 2006
616.89'506—dc22
2006016098

ISBN-10: 1-56924-340-9
ISBN-13: 978-1-56924-340-4

9 8 7 6 5 4 3 2 1

DESIGNED BY PAULINE NEUWIRTH, NEUWIRTH & ASSOCIATES, INC.

Printed in the United States of America

Disclaimer

The information in this book is intended to help readers make informed decisions about their health and the health of their loved ones. It is not intended to be a substitute for treatment by or the advice and care of a professional health care provider. While the author and publisher have endeavored to ensure that the information presented is accurate and up-to-date, they are not responsible for adverse effects or consequences sustained by any persons using this book.

To all of those whose mood swings
challenge their creative dreams

Contents

PART ONE

Examining the Flow

▪ 1 ▪

The Creative/"Crazy" Connection

AN INTRODUCTION

As LONG AS I can remember, family, friends, and associates have praised my creativity. Over the years, they've noted my musical, artistic, and literary gifts. They've marveled at my talent for clear communication. At my expansive imagination. At my dramatic flair. But, because my depressions lowered my self-esteem, my family's support always felt superficial. I *knew* my family was just humoring me and *knew* my gifts were inferior, but I felt desperate to use them.

Toward the end of high school, my parents reinforced that insecurity. They advised me to study something "practical" in college, in case I didn't meet a man who could support me or something happened to this envisioned husband at some point. My father insisted I take typing in high school—a ploy, I thought, to prepare me for a secretarial career.

I began college majoring in interior design rather than in art or theatre, as I'd preferred. Even if I couldn't express my own creative needs, I'd at least be expressing those of other people.

But I couldn't abandon my dreams; they kept stalking me. My second semester, I switched my major to theatre, assuring my parents I'd teach it after graduating. (I never did.)

The switch—and my escalating bipolar disorder(which hadn't yet been diagnosed)—propelled my dreams even further. When hypomanic, I *knew* I'd find success but, when depressed, I *knew* it was hopeless. At times, my gifts seemed a burden, even a curse, because extreme sensitivity and frequent mood swings seemed to accompany them.

I wasn't aware until the mid-1980s that others felt a creative/"crazy" connection. When a traveling exhibit about famous people with mental illnesses came to town, I began more consciously associating creativity and mood disorders.

Since then I've contemplated this link, and I can't help but see a connection. Many of my artistic products were born out of exuberant hypomania or out of depressive episodes. Was this just a coincidence? I doubt it. It didn't fit my experience of creativity.

My questions about this connection—and how to manage it better—finally led to this book.

WEIGHING THE CREATIVE/"CRAZY" CONNECTION

IS THERE REALLY a connection between creativity and mental illness, as many people think? And, if so, why? Psychiatrists and researchers have wrestled with this controversial topic for years.

Many in our society expect creative people to be eccentric or "crazy." This holds true not only for fine artists but also for inventors, "mad" scientists, and even visionary entrepreneurs. But does it represent reality?

*A*rt will remain the most astonishing activity of mankind born out of struggle between wisdom and madness, between dream and reality in our mind.

—Fiber artist and art teacher Magdalena Abakanowicz (1930–), known for her abstract weaving *Abakans*

Nowhere is the idea of this creative/"crazy" connection so prevalent as it is in the creative arts. Many people just assume that artists, musicians, writers, and the like are "nuts." Perhaps the source of this link idea comes from what I call "the creative mystique."

THE CREATIVE MYSTIQUE

PEOPLE EXPECT CREATIVE artists to suffer. To be outcasts. To live in drafty flats in seedy neighborhoods in heartless cities. Or worse, in their cars or on the street. People expect creative artists to chain-smoke and drown their sorrows with alcohol and drugs. Many aspring artists even begin smoking, drinking, and doing drugs in the effort to live up to this mystique.

*W*riting is not a profession, but a vocation of unhappiness.

—Belgian crime novelist Georges (Joseph-Christian) Simenon
(1903–89), known for the Inspector Maigret series

Celebrities—living and dead—who've been diagnosed with a mental illness, or who've had problems with drugs and alcohol, reinforce this view. Might the perceived creative/"crazy" link be an illusion born of the challenges of creative life itself?

DOUBTS ABOUT THIS CONNECTION

IN THE BOOK *Pressure Sensitive: Popular Musicians under Stress*, British psychologist Geoffrey Wills and writer Cary Cooper describe the very real stressors that struggling musicians often face to make a living. These authors say the ways in which musicians deal with these stressors may make them seem a bit "off," but that may not indicate mental illness.

In *Touched with Fire*, psychiatry professor Kay Redfield Jamison writes, "Another argument set forth against an association between 'madness' and artistic creativity is that a bit of madness and turmoil is part and parcel of the artistic temperament, and that artists are just more sensitive to life and the experiences of life than are other people. This is almost certainly true, and it would be foolish to diagnose psychopathology where none or little exists."

Thomas Szasz claims that poverty and rejection, accompanied by mood swings, can reinforce society's false perception that an artist is mentally ill when the true problem is the situation.

Some researchers point out parallels between creative personalities and the symptoms of mental illness, suggesting that these parallels explain the perceived connection.

There's also the chance that what's "crazy" depends more on creative artists' audiences than on the creators themselves. English teacher Dea Mallin illustrates this point by relaying Freud's observations about Edgar Allan Poe. Freud asserted that the obsessions, compulsions, fantasies, and nightmares in Poe's work might not indicate a mental illness. They might instead represent his audience's buried feelings. Perhaps the pleasure readers find in Poe's work relates to the release of their *own* obsessions, compulsions, fantasies, and nightmares.

Creativity expert Mihaly Csikszentmihalyi writes, in *Creativity: Flow and the Psychology of Discovery and Invention*, "Creativity is a systemic phenomenon that involves a new and valuable idea or action that relates to interaction between the creator's subjective belief and the sociocultural context." What's considered "crazy" in one culture isn't in another. We have a long history of shunning all kinds of creative people and their works and calling them "crazy" when we're not yet ready for their ideas.

In *Creators on Creating*, Frank Barron notes that both exceptionally creative people and people with mental illness can tap their heightened sensitivity to produce vivid works of truth and beauty that profoundly touch others' lives. Although healthy creative artists sometimes "push sanity almost to the breaking point" and find their way back, Barron says those with mental illness go far beyond and sometimes can't return.

Might the link be based on choice of occupation? Wayne State University psychiatrist Leon Berman asks: "Is it simply that pathological personalities are more attracted to creative fields? Or is there something intrinsic in the creative process that predisposes to emotional illness? Is madness the risk they run . . . the price they pay for their creativity? . . .

"Yet, this is not the only way in which the artist experiences his creativity. In some it is sustaining, reparative, and even life saving. . . . While psychoanalysts have important contributions to make to this subject, it must be concluded that we know a great deal more about madness than we do about creativity."

Although we can't yet absolutely conclude that the creativity/"crazy" connection is real, some will swear it exists. Others will remain skeptical, no matter what creative people with mental illness say. I suspect that individual experiences greatly influence everybody's point of view. I encourage you to read on and draw your own conclusions.

WHO THIS BOOK IS FOR

FINDING YOUR BIPOLAR MUSE examines the creativity/"crazy" connection and addresses the challenges all creative artists face. It also suggests many options for dealing with them. This book will help:

- People with mood disorders who want to use the creative arts for their own healing and recovery
- People who have submerged their creativity because others have discouraged them from pursuing it
- People who want to express their gifts privately
- People whose creative talents may or may not yet be acknowledged
- People who want to use creativity to supplement their income
- People who intend to rely on the arts to earn their entire living
- People who want to support creative artists with their goals
- People who are simply curious about the potential connection between creativity and mental illness, or about creativity alone

Regardless of your belief about the creativity/"crazy" connection—or lack thereof—*Finding Your Bipolar Muse* will help you better access and manage your own creative flow.

HOW I WROTE THIS BOOK

IN WRITING *FINDING YOUR BIPOLAR MUSE*, I obtained information from creativity experts, psychiatrists, neurologists, psychologists, creative arts therapists, and educators. I surveyed and interviewed both successful and frustrated creative individuals who also have depression or bipolar disorder.

I obtained the personal stories throughout the book in three ways:

- Survey responses obtained through the Depression and Bipolar Support Alliance
- Survey responses from my Web site and from readers of my last book, *Bipolar Disorder Demystified*
- Interviews conducted in person or over the phone

As most of the people I heard from or spoke with have not yet disclosed their mood disorder to others, their contributions are anonymous. When people have made their mood disorders public, their names do appear. If you have a mood disorder, I think you'll understand my logic.

I'll also share stories from a few "normal" creative people whose experiences can help enhance your own potential. The majority of the stories, though, come from creative people with mood disorders. A few of these folks are famous, but most are lesser known or use their talents privately. Some of the short inspirational quotes attributed to famous people come from those with mood disorders, but frequently they don't. They're there to reinforce a point or simply to entertain you.

HOW THIS BOOK IS ORGANIZED

FINDING YOUR BIPOLAR MUSE contains three parts. Part 1 shares opinions about the creativity/"crazy" link. Some questions addressed in this part follow:

- Do you need a bit of "madness" to produce great creative works?
- Is madness the price creative people must pay for their gifts?
- Why do some people think there's a link?
- Are people with mental illness more attracted to creative fields?
- Can we measure creativity?
- Does intelligence affect creativity?
- Does brain chemistry affect creativity or vice versa?
- What part might heredity and life experience play?
- What about personality?
- What about environment and culture?

Chapter 2 shares other people's perspectives on how their mood disorder relates to their creativity. They talk about the joys and advantages their illness brings in relation to creativity. They also talk about its challenges and disadvantages.

Chapter 3 describes researchers' perspectives on the creative/"crazy" connection. It explains views on how heredity, family environment, and culture might affect a creative person's output. It discusses the potential role of IQ and personality. It also briefly describes how researchers test creativity. Finally, it tells how scientists are starting to study creativity by examining the brain.

Part 2 focuses on commitment to creativity and provides guidance and exercises that will help you build more creativity into your life. Some questions addressed in Part 2 follow:

- How do you overcome fears about using your creativity?
- If you have more than one creative interest, where do you start?
- How can you fit more creativity into an already busy or challenged life?
- How do you learn new creative skills or strengthen those you already have?
- Where do inspirations come from?
- Can you tap your creativity just enough to "quench your thirst" without experiencing "droughts" or "floods"?
- Can you be consistently productive when you're living with depression or bipolar disorder?
- How can you find the space to practice your art?
- How do you plan and manage artistic projects so they don't get out of control?
- How do you promote yourself and your art?
- How can you earn money from your art or even make a living?
- Can someone with a mood disorder start and run a creative business successfully?

Part 2 will help you access your creative flow, whether you've turned it off temporarily or haven't yet tried to use it. It offers many pointers on successfully balancing creative endeavors with a mood disorder:

Chapter 4 talks about creative dreams, as well as common blocks, where they often come from, and how to move past them.

Chapter 5 helps you determine your creative focus, establish priorities, and set achievable goals. It also explains the creative process—a process about which people often harbor misconceptions.

Chapter 6 emphasizes the importance of attending to physical needs—to manage your mood disorder while exploring creative activities.

Chapter 7 helps you evaluate and adjust your schedule to fit in more creative time. It also offers ways to keep your creative "faucet" flowing without "depressive droughts" and "manic floods."

Chapter 8 describes ways to build and expand your creative skills, and shares several options beyond conventional schooling.

Chapter 9 addresses ways to set up a space that will support your creative efforts and to organize it for better productivity.

Chapter 10 suggests flexible income options that will help you focus more on your creative dreams.

Chapter 11 explains how to budget for and manage creative projects.

Chapter 12 describes how to promote yourself and your creative work—a task that often surprises and overwhelms creative people.

Chapter 13 focuses on collaboration, work styles, and communication. You'll learn how to communicate with the people you'll need to complete your projects, as well as receive tips about working with a partner or collaborating with a group.

Finally, Chapter 14 offers tips for starting your own creative business, if you wish. Despite the myth that it's impossible to earn a living from creative endeavors—*especially* when you have a mental illness, *Finding Your Bipolar Muse* offers tips for doing just that.

The book concludes with a "Creative Life Toolkit" and helpful resources, as well as a bibliography for further reading.

SOME DEFINITIONS

Before wading in further, I'd like to clarify some terms used throughout this book.

■ Creativity, Talent, and Genius

"Creativity," "talent," and "genius" mean different things to different people. A survey of several standard references and works by noted scholars reveals the following distinctions.

Scholars associate the term creativity with marked expressiveness, inspiration, originality, inventiveness, resourcefulness, and imagination rather than imitation, along with the ability to simultaneously conceive opposites or antitheses.

Some people reserve the term creativity exclusively for outstanding achievements; others acknowledge a wide range of creative achievements that may go unrecognized. Still other people insist that creative achievements must have "positive value." For instance, in *Creativity & Madness*, Albert Rothenberg equates creativity with "the production of something that is both new and truly valuable."

Perhaps, as some researchers and I myself believe, *everyone* has creative potential. These researchers apply the term creativity to almost anything an individual or a higher power brings forth. They don't limit it to the arts or sciences (although this book focuses on the fine arts). They see creativity in many everyday aspects of life: cooking, decorating, entertaining, gardening, parenting (and sometimes, even accounting!).

"Talent" is associated with natural aptitude, artistry, giftedness, expertise, knack, skill, and capacity for achievement or success.

"Genius" is associated with exceptional intelligence or ability, brilliance, distinctiveness, mastery, virtuosity, wit, and influence. The Latin root of genius, *gignere*, relates to a guardian spirit or deity. Historian Jacques Barzun states, that in the 1750s, poet Edward Young (1683–1785) equated genius with "the power of accomplishing great things without the means generally reputed necessary to that end." A generation later, people recognized only geniuses and nongeniuses, and claimed talented nongeniuses could only follow the geniuses.

I see a problem with some of these definitions. What's inspired, imaginative, positive, valuable, brilliant, witty, expert, or successful depends on the eye of the beholder. Such judgments vary with each person, each culture, and the time period in which those judgments are made. Individual viewpoints differ incredibly and also change over time.

Although I do see creativity, talent, and genius in many areas of life, in *Finding Your Bipolar Muse*, I use these terms only as they apply to the creative arts. I also sometimes use the terms interchangeably, as I believe that all three attributes can apply to the same individual from project to project and time to time.

■ ARTISTS, CREATIVE ARTISTS, AND FINE ARTISTS

I DON'T MEAN to discount any type of creativity; however, this book focuses on the creative/fine arts: acting, art, dance, film, music, photography, writing, and so on. When I use the term *artists*, I usually mean it in the traditional sense: painters, potters, sculptors, and such, as opposed to actors, dancers, filmmakers, musicians, photographers, and writers. Other times, the context should make my meaning clear. And because the terms *creative artist* could be contrasted with *noncreative artist*, and *fine artist* with *not-so-fine artist*, I'll avoid them too.

In general, I'll use the terms *creative* and *creatives* as nouns that refer to all types of creative people discussed in this book. I'll stay away from the term *creator*, reserving that for a higher power.

Given that we're looking at connections between creativity and mental illness, I'd like to clarify a few psychiatric terms as well.

■ MADNESS, INSANITY, AND MENTAL ILLNESS

"MADNESS" DESCRIBES SEVERE mental impairment, extreme rage, unbridled lack of restraint, self-destructive behavior, and historically, demonic possession (though few people believe that now). Frank Barron says the ancient Greeks saw madness as "a gift from the gods or possession by one's daemon (genius)"—rather than a handicap.

Some equate madness with "psychosis," during which people can't interact normally with others, and may have delusions or hallucinations that they think are real. These delusions and hallucinations are more common to the thought disorder schizophrenia than to mood disorders (depression and bipolar disorder).

Kay Jamison explains that confusion about what "madness" means and people's understanding of bipolar disorder may have influenced the idea of a creative/"crazy" connection: "Any attempt to arbitrarily polarize thought, behavior, and emotion into clear-cut 'sanity' or 'insanity' . . . defies common sense and it is contrary to what we know about the infinite varieties and gradations of disease in general and psychiatric illness in particular. 'Madness,' in fact, occurs only in the extreme forms of mania and depression: most people who have manic-depressive illness never become psychotic. Those who do lose their reason—are deluded, hallucinate, or act in particularly strange and bizarre ways—are irrational for limited periods of time only, and are otherwise well able to think clearly and act rationally."

Sometimes used interchangeably with the terms madness and psychosis, "insanity" is an intermittent state of derangement, frenzy, lack of willpower, unreasonableness, and uncontrollable emotions and instincts.

The term "mental illness" is not completely accurate because our minds and our bodies are deeply intertwined. What we call mental illnesses bring physical signs people tend not to associate with the mind. Western medicine conceptually separated our bodies from our minds a couple of centuries ago and is now slowly retracting that view.

In this book, I'll keep it simple and just say mental illness involves extreme thoughts, behaviors, moods, and perceptions that alter the way you typically live. And other people find these thoughts, behaviors, moods, and perceptions unusual or strange.

Mood disorders primarily involve extreme changes of mood but also pronounced changes in the following:

- Appetite and sleep patterns
- Energy and activity levels
- Thoughts and feelings
- Self-esteem and confidence
- Concentration and decision-making abilities
- Occasionally, psychosis

The two major types of mood disorders are depression and bipolar disorder (manic depression). Depression (unipolar disorder) may bring sadness and despondency or lack of feeling and a sense of numbness. In most cases, bipolar disorder involves both depression and mania or hypomania (mild mania). Both mania and hypomania can bring delight and euphoria, or anger and irritability.

While everyone experiences sadness, numbness, delight, euphoria, anger, and irritability from time to time, when you have a mood disorder, the intensity and duration of these feelings change. They last for days or even weeks and dominate your life. And many of the symptoms listed above accompany those intense, persistent moods.

Of course, just as with creativity, talent, and genius, what's considered mental illness also varies with different interpretations, cultures, and time periods.

■ RECOVERY AND HEALING

TWO FINAL TERMS I need to clarify are "recovery" and "healing." For now, we don't know how to *cure* mental disorders, just as we don't know how to *cure* many other types of illness. But we do know ways to manage them successfully. In this sense, "recovery" and "healing" mean managing a disorder in a way that helps you function better and reclaim your life.

COMMITTING TO CREATIVE FULFILLMENT

WELL-MEANING PEOPLE often discourage us from pursuing our creative interests, just as my parents did with me. They warn that we'll never make a living from our talents. They say there's too much competition. That we'd have to know some "insider" who would help us break into our field. They insist we get day jobs and then dabble in our passions on the side. This is especially true for those of us with mental illness, even if we possess extraordinary talents. Obviously, this doesn't encourage creative fulfillment. And that troubles me.

When I finally committed to becoming a writer (after fearfully circling that dream for years), I began to experience hope. I began to heal. I began to reclaim my life. Expressing creativity played—and still plays—a huge role in my recovery. I hope to help you capture your creative dreams and to reclaim your life as well.

As mentioned before, part 1 examines the creativity/"crazy" connection. Because it shares authoritative research and other people's experience of this link, it's the more theoretical part of the book. If you're already thoroughly familiar with the connection and want to plunge directly into the heart of this book, feel free to skip over part 1 or to read it later. But please *do* read it at some point because it contains many interesting insights.

I've learned a lot from my exposure to several types of creative fields and from observing my own creative process. I've learned even more during my research for this book. I'm eager to share it all with you, and I believe you'll find the information in this book useful as well.

*H*e who has a 'why' to live, can bear almost any 'how.'
—German philosopher Friedrich Nietzsche (1844-1900)

· 2 ·

The Faucet of Creativity

EXPERIENCES OF THE CONNECTION

FOR ME, TAPPING creativity when you have a mood disorder is like trying to quench your thirst. You turn on the "faucet" for a "cup" of creativity, and sometimes magic gushes forth and threatens to overflow; other times it drips and trickles—or doesn't flow at all. Some folks can easily twist the "knob" to coax out what they want, but such control eludes others of us entirely.

All creative artists experience such "droughts" and "floods" from time to time, but many of us believe these experiences occur more frequently and more intensely for those of us with mood disorders. With depression or bipolar disorder, we may go for months without a drop and then suddenly find ourselves floundering in an uncontrollable surge.

When we're manic or hypomanic, our "sinks" overflow and we feverishly try to capture every cup. We pour inspirations and energy into way too many different "buckets," spilling most in the process. The water rises, carries us out the door, and propels us down the street. We plunge into the river, ride the rapids, barrel over the falls, and plop into the sea.

Although depressive states usually bring drips and trickles, they can also release dark, roiling streams that overflow. The difference is, we sink beneath the surface or bob around at nostril level. Then, if we're lucky, we'll float around or tread water until, thoroughly exhausted, we're washed ashore.

WHAT MOOD DISORDERS BRING TO THE CREATIVE MIX

MANIA OFTEN SPEEDS and colors speech and inspires bright, expansive, unusual thoughts. Depression tends to slow down speech, drain its color, and shift our creative focus to sadness or death. Mania can dramatically increase creative output, whereas depression most often reduces it.

Creative artists with mood disorders not only suffer unparalleled distress and misery but also experience profound joy and fulfillment.

I've met many others who have battled with the effect of their illness on their own creativity. As a long-time facilitator of support groups for DBSA Austin (an affiliate of the Depression and Bipolar Support Alliance), I know a surprisingly large number of other creatives with mood disorders. The following segments, based on survey responses and interviews with others who have depression or bipolar disorder, share some perceptions about the creative advantages and disadvantages that seem to accompany mood disorders.

DISADVANTAGES OF MOOD DISORDERS

DEPRESSION IN PARTICULAR brings a wide range of complaints that can impact creativity, as well as increase stigma, stress, and shame. In others' words:

■ LOW ENERGY AND APATHY

"The depression squelched any real thought of using any creative energies I possess. Depression exhausts me, makes me sad. . . . I live in my bed twenty-four hours a day."

"Depression has challenged my career, because as a graphic artist, I was expected to not only be creative, but quick with ideas and execution. When I was having a bad day, I had to force myself through it to get my job done."

"When I am severely depressed I have no interest in writing, and can't be bothered to play music, let alone write it. I'm no longer under emotional pressure because I don't feel anything."

■ FEAR AND PARALYSIS

"Depression often instilled irrational fear into me, which made it difficult for me to perform at times, being incredibly nervous."

"Even playing a tape, reading a finished written work, or showing a drawing is terrifying."

"When I come back to the blackness I rarely pick up my needle and threads; there are absolutely no desires in me to create anything at all. I feel completely lost when I don't want to make things or paint."

■ SHAME AND STIGMA

"I am sidelined when I fall into major depressions. They cause me to become catatonic and ashamed."

"I'm ashamed to be dysfunctional and mental illness has a stigma in Hollywood. . . . drug and alcohol abuse is acceptable. . . . everyone goes into 'rehab.' Mental illness ruins a reputation faster than you can say the words."

■ SELF-DOUBT AND LOW SELF-CONFIDENCE

"Depression can often dull my senses, thus stunting my creativity at times. I feel incompetent at just about everything, even artistic pursuits which usually give me satisfaction and a feeling of competency."

"I doubt even the positive feedback I get from most qualified sources."

"The sense of worthlessness . . . begins to affect my art, my music, my words, and I begin to think them useless and ugly. I become angry at my work, to the point where I've literally destroyed my creations."

 THIRTY-NINE-YEAR-OLD *Virginia writer, actor, dancer, artist, and photographer LW has been bipolar since her late teens. However, she's been in treatment only five years. LW says she's hypomanic or manic most of the time. "Mania definitely sets off my 'comedic' acting abilities. I become so 'hysterically funny' everyone thinks I should quit my job and become a comedian. . . . But the sad part is, when I am not manic, everyone wants to know what is wrong with me, why I am not funny anymore!"*

Her illness and her racing mind make it hard for her to sit still,

> *focus, and organize her thoughts. "I am naturally creative, always have been. Always writing, drawing, joking, moving, doodling. Did hair, nails and tattoos for years. Dance was my exercise, hours at a time. Always writing things down, only problem is it's a jumbled mess because I can't concentrate enough to organize my thoughts."*
>
> *LW says hypomania and mania take her talents "to the nth degree." As with many of us during such episodes, her work feels like her calling.*
>
> *When she starts coming down from her high, LW feels "lost and unsure, not really clear on why I decided on that particular 'calling,' and oh boy! Here comes the depressive cycle." At that point, LW says, she often discards her work.*
>
> *LW has used her talents both professionally—as a copywriter for a marketing firm—and for her own satisfaction. She expresses herself and releases her emotions through writing, dance, and photography.*

Creative artists also experience problems during mania and hypomania:

■ IMPATIENCE AND FRUSTRATION

"It causes a lot of frustration when my students aren't as passionate, excited, and downright high as I am about the art form."

"I sometimes get extremely frustrated with myself at not being able to get anything out worth putting on paper, this is because I know that I can write well, but for some reason even though there are still a thousand thoughts running in my brain, I just can't make sense enough of them to get it out."

"I have been overly frustrated when certain sculptural processes aren't instantaneously achieved in the short period of time I allow for them while manic. I have destroyed quite a few pieces in rage. I have also made these, what I thought were beautiful, photographs; however, I didn't leave them in the chemicals long enough, so they are slowly fading to black."

■ SCATTEREDNESS AND OVERCOMMITMENT

"I do ten things at once but nothing gets completed until I get 'normal.'"

"With bipolar it is challenging to finish a project without a new idea replacing the first one."

"I often start many projects with unbelievable enthusiasm, but often this enthusiasm will suddenly decrease into nothing, and then I completely give up."

■ Unreasonableness and Defiance

"I often get agitated and angry when I am in a manic state and alienate people by speaking without thinking."

"When you get irritable and angry with people—they fire you, no longer accept your writing, and become rude, crude, or indifferent."

And depression, mania, or even hypomania can bring other challenges:

■ Lack of Focus and Concentration

"When I am depressed, I can't concentrate enough to work on my creative endeavors. I find focusing on a piece of writing difficult and I have little interest in doing so."

"I don't finish the projects I start, and then I change them again."

"When I am manic, I find it hard to sit down and write because I just can't sit still."

■ Disorganization and Chaos

"[During mania], the biggest challenge was staying focused—my mind was constantly racing, having several conversations at the same time—I liken it to having seven televisions in my head, all on different channels, all going at the same time."

"Beginning mania is the point at which I think of new ideas, am among the world's greatest drama queens, the life of any party, and have boundless energy to act on every one of the million new ideas I have for making things in my world better, more attractive and more interesting, plus writing important information for posterity, to benefit all future mankind. . . . The higher I become, the more scattered I become. The more depressed I become, the more immobilized I become."

"My creativity can be fueled by mania as I am so bursting with ideas. I get so frantic, however, that I write hundreds of pages of notes on ideas for a play . . . and will never actually sit down to the disciplined task of writing it."

"In a 'mixed state' [simultaneous mania and depression], I find myself in bed for hours, unable to get up to do anything—nothing seems interesting or worthwhile. At the same time, I may be having these creative ideas streaming through my head—lyrics about what I'm experiencing, ideas for paintings, patterns for a patchwork bag. I don't even have the energy, or I don't care enough, to jot them down. The day goes by, and the precious time I'd been complaining never to have to do my artwork is gone."

Toward the end of my graduate school career in the late 1970s, I designed a simulation game for young women transitioning from high school to adult life. Its purpose was to introduce the players to the concept of continuous learning beyond formal education and to the notion that we still keep growing as adults. I wanted to help them examine any expectation that they'd be "all grown up" when they turned eighteen or twenty-one, or completed college, or obtained their first "real job," or married, or had children.

The inspiration for my game came from my own delusional expectation that, once I'd finished college and married, I'd be "all grown up" myself. I entered an ill-advised marriage the very day after my college graduation purely because I'd panicked about my future as an adult. In my defense I must say that, in the early '70s, most women my age expected to become full-time housewives and mothers, or teachers, nurses, or secretaries after finishing school. Society did not yet widely accept women in other careers. I expected to magically transform once I came of age. Of course that didn't happen.

In my game, players took on various roles to introduce them to other possibilities: pursuing nontraditional careers, lobbying for flexible schedules, remaining single, having families later, returning to school. I piloted the game in an Austin high school and presented the results at a National Association for Simulation and Gaming conference. A brief, positive review appeared in the association journal, after which

I set the project aside. I was pleased by my results but discounted the importance of my product.

Not long after, I fell into a crippling depression. Then, in the midst of it, about six months after the conference, a British woman called to say her company wanted to publish my game. Normally such news would thrill me, but due to depression, I had no positive response. My self-confidence had fallen so significantly that I thought she was delusional and would never follow through. I was certain she'd soon discover what a worthless person I was and change her mind. I didn't even write down her name. That was only one of my lost opportunities.

Many creative artists, however, believe their mood disorders bring great advantages.

ADVANTAGES OF MOOD DISORDERS

> *The* deeper that sorrow carves into your being the more joy you can contain. Is not the cup that holds your wine the very cup that was burned in the potter's oven?
>
> —Poet, painter, and novelist Kahlil Gibran (1883–1931), best known for the inspirational book *The Prophet*

In contrast to the challenges, we creative artists with depression or bipolar disorder appear to have unique perspectives, heightened intuition, and a depth of feeling other people apparently don't share. We can more easily think outside the box and capture our feelings in our work.

■ UNIQUE PERSPECTIVES

"I see beauty in things as a child or seeing it for the first time. I use a lot of analogies, in awe of small taken-for-granted things."

"It [my mood disorder] has furnished a wellspring of ideas, images, connections, and abilities. Hypersensitive awareness of light, color, sound, mood, temperature, essence. Incredible intuitive awareness and understanding. Lightning-fast reflexes and fast grasp of complex ideas. High energy level to complete projects. Deep emotional and visceral sensing. Cinemagraphic and vivid imagination. Command of language and writing. Use of 'body memories' for storing information. Ultrasensitive proprioceptive/balance abilities. Strong enthusiasm and risk-taking abilities."

■ SELF-ESTEEM AND CONFIDENCE

"My bipolar illness has allowed me to break out past any inhibitions [to have] complete power over an audience . . . [but there's] a lack of consistency, and sometimes the opposite happens in terms of crowds—[I have] fear and anxiety."

"When I was in middle school, I believe it helped me be much more creative in my acting. I felt as if I was the only one onstage. It also helped to let myself be myself, and not hide the child I was inside."

 FIFTY-YEAR-OLD *Texas writer and singer BJ believes bipolar disorder heightens her creativity. "It has helped me to look inside and see that I am an important person—despite my disorder." She writes about "the truths we all hide—in a colorful, useful way." Sometimes intense and dark, BJ's writing reveals what she feels, and that's how she relates to others.*

"When I am too depressed," she says, "the words tend to trickle out of me," but when depressed "just enough," a "torrent of ideas are released." To manage her depressive episodes, BJ sings or writes, and the "veil of depression" eventually lifts. "I do tend to push myself in that direction, as if by an unseen force. . . . Sheer will drives my creativity. Intense emotions of an event keep me moving forward to my eventual goal."

BJ uses her talents for her own satisfaction and that of the few friends with whom she shares her work. "They get immense pleasure from my writings and poems."

■ HEIGHTENED ENERGY

"When I am in a hypomanic state, I write all the time. Whether I am in school, at work, or in bed, I always am writing. I am more likely to start and finish poems during these states. Typically, I write from start to finish within a matter of minutes."

"I am a high-energy person with a rapid-fire brain, lots of ideas. . . . frontal lobe energy is high—I have friends who tell me they feel the energy in my forehead."

■ INTUITION

"I think my depression allows me to see the world with a very broad perspective and I can problem solve and analyze very well, which in turn helps me to be able to teach myself many creative things."

■ DEPTH OF FEELINGS

"I use [the arts] to release my inner thoughts, feelings, and visions. . . . If you can't share it with the world at least share it with those that you love."

 SIXTY-TWO-YEAR-OLD *Illinois musician and actor EK pours experiences from his depression into his music: "Being depressed is like being confined in a black cyst of hopelessness, which forces attention inward to self-reflection. . . . After a period of depression, I am able to use those reflections as tools to express my thoughts and feelings in an artistic manner."*

EK says his feelings overtake technique when he conducts music. "My attention is directed less to correct notes and rhythms, and more to phrasing and bringing out a visceral reaction to the text and music. The confluence of text and music becomes of greater importance to me because of the intense reflection that depression has forced upon me."

Always driven to express his feelings through art, EK focuses on music and theatre. He finds great satisfaction as his church's choir director, for which he is compensated, but he doesn't yet charge for his singing. "Until I have the time to work my voice to its full capability," he says, "I don't feel right taking money for singing."

Some people experience a shift of focus when their episodes change from mania/hypomania to depression or vice versus. The change suppresses one art and enhances another. As one creative explained it:

"For many years I endured periodic [three to four times per year] episodes of depression that lasted for about a month. Generally, during those times, my musical creativity increased significantly while my design work ground to a halt."

Even depression can bring advantages for creative productivity. Kay Jamison believes, "depressions may have an important cognitive influence on the creative process. Depression may slow the pace, put thoughts and feelings into perspective; and eliminate excess or irrelevant ideas, increasing focus and allowing structuring of new ideas."

Clearly, many of us with depression or bipolar disorder are convinced that creativity and mood disorders are linked.

*W*hen one door of happiness closes, another opens; but often we look so long at the closed door that we do not see the one which has been opened for us.

—Author and advocate for the blind, Helen Keller (1880–1968)

· 3 ·

Research on the Connection

$\mathcal{T}$HE IDEA THAT creativity and mental illness are linked goes back several centuries. Plato (427–347 bc) viewed creativity as a "divine madness . . . a gift from the gods," and Aristotle (384–22 bc) thought all poets and artists were melancholic.

Renaissance classical translator and philosopher Marsilio Ficino (1433–99) combined Aristotle and Plato's theories and introduced the idea that creative genius and manic-depression (or bipolar disorder) are linked. The 1700s brought theories that:

- Everyone has creative potential.
- Creativity does not depend on the supernatural.
- Fulfilling creative potential depends on one's environment.

The 1800s ushered in the idea that people's creativity could be inherited. Italian physician, professor, and criminologist Cesare Lombroso (1835–1909) saw genius and madness as "closely connected manifestations of an underlying degenerative neurological disorder."

The nature versus nurture debate—pitting genes against

upbringing—surfaced in the early 1900s. Then, in the 1950s, human-istic psychologists proposed that ideas and beliefs are self-fulfilling and creativity can grow over a person's lifetime. In the late twentieth century, the emphasis shifted to brain biology.

Over the years, theorists have linked creativity to attention deficit disorder, bipolar disorder, depression, personality disorders, and schizophrenia. Suffice it to say, the research that's been done on the creativity/"crazy" link could easily fill another book. This chapter therefore distills some prominent theories concerning what intelligence, personality and behaviors, genes and family environment, culture, and brain biology appear to bring to the creative/"crazy" mix.

ASSESSING CREATIVITY AND MENTAL ILLNESS

IN A 2005 article in *Psychiatric Times*, University of California-Davis psychologist Dean Keith Simonton described three general types of creativity/"crazy" research that have been done over the years: historical, psychiatric, and psychometric.

1. *Historical* (posthumous or historiometric) studies systematically analyze biographical information about eminent creatives for psychiatric symptoms. Such studies indicate that better-known creatives are more likely to display such symptoms and to experience them at a greater intensity than other people. These factors vary with different types of creatives, poets showing the most and most intense symptoms.

   The most frequently cited historical study is one conducted by John Hopkins University School of Medicine psychiatry professor Kay Redfield Jamison. Jamison studied prominent eighteenth- and nineteenth-century British and Irish artists and writers and their families, to explore the link between creativity and mood disorders. She shares her results in *Touched with Fire*.

2. *Psychiatric* studies use modern diagnostic standards to look for evidence of clinical diagnoses and therapeutic treatments for contemporary creatives. These studies also indicate that distinguished creatives display more symptoms and symptoms of greater intensity than the general public does. Psychiatric studies have relied on the psychiatrists' "bible," the *Diagnostic and Statistical Manual of*

Mental Disorders (DSM), published by the American Psychiatric Association.

3. *Psychometric* studies of contemporary creatives use standard assessment instruments to search for clinical indications of mental illness. These studies indicate elevated rates of certain psychopathological symptoms among highly creative people, but those symptoms aren't severe enough to be considered psychopathic. When moderate, these symptoms may actually enhance creative behavior.

Education professor Jonathan Plucker and psychology professor Joseph Renzulli say psychometric tests measure creativity by exploring one or more of the following:

- A person's creative products
- A person's personality and behaviors
- A person's creative process and creative potential
- Environments that foster creativity

Most studies in this chapter combine psychiatric and psychometric methods. An example is some research conducted by University of Iowa psychiatrist and neuroscientist Nancy Andreasen. Andreasen conducted a small but groundbreaking fifteen-year study through the famed Iowa Writers' Workshop. Rather than interview subjects and collect anecdotes, as other researchers had done, Andreasen used modern diagnostic criteria, creativity assessment instruments, and structured interviews.

Andreasen compared thirty workshop faculty members and their first-degree relatives (those who share one-half of your genes) to a control group of socio-demographically matched nonwriters and their first-degree relatives. She found that 80 percent of the writers and 30 percent of the control group had mood disorders.

More writers than nonwriters had creatively gifted relatives, many of whom were artists, dancers, or musicians. Andreasen therefore concluded that genes play a crucial part in creativity.

Those of us with mood disorders—especially bipolar disorder—already know how difficult it often is to obtain an accurate diagnosis. Although mood disorders bring outward signs and symptoms (shifts in sleep and appetite, energy and activity levels, and so on), much of what happens occurs within. Can we measure creativity any more successfully? Many researchers seem to think so.

CREATIVITY AND INTELLIGENCE

MODERN RESEARCHERS HAVE found that intelligence only slightly influences creativity. Frank Barron says, "After an IQ of 115 or 120, there appears to be hardly any relationship at all; other factors of personality and motivation take over." According to Barron, these factors include:

- Ability and motivation for independent, autonomous work as opposed to mindless conforming
- High energy level—particularly, high psychic energy
- Drive to comprehend contradictory or divergent facts through a single theory or perception
- Flexible thoughts and actions

In *Creators on Creating*, Barron notes that most IQ test items call for single, predetermined answers and asks how such tests can address creativity, which is open-ended. We don't know the solutions to creative problems before we start our work; surprises nearly always appear. Both intelligence and creativity involve more than previously identified answers about numbers, words, spatial relationships, and visualizations.

World expert on creative thinking, Edward de Bono, Harvard psychologist Howard Gardner, art educator Constance Wolf, and Mihaly Csikszentmihalyi agree that creativity doesn't require an extraordinarily high IQ. Instead, a high IQ may be a hindrance. According to John Dacey and Kathleen Lennon, coauthors of *Understanding Creativity*, "personality traits, brain function, intrinsic motivation, and the ability to recognize and act on opportunity are also involved."

The environment in which IQ tests are administered influences test outcome, as some very creative people may experience significant test anxiety. In *Modes of Thinking in Young Children: A Study of the Creativity-Intelligence Distinction*, psychologists Michael Wallach and Nathan Kogan assert, "When creativity tests are untimed and are administered in a relaxed, gamelike atmosphere, the usual correlation between intelligence test scores and creativity test scores disappears."

So, what types of tests measure creativity?

CREATIVITY TESTS

RESEARCHERS HAVE CREATED all types of tests to measure creativity. These tests, explains educational psychologist Gary Davis, assess "music . . . motor activities, creative writing, creative drama . . . and play; . . . curiosity, humor, risk-taking, and regression; . . . creative activities and background (family, education) characteristics." Open-ended creativity tests, he says, ask for product improvements or explore what's "round or purple."

One of the most important creative measures that researchers agree on is divergent thinking—the ability to produce several different responses to a single prompt or obscure problem. These prompts may be verbal (completing stories, describing various ways you might use an object, and so on) or visual (finding embedded figures, interpreting patterns, and so on). Certain other personality traits and behaviors appear to relate to divergent thinking as well.

PERSONALITY TRAITS AND BEHAVIOR

MANY PERSONALITY TRAITS and behaviors that creatives display overlap symptoms of mood disorders. As Kay Jamison notes, "Many . . . changes that characterize mania and hypomania are also typical of creativity: restlessness, grandiosity, irritability, intensified sensory systems, quickening of thought processes, and intense feeling." Both creative and hypomanic thinking display "fluency, rapidity, and flexibility of thought on the one hand, and the ability to combine ideas or categories of thought in order to form new and original connections on the other."

Expanding on this idea, I compiled the following table of creative traits and behaviors from the sources used to write this book.

Creative Traits and Behaviors

Absentminded	Enthusiastic	Outspoken
Adaptable	Flexible	Perceptive
Adventurous	Focused	Persistent
Alert	Humorous	Rebellious
Ambitious	Hurried	Reflective
Argumentative	Idealistic	Reserved
Assertive	Impulsive	Resilient
Attracted to novel connections	Independent	Resourceful
	Individualistic	Restless
Capable	Industrious	Risk-taker
Careless	Insightful	Sarcastic
Clever	Insomniac	Self-centered
Complicated	Intense	Self-disciplined
Confident	Introspective	Sensitive
Curious	Introverted (slightly)	Serious
Cynical	Intuitive	Sharp-witted
Demanding	Irritable	Sociable
Disorderly	Logical	Spontaneous
Dissatisfied	Moody	Tactless
Distractible	Nonconforming	Tolerant of ambiguity
Egotistical	Open to new experiences	
Emotional		Unconventional
Energetic	Optimistic	

These traits and behaviors alone don't necessarily indicate mental illness. In *The Creating Brain,* Nancy Andreasen says that the intense concentration and focus many creatives display when working on their art resembles what psychiatrists call a *dissociative* state. In such a state, a person mentally separates from his or her surroundings and appears out of touch with reality. Sometimes such a state signals psychosis. But sometimes it's actually productive.

Oxford biological psychologist and author Daniel Nettle says people with mood disorders are "unrealistically pessimistic in depression, and unrealistically optimistic in mania. The high mood of mania is too high to be productive or in any way positive, but the good mood that lies a little way below it [hypomania] is associated with great energy to work, and optimism that tasks can be completed. This is immensely valuable for the long, frustrating period of development intrinsic to any worthwhile creation."

When you have a mood disorder, you may feel like a completely different person, based on whether you're experiencing an episode, and, if so, what type. If you have unipolar depression, you may feel like one person when you're depressed and another when you're balanced. If you have bipolar disorder, you may feel like three: a depressed person, a manic/hypomanic, and a balanced person.

A study conducted by Connie Strong, research manager at Stanford University School of Medicine's Bipolar Disorders Clinic, and Stanford University psychiatry professor Terence Ketter revealed other clues. Participants in the study included forty-eight people with bipolar disorder, twenty-five with depression, thirty-two graduate students pursuing creative degrees, and forty-seven healthy, relatively uncreative people.

Strong and Ketter found that those with bipolar disorders shared traits with the highly creative students: they were more moody and neurotic; they felt anxious, resentful, alienated, victimized; and they had lower self-esteem and less ability to tolerate stress. However, they were also more open. Strong defines such openness as "a willingness to embrace new experiences, as well as being imaginative, curious and unconventional."

The creative tendencies that bipolar people display, Strong says, may come from viewing the same surroundings in two different ways: one during depression and the other during mania/hypomania. In the Stanford study, the "creativity among treated bipolar patients matched that seen in the graduate students pursuing creative degrees." The correlation was much higher than that seen in their subjects with depression, and even higher still than that seen in the participants who displayed no mental illness.

CREATIVITY AND COGNITION

MANY RESEARCHERS BELIEVE that creatives think in a distinctive way. Andreasen says, "As we understand more and more about how the brain works . . . we are observing that highly creative people are likely to have brains that think somewhat differently. . . . Within the creative individual, 'the wandering mind' is experienced as producing a steady input of ideas that may be somewhat fragmented and formless. To the outside observer, the person may seem to move rapidly from one topic to another," an indicator of bipolar disorder that psychiatrists call "flight of ideas."

But this indicator might be common to "normal" creatives as well. Harvard neurologist Alice Flaherty, author of *The Midnight Disease*, notes that creative people "fantasize more, have better memory of their dreams, are more easily hypnotized, and score higher on measures of mildly psychotic traits."

Manic, psychotic, and creatives appear to think in similar ways. "Psychotic thinking rarely turns into creative production without some abatement of the psychosis," explains clinical child psychologist Maureen Neihart, "but there is evidence that creative processes sometimes turn into psychotic ones." The work of psychologist and author (*Creativity and Psychopathology*) Robert Prentky, and of Harvard psychiatry professor Albert Rothenberg and psychologist P. E. Burkhardt, supports this finding.

Rothenberg's research discusses a type of thinking common to both people with psychosis and people who are highly creative. During what he calls *translogical thinking*, the mind combines "paradoxical or antagonistic objects into a single entity" and brings "multiple, discrete objects" together.

Studying a sample of writers, people with bipolar disorder, and people with schizophrenia, psychiatrists Pauline Powers, Chris Stavens, and Nancy Andreasen investigated "conceptual overinclusiveness" (the tendency to combine things into categories that blur conceptual boundaries). Only the first two groups in their study had similar conceptual styles, and the subjects with bipolar disorder had less control over their thought processes than the writers did.

Studies by Frank Barron and by psychologists Raymond Cattell and Harold Butcher note that strong egos and self-sufficiency help some creative people control symptoms and exploit their bizarre and unusual ideas rather than having those thoughts control them.

 MUSICIAN/SONGWRITER, ACTOR, *artist, and writer WR, age forty-one, describes the "incredibly creative connections" he sees during mania by comparing them to a tapestry. "On one side you've got these clumps of tangled thread {the chaos of everyday life}, and on the other, you've got this perfection, where everything fits together {the manic experience}."*

For months, WR recalls, he saw connections between certain numbers, words, and phrases, all of which he thought held hidden meanings. Particularly significant were the number eight and a black widow spider with "all eight legs spread out." WR says he saw the crimson hourglass on the spider's abdomen rotate to produce the symbol for infinity, which he connected to time travel. Because spiders can eat the damaged part of their web and cast it again, he explains, they could change past events and thereby change their lives. "Life is like a multilayered story. If you don't like the ending, you manipulate things until you get what you want."

WR also saw "symmetrical quadrants" with mirrored opposites, like complementary colors on a color wheel. Contrasting emotions, different races, and various geometric shapes. Synonyms, antonyms, homonyms. God and Satan. "All had new significance and different realities," he says. . . . Life was a complex puzzle, all people and animals and buildings interrelated, and I had ability to see how. . . . {It was} like a whole new viewpoint of the universe. . . . Three-dimensional multi-universes existed on so many levels, so many realities."

But others didn't share his perspective, he explains: "It's like several people working a jigsaw puzzle. Different people see different parts of the puzzle. I was seeing a larger piece than most people — though not the whole puzzle. It was too complex." But this complexity also reassured him. "I felt important," he says. "If every person is a piece of the puzzle, any piece lost would cause the whole thing to unravel."

But how much do genes and upbringing contribute to creativity, as opposed to personality and cognitive traits?

GENETIC FACTORS

CREATIVITY AND MENTAL illness both often appear throughout a single family.

Psychoanalyst Alma Bond illustrates this point with England's famous Virginia Woolf's family: "Virginia's great-grandfather, grandfather, uncle, and cousin were all prominent authors. Her mother was Julia Jackson, herself a published writer. . . . Virginia's sister, Vanessa, became a celebrated painter who married the critic, Clive Bell, while her brother, Adrian, was a distinguished psychoanalyst, writer, and editor."

However, psychotic illnesses were prevalent in Virginia's family. Her father had "a series of 'nervous collapses,' one poet cousin suffered 'floridly psychotic' bipolar disorder and committed suicide, and her uncle 'became unable to function' after his son's death." Woolf herself also committed suicide.

Kay Jamison finds similar patterns in other artistic families, including:

- Composer Robert Schumann, whose mother suffered depression, whose author/publisher father showed bipolar behaviors, and whose sister and cousin committed suicide.
- Novelist Henry James, whose writer-father "passed on his melancholic strain, as well as his vastness of spirit and energies, to at least four of his five children." Henry's youngest brother wrote and painted, had "wild mood swings," and was hospitalized several times. Their artist sister suffered "breakdowns" and obsessed about suicide.
- Painter Vincent van Gogh, whose youngest brother, Theo, had "recurrent depressions . . . delusions and hallucinations," whose sister was chronically psychotic and whose two art dealer uncles "suffered from unspecified recurrent illnesses" [one apparently having seasonal affective disorder.]

Dean Keith Simonton concludes, "Even though there is some evidence that the lifestyle of creative activity can have adverse consequences for mental health . . . it remains the case that there may be a common genetic component to both creativity and psychopathology (Ludwig, 1995)."

Stanford University researchers Diana Simeonova, Kiki Chang, Connie Strong, and Terence Ketter recently conducted a groundbreaking study that revealed a high level of creativity in the forty children of parents diagnosed with bipolar I or bipolar II, against eighteen born to healthy parents. The study compared:

- Twenty children of bipolar parents, who also had bipolar disorder
- Twenty children of bipolar parents, who had attention deficit hyperactivity disorder (ADHD), half of whom also had major depression or dysthymia (mild but chronic depression)

■ Eighteen healthy children who had no first-degree relatives
with mental illness and who had no bipolar disorder among
first- and second-degree relatives

The bipolar parents scored more than twice as high as the healthy
controls on one subscale of Barron Welsh Art Scale creativity test and
about one-third higher overall. The bipolar children scored more than
twice as high (but not quite as high as their parents) as the healthy controls on the same subscale, and the children with ADHD scored nearly
twice as high. Overall, the bipolar children scored well over one-half
higher than the controls, and the children with ADHD nearly two times
higher than the controls.

However, the study's authors point out that their findings don't
necessarily indicate the genetic transmission of creativity. The family
environment could influence the children's creativity as well. Few
results in life come from a single cause.

"It appears likely that a mix of genes and environments indeed
affects creativity," says Frank Barron. "Genetic influences are very difficult to separate from environmental ones. My personal preference is to
put aside genetic differences, if any, and to look to environments."

So let's follow Barron's lead.

FAMILY ENVIRONMENT

THE FIRST PERSON to suggest that the interaction between genetics and
the family environment in fostering genius and creativity was psy-
chologist/philosopher William James (1842–1910). In fact, he argued
that creatives' upbringing and parents' philosophies played a larger part
than their genes.

Most every child has the potential for creativity, but it seems more
likely to flourish in certain kinds of family environments. Dacey and colleagues conducted a thorough study of highly creative young people's
family environments. A few of their findings follow:

■ Parents recognized their children's creative abilities, superior
problem-solving skills, and distinctive thought patterns when
the children were very young.

■ Parents reinforced their children's creativity by supporting their interests and goals, and by providing opportunities to develop creative talents.

- The families modeled values like self-control and sensitivity, and valued traits like imagination and honesty much more than grades and health.

Parenting style and family rules also appear to play an important role in developing a child's creativity. Children of parents who discipline them only when they're endangering their own or another's safety (but don't *fail* to discipline them) tend to develop the most creative personalities. Likewise, children whose parents guide rather than direct them tend to be more creative than those whose parents impose lots of rules.

> *D*EAN KEITH SIMONTON estimates that *only 1 percent* of children with the potential for exceptional creativity get an opportunity to fulfill that potential. But that doesn't rule out fulfilling it later on!

Because creative endeavors involve significant risk taking, a family that allows children to take reasonable risks builds creative skills. Psychologist Robert Albert believes that the most decisive environmental factor in developing creativity is the family's willingness to take risks and let the children learn from experience. Such families tend to be less concerned with "conventional success, acceptability, and status."

This doesn't mean you can become creative only if you come from the "right" kind of family. In fact, creativity sometimes grows out of trauma, anger, or grief. Maureen Neihart says, "Many artists report that their motivation for engaging in their creative endeavors is to work through, release, or better understand their own destructive urges." Perhaps that explains the drive so many of us with mood disorders have to express ourselves.

 COMEDIAN RICK REYNOLDS *was challenged not only by genes and bipolar disorder but also by the trauma of childhood abuse. His family lived in poverty, and his mother was deeply depressed. "I listened many nights to my mother being beaten by men who picked her up, or stepfathers." Reynolds says his mother, apparently envious of his highs, "went crazy quite often and beat me." He believes that, if his*

kids went through even one night of what he went through, it would "just horribly scar them."

Reynolds used his creativity to cope with the pain. In high school, he was awarded best actor, sang in the band, became the class clown, and put out a humorous newspaper. But he was still often "hugely depressed."

"In the throes of my depression is when I'm most creative, which is ironic because depression brings this lethargy, when you'll just sit there and you'll go, 'there's not one thing in the world I want to do.'"

Later, Reynolds says, "I was like a Bohemian, making $8,000 a year and living in hovels. . . . Then comedy presented itself." He entered a standup comedy competition when he was twenty-nine, then moved to the Bay area.

He did standup until he was forty, and then started writing for television. When he wrote a ninety-minute Showtime special called "Only the Truth," he got nominated for an Emmy. "This brought in millions of dollars," he reports.

Now fifty-four, Reynolds is best known for his one-man shows. "I went from being a standup to doing these incredibly cathartic one-man shows. I'd actually cry on stage many nights," he admits. "They were hugely successful. I won many awards, and they spun off books and CDs and all these things."

"I think if you trace most—what I consider to be the great comics—all of them are depressed. So that just can't be a coincidence. The greats, you know, Woody Allen, Steve Martin—many, many of them talk about being depressed. . . . If you can get a laugh, that's a huge instant reinforcement."

Reynolds is now working on a new show called Happiness.

CULTURE

DIFFERENT CULTURES HAVE supported different levels of creative freedom. For instance, historian Moses Hadas (1900–66) said the ancient Greeks could be creatively prolific because they were economically secure, slaves took care of daily needs, and their civilization didn't impose cognitive and religious restraints on their creative output.

Many U.S. creatives complain about the country's dwindling support for the arts. In *Flow: The Psychology of Optimal Experience*, Mihaly

Csikszentmihalyi explains how this lack might trigger mental illness: "If to survive as an artist in a given social environment a person has to put up with insecurity, neglect, ridicule, and a lack of commonly shared expressive symbols, he or she is likely to show the psychic effects of these adverse conditions.

"What sets creative individuals apart," Csikszentmihalyi continues, "is that regardless of whether the conditions in which they find themselves are luxurious or miserable, they manage to give their surroundings a personal pattern that echoes the rhythm of their thoughts and habits of action. Within this environment of their own making, they can forget the rest of the world and concentrate on pursuing the Muse."

CREATIVITY AND LATENT INHIBITION

MANY RESEARCHERS LINK creativity with decreased latent inhibition— your brain's unconscious ability to ignore a stimulus once you've determined it's not threatening and not relevant to your needs.

"Having low latent inhibition allows you to remain in contact with the extra information constantly streaming in from the environment," says University of Toronto psychology professor Jordan Peterson. "The normal person classifies an object, and then forgets about it, even though that object is much more complex and interesting than he or she thinks. The creative person, by contrast, is always open to new possibilities."

"Creative people are more prone to be flooded with ideas and thoughts, and also less likely to censor them, because these are the stuff of which their art or science is made," adds Nancy Andreasen. Creatives with a high lifetime achievement display significantly less latent inhibition than low creative achievers do. Eminent creatives who excel in a single creative specialty, researchers say, are seven times more likely to show low latent inhibition scores.

Researchers have generally associated low latent inhibition with psychosis; however, it's also possible that low latent inhibition is an important factor in creative thinking.

Latent inhibition may be positive when combined with high intelligence and the capacity to think about many things at once, but negative otherwise. "If you are open to new information, new ideas, you better be able to intelligently and carefully edit and choose," Peterson says. "If you have fifty ideas, only two or three are likely to be good. You have to be able to discriminate or you'll get swamped."

CREATIVITY AND NEUROTRANSMITTERS

AS MENTIONED EARLIER, researchers have long associated creativity with the capacity for divergent thinking and the ability to develop alternative solutions. Neurology professors Kenneth Heilman, Stephen Nadeau, and David Q. Beversdorf say both clinical and functional-imaging studies suggest that the brain's frontal lobes influence these activities. The frontal lobes are strongly connected to regions where the brain stores concepts and knowledge.

In addition to influencing the norepinephrine system (which controls attention, impulsivity, and stress response), the frontal lobes in creative people's brains seem important to divergent thinking. Heilman, Nadeau, and Beversdorf say, "These connections might selectively inhibit and activate portions of the brain's posterior neocortex and thus be important for developing alternative solutions."

Linking knowledge with divergent thinking may therefore require increasing communication between regions of the brain that normally aren't strongly connected. Because creatives often get ideas when relaxed or disengaged and depression sometimes brings creative inspirations, altered neurotransmitters may play an important role.

In *Exuberance*, Kay Jamison describes the role of dopamine: "Dopamine, which is concentrated in the frontal lobes of the brain and in the limbic system, or 'emotional brain,' strongly influences the emotional system that motivates both exploratory and anticipatory behaviors." Because dopamine is associated with pleasurable sensations, it plays a significant role in addiction and may also make us "addicted" to creativity.

Scientists, Jamison says, also correlate dopamine with extraversion. Dopamine increases both during acute mania and with high energy and ecstatic moods. Perhaps this explains why getting overly involved in creative work sometimes makes people "crazy."

THE BRAIN AND CEREBRAL BLOOD FLOW

NEUROPSYCHOLOGISTS INGEMAR CARLSSON, Peter Wendt, and Jarl Risberg, at Sweden's Lund University, investigated the relationship between creativity and cerebral blood flow. They took measurements in the brain's anterior prefrontal, frontotemporal and superior frontal regions both during rest and during completion of three verbal tasks, including a divergent-thinking task.

Their subjects, grouped by creativity level, showed different rates of blood flow in all three regions examined. Blood flow activity in the highly creative group increased or remained unchanged, and usually decreased in the less creative group. IQ measurements for logical-inductive ability and perceptual speed were higher in the less creative group. Both groups, however, scored equally well on verbal and spatial tests.

So which most influences the creative/"crazy" connection? Intelligence? Personality and behaviors? Genes? Family environment? Culture? Brain biology? For now, no one truly knows.

I sincerely believe that *all* of these factors play a part. Attributing a single cause to *anything* in life seems shortsighted. This brings us to the biopsychosocial view.

THE BIOPSYCHOSOCIAL VIEW

"THE MYOPIC FOCUS on just one factor as the cause of anything is now taking a backseat to a more holistic view," according to Dacey and Lennon. "Instead of believing that *just* biology *or* psychology *or* social factors determine a particular ability and behavior, the biopsychosocial view acknowledges that three factors interact and influence the outcome. One can therefore only understand these factors in the context of the others."

We must remember too that not all creatives have a mental illness. Simonton says, ". . . outright psychopathology usually inhibits rather than helps creative expression. . . . a very large proportion of creators exhibit no pathological symptoms, at least not to any measurable degree. . . . It is probably more accurate to say that creativity shares certain cognitive and dispositional traits with specific symptoms, and that the degree of that commonality is contingent on the level and type of creativity that an individual displays."

*W*hen you are *insane*, you are busy being insane—all the time. . . . When I was *crazy*, that's all I was.

—Poet Sylvia Plath (1932-63)

Regardless of your own conclusion—or confusion—about the implications of this research, I suspect you sense some connection between mood disorders and creativity. I feel certain there is one. And I'm convinced you can consistently access your Muse by carefully managing your mood disorder and taking on only well-defined goals. You need not risk mania or plunge into depressive depths to call forth your Muse.

Part 2 provides concrete, practical steps to help you use your creativity more consistently, while successfully managing your mood disorder. You'll learn how to:

- Confront the fears that threaten to drown your creative dreams
- Determine your creative focus and set reasonable goals
- Find a balance between depressive "droughts" and manic "floods"
- Locate and organize your studio or workspace
- Explore options for building and expanding your creative skills
- Manage your creative projects more easily
- Promote yourself and your creative work
- Communicate and collaborate with others effectively
- Survive financially while pursuing your creative interests
- Use your gifts to generate income or even to start a creative business

Are you ready to embrace your unique, creative gifts?

*G*enius means little more than the faculty of perceiving in an unhabitual way.

— Psychologist and philosopher William James (1842-1910)

■ PART TWO ■

Taking the Plunge

· 4 ·

Clearing Creative Clogs

USING ARTISTIC TALENTS can mean anything from spending more time on a creative hobby to running a thriving business. For instance, you might decide to learn ballroom dancing or to devote more time to writing poetry. You might wish to design greeting cards to send to family and friends. You might want to take photos suitable for framing. Or, you might hope to lead workshops on animation or to start an improv group.

Perhaps your creative dreams are more aggressive. Maybe you hope to sing on *American Idol*. Or to exhibit your art all over the country. Or screen an independent film at the Sundance Film Festival or write a novel that gets nominated for the Pulitzer Prize!

You might be dreaming of getting excellent reviews, winning prestigious awards, or obtaining enough funding from a patron or foundation that you can pursue your creativity for years!

Whatever your desires, it will take hard work to achieve them. If you expect big results without investing the time, energy, and money they require, you're setting yourself up for *big* disappointments.

I'm a great believer in luck and I find the harder I work, the more I have of it.

—Irish playwright George Bernard Shaw (1885–1950),
recipient of both a Nobel Prize in Literature and an
Academy Award for Best Screenplay for *Pygmalion*

Prepare yourself for frequent frustrations, multiple rejections, and bad reviews—even if your work is stellar. You might need a moment—or considerably longer—to lick your wounds, but if you truly want to follow your dreams, you must keep moving forward. You can't let such disappointments stop you.

Succeeding in any creative endeavor is challenging enough, but it becomes much more so with a mood disorder. I know because I've been there, and still am. Being unable to move forward or to stay focused at times doesn't mean you must abandon your dreams. Just keep your eye on the prize and take whatever steps you can—whenever you can.

Where you go with your creativity is entirely up to you. In this chapter, we'll examine your creative dreams and the "clogs" that may be blocking you from pursuing them. One of these could be "being" versus "doing."

"BEING" VERSUS "DOING"

MANY PEOPLE'S CREATIVE dreams revolve around what they want to *be*: an actor, artist, dancer, filmmaker, musician, photographer, writer or any other type of creative. But becoming any of these depends more on *doing* than *being*. When you act, you *are* an actor. When you dance, you *are* a dancer. When you sing, you *are* a singer. When you write, you *are* a writer. Being an actor, dancer, singer, or writer means *taking action*. It means immersing yourself in the creative process by acting, dancing, singing, or writing.

If your focus is on *being* rather than *doing*, it's time to reexamine your dreams. For instance, when someone expresses interest in being a travel writer, that person's real interest might be to travel and have travel pieces published—but not to actually *write* them. You don't get the perks if you don't do the work! So carefully consider whether your interest lies in *doing* or only *being*.

DELIBERATING YOUR DREAMS

WHAT ARE YOUR creative dreams? A close examination of them will lay the groundwork for you to find ways to reach them.

What do you envision when thinking about your creative passions? Do you see yourself creating something with others—such as a play or a film? Or are you working on your own—say, taking photos or playing an instrument?

Are you sharing your creativity with others? Or are you using it solely to get in touch with your feelings—sketching what you see in your mind, or writing a poem or song?

Do you hope to use your talents exclusively within your family? Or publicly in your hometown, state, or region? Or all over your country or throughout the world?

Take a moment to describe your dream as clearly as you can. Answer whether you'll work alone or with others, whether you'll keep your work private or share it, and where you'll work. An example follows. The Creative Life Toolkit at the end of this book contains a blank form you can use.

SAMPLE CREATIVE DREAM

MY CREATIVE DREAM: To design & produce hooked rugs for my family

☐ WORKING ALONE? ☑ WITH OTHERS? WHO? With input from family

☐ FOR MYSELF? ☑ FOR FAMILY/FRIENDS? ☐ FOR THE PUBLIC?

WHO? My parents, sisters, aunts, & uncles

WHERE? In my home

Succeeding in any type of creative art takes a lot of work. I don't mean to discourage you from pursuing your art. Far from it. I just want to ensure that you reach for your dream with open eyes. Most of us have expectations that fall somewhere in-between instant fame and fortune, and simple self-satisfaction. And most of us also have a long list of things, real or perceived, that keep us from pursuing our creative dreams. Let's take a look at what I call the "Terrible Too's."

COMMON "TERRIBLE TOO'S"

WHAT'S STOPPED YOU from pursing your creative dreams? Grim realities or merely unchallenged fears? Be honest with yourself. To get things rolling, here are some common reasons why creatives with mood disorders, as well as without them, don't follow their hearts. We believe:

- We're too ill.
- We feel certain our medications will drain our creativity.
- We'll have too few inspirations. Or too many to choose from.
- We have too little time, too little energy, or too little money.
- We're burdened with too many responsibilities.
- We're too old or too young.
- There's no use in setting creative goals because we'll never achieve them.
- We're too unfocused or too disorganized.
- We have too little skill or too little knowledge.
- We don't have enough talent and won't be able to compete. Or perhaps be so competitive that we lose our creative friends.
- We're too shy or intimidated to perform in front of others or to promote ourselves and our work.
- We'll receive too much criticism and won't be able to take it. Or we'll be so critical of others' work that those we criticize will ostracize us.
- We know too few (or none) of the "right" people and we'll have too little support.
- We have too little space, too little equipment, too few supplies—and we'll never be able to afford more.
- Committing to our creativity is just too financially risky. We'll surely go broke and wind up on the street!

Anything here sound familar?

The following list covers most of my old Terrible Too's, many of which I've overcome. But I didn't overcome them all at once; it took quite a while. I'm still working on a couple, and I'm getting lots of ideas how to tackle them. I suspect the same will be true for you. We'll use my Terrible Too's as examples to help you work through your Terrible Too's.

SAMPLE TERRIBLE TOO'S

✔ TERRIBLE TOO	SOURCE	SUPPORTING FACTS	REJECTING FACTS
☑ Too ill			
☑ Too few ideas			
☑ Too little energy			
☑ Too many demands			
☑ Too unfocused			
☑ Too little knowledge			
☑ Too shy/intimidated			
☑ Too financially risky			

Now draw up your own list of Terrible Too's. The Creative Life Toolkit contains a blank form you can use. If the list on the form isn't complete enough, feel free to add your own Terrible Too's! If you prefer, create your own form.

If you use the form from the toolkit, place a check to the left of each Terrible Too that applies to you. Then list any other Terrible Too's you might have. Wait to fill out the other columns until you've read through the next dozen pages. Then we'll see how many we can knock out of the way.

Your Terrible Too's list need not be perfect. You can always return to it later.

■ Too Ill

Mood disorders and other illnesses don't have to suppress your creativity. There are always ways to keep your creative flow running, even if not as steadily as you wish.

The Healing Power of Self-Expression—

Self-expression can be tremendously beneficial—as well as fun—and can help alleviate some of your symptoms. Here's what one creative says about it:

"I find that pursuing creative activities can be somewhat cathartic for me, channeling my energy in a positive direction. It takes me to a 'different place,' which is beneficial when I'm especially struggling. It can be one bright spot in otherwise murky waters."

*A*rt is our one true global language. It knows no nation, it favors no race, and it acknowledges no class. It speaks to our need to reveal, heal, and transform. It transcends our ordinary lives and lets us imagine what is possible.

—Richard Kamler, artist and creator of the Seeing Peace Project

Here's another creative's perspective:

"During a hypomanic state, I'll get my painting supplies out and paint with joy and enthusiasm. I don't produce anything that I'm particularly proud of, but the process is so enjoyable and relaxing. . . . I write and paint for my own satisfaction because I gain a certain peace from these activities. . . . I am only becoming aware of the toll that depression has taken on my life. But that is a start. I am now looking at self-expression as a method to treat this illness with a playful approach."

The Healing Power of Arts Therapy—

Various types of arts therapy can also speed your recovery, and you don't have to be in the hospital to do them. Ask your therapist to recommend an arts therapist near you. If you're not comfortable doing that or want another option, call a mental health organization for a referral.

Art therapist Evelyn Virshup talks about the power of self-expression: "I saw, time and time again, that when my clients had found their images through projective techniques and then wrote or talked about the significance of the image, they reached powerful truths about themselves, long denied, or forgotten. In addition, they found self-esteem when they discovered their 'latent' creativity and received praise from their peers."

Another important type of art therapy, dance, has proven especially beneficial for those with mental illness who need to release painful feelings. Dance is also a great way to exercise and get those endorphins jumping, a clear benefit for easing depression.

Over ten years ago, a researcher named Sarah Cook, at England's University of Sheffield, discovered she could literally dance grief, sorrow, and stress out of her system. Cook recently completed a study that examined the benefit of dance. The nineteen women in her study who were experiencing "varying degrees of mental illness" all felt "positively transformed" after dance therapy. Dance, Cook says, helps those with overwhelming feelings communicate what they can't say through words or other arts.

The therapeutic effects of music are widely known. For instance, those of us with mental illness can sometimes calm or energize ourselves by listening to music or playing instruments or singing. Authors Phyllis and James Balch note that "music can reduce anxiety and lessen irritability," and that playing an instrument can improve self-confidence.

Kay Jamison says, "Music and dance . . . paralyze the ability to think logically. . . . Dance energizes and unites; it quickens, it exhilarates, it liberates. . . . Music has an infectious, and on occasion, transformative effect." Jamison explains that "brain imaging studies conducted while a person is listening to music show . . . increases in cerebral blood flow in the same reward areas of the brain that are active when food, sex, or highly addictive drugs are involved." Music also "decreases activity in brain structures associated with negative emotions," Jamison adds.

Here's what another creative says about the value she's gained from expressing herself:

"Artistic therapy, especially if done with some freedom to choose your form of expression, be it music, dance, writing, collage, or art, has been very helpful. Even if I do not feel very creative and can't come up with much on my own, using my creative talents therapeutically has been very helpful."

These opinions provide a good argument for dealing with people who don't understand your creative dreams or say you're "too sick" to pursue them. And they provide a good argument to convince yourself, too!

▪ TOO MEDICATED

The biggest concern of creatives with mood disorders is the fear that psychotropic medications will dry up their creative inspirations. That they'll never be able to enjoy their art again. Medication sometimes does make it challenging, but not always. The problem may rest more in the belief that it will and in the belief that creativity depends entirely on magical inspiration. It doesn't.

This fear may be partially based on misconceptions about how the creative process truly works. Chapter 5 will help you better understand it.

Waiting for an illusive Muse to inspire you will needlessly suppress your unique gifts. Instead, lure that Muse in by starting without it. Usually, creating in spite of its absence makes it jealous enough to show up!

■ TOO FEW OR TOO MANY IDEAS AND INSPIRATIONS

The word *inspire* comes from the Latin *inspirare*—to breath in or draw in—and, according to the *American Heritage Dictionary,* involves "divine guidance or influence exerted directly on the mind and soul of humankind." The idea that the gods channeled creative inspirations through personified Muses came from Greco-Roman mythology, which mentions nine.

Calliope (also spelled Kalliope), the chief Muse, brought ideas for epic or heroic poetry. Erato channeled love and lyric poetry; Euterpe, music and flutes; Melpomene, tragedy; Polymnia (or Polyhymnia), sacred poetry and hymns; Terpsichore, dance and choral song; Thalia, comedy. The other two muses were Clio, who channeled history, and Urania, who channeled astronomy.

One of the earliest creatives to attribute his gifts to the Muses was the Greek epic poet Hesiod (about 700 bc), who claimed the Muses appeared before him, gave him a poet's voice and staff, and told him to "sing of the race of the blessed gods immortal." Since that time, creatives desiring inspiration have tried to invoke a Muse to assist them, and some still do.

Many creatives fear their Muse will abandon them, and that's especially true for creatives with mood disorders. As stated before, that's a major reason why some are concerned about taking medication.

> *I*nspiration only knocks. Some writers expect it to break down the door and pull them out of bed.
>
> —Composer, pianist, and conductor Leonard S. Bernstein
> (1918–90)

Do you fear you'll lose the inspirations that strike like lightning when you're manic or hypomanic? Or the depth of feeling depression sometimes brings? That's not how the creative process really works—at least if you tap it regularly. Once you understand the process, you'll be able to access your creative flow nearly anytime you want—even when you feel uninspired.

When my first one-act play, *The Guest*, was produced in college, I couldn't have been more thrilled. It was magic to see my words come alive onstage so perfectly. Even the pauses were perfect. *The Guest* even got nominated for an award! For awhile, I was on Cloud 9.

But my inspiration for the play had come a few years earlier, and afterward, no earth-shattering inspirations came. I kept waiting for my muse, and my fear stopped me cold. I turned my back on my passion—all because of an unsubstantiated Terrible Too! Don't let the same happen to you. You need not wait for inspirations when you truly commit to your art.

We'll reutrn to the inspiration issue down the line. Chapter 6 discusses the medication controversy. Chapter 8 suggests ways to develop your innate talents. Chapter 5 discusses the creative process. And chapter 7 suggests a few "creative workouts" to keep those inspirations flowing.

■ TOO LITTLE TIME OR ENERGY OR MONEY

We all have twenty-four hours a day, even though it often feels as if we don't. Those of us with mood disorders *do* have a few more demands on our time than others (doctor appointments and therapy, dealing with medications and lab tests, possibly attending outpatient programs or support groups). But even these don't consume all of our time.

Not having as much energy or money as we want or need may bring greater challenges, but not insurmountable ones.

Certainly, when you're depressed, your energy level will be down, but you can nonetheless take small steps toward your goals. Spending time on your creative dreams does take energy, but it usually generates much more. Using your creativity will boost your self-esteem and help you keep from feeling so drained.

Financial challenges are often prevalent when you have a mood disorder. You may be unable to work, as I've been at times. You may owe lots of money, as I have and still do. You may see few opportunities to produce some (or more) income. I've been working on my writing career over twenty years, and I'm *finally* finding more ways to bring in money through my personal writing interests.

Chapters 6 and 7 take a closer look at time commitments and suggest ways to boost your energy. Chapter 10 suggests ways to stay afloat financially.

■ Too Many Responsibilities

What about when you have a full-time job, a family, and community commitments? What if you're deeply involved with your friends? (And friendships aren't that easy when you have a mood disorder.) Is it possible to juggle even more responsibilities brought on by actively pursuing creative dreams? With a shift of perspective, it often is!

Chapters 5 through 8, 10, 11, 13, and 14 offer ideas to help you adjust responsibilities so you can clear room for more creative time.

■ Too Old

Do you think you're too old to explore and enjoy your creativity because you've completed your formal education or you have children (or grandchildren). Do your creative dreams seem "immature"?

University of Kentucky psychiatrist and professor Arnold Ludwig conducted a ten-year investigation with 1,004 creative people and examined their lifetime achievements. Although his study also included athletes, explorers, military officers, scientists, social figures, and businesspeople, a large number of his subjects were creative artists. There were:

2 lyricists	21 nonfiction writers
5 conductors	23 playwrights
5 sculptors	26 journalists
6 cartoonists/caricaturists	27 singers
6 choreographers	27 other kinds of writers
7 designers	38 composers
8 dancers	53 poets
11 theatre/film directors	54 painters/illustrators
11 photographers	57 actors
12 other kinds of performers	130 fiction writers

Ludwig states that "members of the various creative arts professions, as a whole, display greater creative achievement *over the entirety of their lives* than members of most other professions."

Here's a story to consider if you think you're "too old" to pursue your creative dreams:

Artist Elizabeth Layton's (1909–93) first depression came after her first child was born, and it didn't go away. Many years later, when Layton lost a son to liver disease, "her grief was all-consuming and prolonged," relays UCLA psychiatrist and professor Sara Epstein.

At her sister's suggestion, Layton—then sixty-eight—began taking a contour drawing class. In contour drawing, the artist draws while looking at the subject rather than the paper. This technique helps artists better tap their feelings because they're not judging their work in progress.

According to Epstein, drawing made it possible for Layton to deal with her grief and experience an "explosive catharsis." The year after starting classes, Layton "worked feverishly, obsessively, as long as ten hours a day," Epstein says. Within nine months, her depression lifted and never returned. Layton's art provided a creative purpose that she enjoyed until she died at age eighty-four. Are you truly too old to pursue your creative dreams?

■ Too Young

Or do you believe you're too young and that you'll have to wait until you're older—that you must know "everything" about your field? Consider this: As a young person, you actually have a great advantage. Talented and skilled children, teens, and young adults tend to attract a lot of attention. With strong support from a family member or mentor, you need not wait until you're older or completely on your own.

One impressive example of young creatives is the more than 400,000 students in thirty-four countries (as of the late 1990s) who have learned to play

*G*ERMAN CLASSICAL COMPOSER and conductor Felix Mendelssohn (1809–47) began his musical career at the ripe old age of *nine*. At seventeen, he composed his overture to *A Midsummer Night's Dream,* the source of what we call the Wedding March. Although Mendelssohn battled with pronounced mood swings, he enjoyed a successful career, composing and conducting in England and throughout Europe. Among his many compositions are the Symphony No. 1 in C Minor, and Symphony No. 3 in A Minor (the "Scottish Symphony").

stringed instruments through the Suzuki method. Shinichi Suzuki (1898–1998) was a Japanese violinist and teacher who, after World War II, developed a method to teach violin to young children. Instead of teaching them to read music, he encouraged them to listen, imitate, and repeat songs. More than eight thousand teachers have successfully used the Suzuki method to teach children as young as *two years old* how to play the violin, viola, cello, or piano.

When it comes to using creativity, age is not an issue!

■ TOO UNACHIEVABLE

The fear that creative goals are unachievable often comes from the low self-esteem depression brings. When others say your goals are unreasonable, you *might* possibly be hypomanic/manic. In either case, better understanding what creative success involves will help.

> *Y*ou gain strength, courage and confidence by every experience in which you really stop to look fear in the face. You are able to say to yourself, 'I have lived through this horror. I can take the next thing that comes along.'
>
> —Author, speaker, and former First Lady
> Eleanor Roosevelt (1884-1962)

By committing to your dreams and working through this book, you'll vastly improve your self-esteem and overcome many other fears. Chapter 5 explains the creative process, and chapter 7 helps you build a schedule that makes time to work on your creative dreams.

■ TOO UNFOCUSED, TOO MANY GOALS

It's quite common for those of us with mood disorders to have multiple creative interests. When you do, how do you decide what to explore first? Do you have to limit yourself to just one? (Despite what you think now, if you're manic or hypomanic, you can't pursue them all simultaneously. That approach backfires pretty fast.) It's usually best—and easier and more effective—to examine your interests and set goals and priorities.

Chapter 5 talks about setting goals and prioritizing them to improve your chances of success.

■ TOO UNSKILLED OR UNKNOWLEDGEABLE

In grad school and in the working world, I discovered that learning is a lifelong process. I could reinvent myself many times. This came as a wonderful surprise. You don't have to resign yourself to a role or job that you assumed when you first became "all grown up."

Do you feel capable of learning more? Or do you think you know more than enough already? How many times have you come out of a depression or a manic (or hypomanic) episode to learn that something you were *convinced* of during that episode simply wasn't true?

While in a depressive state, you probably think you're incompetent and have no skills at all. That you can't even dress yourself properly, let alone learn how to don a costume and appear onstage. That you can't draw a stick figure, play an instrument, shoot a decent snapshot, or write a simple poem.

While in a manic or hypomanic state, you may have thought that no one on the planet had better skills and knowledge than you did. That you were the best at *all* types of art. You have to accept that that's not true.

It will take a while to learn a new skill or to improve one you already have, but I'm sure you can. You may have more to learn than you'd ever imagined, but you can soak up that knowledge if you try. However skillful you are at something, you can always refine your skills and become even better. You could very well become an expert!

If you're concerned about having too little skill to achieve your creative dreams, remember that no one is born with perfect skills or complete knowledge. Even the most talented among us had to learn their art somewhere. And sometimes it doesn't take all that much skill or knowledge to make significant progress toward a goal.

We develop skills through experience—by taking classes, talking with people in the field, reading about our art, watching videos about it, dabbling in it ourselves. You don't have to start big. In fact, skills are often much more solid if you move slowly and absorb things at your own pace.

Chapter 8 suggests ways to develop your creative skills and to expand your knowledge.

■ Too Little Talent or Too Much Competition

Most of us think we have much less talent than we actually have when we're depressed, and much, much more when manic/hypomanic. Those of us with mood disorders are even more challenged than other creatives to see our talents as others see them.

But how much do other people's opinions really matter? As Nancy Andreasen says in *The Creating Brain*, "Must we require that a creative person, and creative work, win external confirmation by publishers, critics, and other arbiters in order to judge the presence of genuine creativity?"

Success doesn't have to mean making it big. Your creative pursuits can be completely personal, meant for your eyes alone. Or, if you wish, you can share your achievements with friends and family. There's no rule that says you have to go public. Sometimes it's better, even more satisfying, if you don't.

There is only one success—to be able to live your life your own way.

—Writer and editor Christopher Morley (1890–1957), author of the novel *Kitty Foyle*

I believe that pursuing your creative interests will play an enormous role in your recovery. It certainly has for me, whatever results I achieved. I suggest that you carefully determine what success means for *you*.

TWENTY-FIVE-YEAR-OLD *musician, writer, dancer, actor, artist, and photographer NB of Georgia says she creates only for herself, that her works are too personal to share with the public: "I think they're . . . sometimes too stark. I've written music to lament an entire summer wasted in emotional turmoil that I couldn't give a proper name to, taken nights where my thoughts were so black that the ink dripped through my fingers and onto the paper in painful gashes of words, sung my undefined elation to an uncaring sky for the sheer wonder of feeling the notes resonate in my body, but always, 'always' for me."*

NB seeks outlets to release what seem almost unbearable emotions, she explains. "I feel that this has enriched my artistic expression, making it more poignant and perhaps somehow more real."

"My drive to create is caused by a need to express. It's my way of taking the abstract thing inside of me that I can't control or completely explain, and making it concrete. The blocks I don't have a clear understanding of yet."

NB *advises others to use their creativity when they can. "When you can't . . . find someone you trust to talk to. Having a mood disorder can be a blessing, but it can also be a curse. Keep someone close, even when you feel most like shutting the world out; a confidante can sometimes help you through the darkest parts."*

Even a low level of talent doesn't have to stop you from enjoying your creativity. You can immerse yourself in all sorts of creative hobbies, regardless of how talented you are. Such activities can relieve stress, too.

Creative fields will always be competitive. Some people will always think that someone else's work is better than yours or mine, but they'll always think that someone else's work is worse as well. Notice that I said "someone else's work," not "someone." Remember, as much as you may identify with your creative work, you are not your work. There's much more to you than that!

Chapter 8 addresses ways to expand your talents and chapter 13 talks about using them collaboratively.

■ TOO SHY OR TOO INTIMIDATED

People often become shy when they stretch their comfort zone, but it's necessary to do so. Creative artists must learn to promote their work and to overcome their intimidation. Here's what one creative has to say:

"Depression often instilled irrational fear into me, which made it difficult for me to perform at times, being incredibly nervous."

These feelings are often a product of poor self-esteem. If you work diligently at your art, though, you can overcome them. It takes a lot of time and conscious effort, but you can do it. Chapters 8 and 10 through 14 offer tips that will help.

■ TOO AFRAID OF CRITICISM OR TOO CRITICAL

Criticism is something you simply have to adjust to. And you will as you gain more experience. Even the greatest creatives get criticized and rejected. After all, no one can please everyone (despite what we think when manic or hypomanic). We all have different tastes, and that's truly a blessing.

*E*MILY DICKINSON (1830–86), born in Amherst, Massachusetts, was a prolific poet, now lauded by critics for her ability to capture emotional extremes. She wrote the bulk of her work between ages twenty-eight and thirty-five, producing considerably more in spring and summer than in fall and winter.

During one highly productive four-year period, she began experimenting with language stripped of superfluous words and by placing familiar words in unusual contexts. But the world was not yet ready for her style.

Dickinson had corresponded with two editors at a Springfield, Massachusetts, newspaper, but they gave her little encouragement. She became quite discouraged but still continued to write. Eventually, the paper published five of the seven poems published during Dickinson's lifetime—most likely due to the interest of one editor's wife. But the bulk of her writing went unpublished.

By 1870 she began dressing only in white and became extremely reclusive. The deaths of her father, her eight-year-old nephew, and some friends in the 1880s caused her great grief. Dickinson and her siblings remained close throughout her life.

After Dickinson's death, her sister led the effort to publish her poems. Altogether, 1,175 of Dickinson's poems and nearly as many letters survive.

Criticism and rejection hurt, but they're not fatal. Provided the criticism is constructive and you don't take the rejection personally, they actually help. If you actively perform or produce creative works, you will get criticized or rejected from time to time. Expect it. Then expect yourself to look past it and refocus on your goal. View criticism and rejection as opportunities to learn and improve your work.

Chapter 8 offers more ideas for handling criticism and rejection.

■ TOO FEW (OR NO) CONTACTS, TOO LITTLE (OR NO) SUPPORT

Many people say success is all in who you know—particularly in the arts. That you can't get your foot in the door without knowing someone "important." But it takes much more than social contacts to get ahead. Remember: *You're also important,* and the people you *do* know are as well! But it's possible to move forward without having all of the support you want.

 TEXAS ACTOR KK, *age forty-two, initially thought he'd be an athlete. His father was a coach and encouraged him to play sports. KK says he became obsessed with sports. "I hoped I'd get good enough to be recruited. That I'd get on television."*

However, KK's talents didn't lie in sports. Plus, other players picked on him because of his disorder. Because of his obsession and his lack of success, KK believes, sports contributed to his big breakdown. He finally realized that sports weren't a good option for him.

So KK turned from sports to theatre. "I didn't feel very successful in other things, but with acting it all came together."

KK says he learned a lesson from his sports experience: "I did not allow myself to enjoy the journey. I was always worried about getting to the top." When he began acting, he says, he quit worrying about fame. He's now "enjoying the journey and having fun." Theatre has and still is helping him significantly in his recovery.

Chapters 6 through 8, 10, 13, and 14 share ideas to help you obtain support and to meet and interact with others who can help you move ahead with your creative goals.

■ TOO LITTLE (OR NO) SPACE, EQUIPMENT, OR SUPPLIES

Not having the space, equipment, or supplies they need for their art stops many people. After all, who can be a pianist without a piano or a photographer without a camera, lights, and a darkroom or photo printer, right? But even that doesn't have to stop you!

Chapter 9 provides ideas for acquiring and setting up whatever you need.

■ TOO FINANCIALLY RISKY

You have to work for a living, rely on others' generosity, or collect disability, right? How else will you have a roof over your head, put food on the table, or pay for the medical care you need? There never seems to be enough money, and you're probably already overloaded with bills. What do you do? How do you survive when you focus on your art?

Chapters 6 through 8, 10 through 12, and 14 offer ideas to help you meet basic needs and pay for your creative efforts.

■ "SUCCESS" AND "FAILURE"

In general, all that Terrible Too's are is fears. And fears are just, well, fears! They're scary, but they don't necessarily represent reality. Fears don't *prove* you can't reach your goals. In fact, they don't prove anything. How many times have you worried about something that never occurred?

Underlying most fears is the fear of failure—or even success, when you think you can't deal with that. If you "fail," it's not the end of the world. Really. Think of it merely as disappointment or as an opportunity for growth.

Get up, consider what you might do differently, and then try again. I know that's not easy, but it is doable.

> *D*on't think of it as failure. Think of it as time-released success.
>
> —Comedy writer and musician Robert Orben (1927–)

What constitutes failure or success is up to you. We all must find our own path. Consider what success means for you, then go for it.

It's very important to confront your Terrible Too's, and if necessary to do so multiple times. So let's see what you might do about them.

TACKLING YOUR TERRIBLE TOO'S

PULL OUT YOUR list of Terrible Too's so we can examine them more closely. If you haven't made a list yet, take time to do so now. Remember, the Creative Life Toolkit contains a blank form.

Let's explore where all those Terrible Too's came from. A negative message you absorbed from others? A negative family member, friend, or teacher? An unquestioned assumption? Here are some of my sources.

SAMPLE TERRIBLE TOO'S SOURCES

✔ TERRIBLE TOO	SOURCE	SUPPORTING FACTS	REJECTING FACTS
☑ Too ill	Reality, sometimes		
☑ Too few ideas	Naïve about process		
☑ Too little energy	Overcommitted		
☑ Too many demands	Parents & sisters		
☑ Too unfocused	Indecision		
☑ Too little knowledge	Insecurity		
☑ Too shy/intimidated	Poor self-esteem		
☑ Too financially risky	Fear of failure		

Now consider if you *must* accept others' opinions? Are they any more valid than your own? Do you *have* to accept these messages and abandon your creative dreams? I doubt it. No matter how well meaning people were, their messages probably limited your belief in yourself or discouraged you from reaching your potential. That's often all such messages amount to.

If the negative message came from *you* or from an *unquestioned assumption*, it may be more difficult to ignore. You'll need to turn your thinking around. This takes more time if you've been feeding yourself such messages for years.

Now examine what facts support those fears and write the facts in the next column. What do you absolutely know to be true about those fears? What evidence can you provide? Facts aren't the same as beliefs or assumptions. They don't hold emotional weight. Facts are just facts, and nothing more.

Next, write some ways to reject your fears. What facts can you provide to help you overcome them? When you're done, consider which column seems more realistic: the column that supports that fear or the column that rejects it? Here are some of my supporting and rejecting facts.

SAMPLE TERRIBLE TOO'S SUPPORTING & REJECTING FACTS

✔ TERRIBLE TOO	SOURCE	SUPPORTING FACTS	REJECTING FACTS
☑ Too ill	Reality, sometimes	Often feel drained	Could energize me
☑ Too few ideas	Naïve about process	Had work rejected	Haven't tried since
☑ Too little energy	Overcommitted	Volunteer too much	Could try saying no
☑ Too many demands	Parents & sisters	Have a job & kids	Could ask for help
☑ Too unfocused	Indecision	Want to do too much	Could do some later
☑ Too little knowledge	Insecurity	Don't know how to start	Could learn how
☑ Too shy/intimidated	Poor self-esteem	Afraid of everyone	Not afraid of some
☑ Too financially risky	Fear of failure	Could lose money	Could budget better

If the "supporting" column seems much more realistic, try running it by someone you trust. This could be a family member or a friend, your psychiatrist or therapist, people in a support group, others who share your creative interests, a teacher, a person in your religious community, or nearly anybody else you think might help. What do they think? If they share your concerns and think you'll never overcome them, you've got at least three options:

1. Accept their opinions and abandon your creative dreams.
2. Slowly work on changing those fears and facts you think you can change.
3. Reject those opinions and do all you can to prove them wrong.

Choose whatever feels right in your heart, but know that choosing the first option means you'll be abandoning your dream. I hope you'll chose the second or third and will commit to working toward realizing your creative goals.

I expect the results of this exercise will surprise you and help you move on. If not, try this variation.

LOSING YOUR "BUTS"

THERE'S A LOT of power in a single word, particularly the word "But." "Buts" negate positive thoughts and possibilities and keep us from moving forward. They barge their way into our brains and cause disastrous results.

I once shared the news that I landed a new project with my therapist, who replied, "That's wonderful! I knew someone would love your idea!" Then I began explaining why the news wasn't all that great, starting all my reasons with "But." She interrupted to say, "Lana, listen to yourself. Are you aware that you use 'Buts' to negate every positive thing that happens in your life?" Whoa!

Do you, too, negate the positives in your life by allowing "Buts" to butt in? Perhaps that's why you're not doing more with your talents. Let's shove those "Buts" out of your way!

Start by listing creative things you'd like to do. The Creative Life Toolkit contains a form like the following for your use. List the things you'd like to do in the first column of the form and your "Buts" in the next. Do your "Buts" truly represent reality? Challenge them if they don't.

SAMPLE LOSING BUTS

I'D LIKE TO . . .	BUT . . .
Learn how to use a potter's wheel.	It probably takes too much skill.
Join the church choir.	I can't carry a tune.

So what if you're not skilled at pottery or if you don't believe you have a great singing voice? You can still *learn* to throw pots or sing. It takes time to pick up any new skill. Keep trying, and you'll improve.

I have this policy about trying new things: Even if I'm uncomfortable—as we all tend to be when approaching something new—I'll try something three times before deciding whether to move on. In this case, I'd go to at least three pottery classes or three singing lessons or three choir practices before deciding whether to continue.

New experiences take *everyone* out of their comfort zones—not just people with mood disorders. Expanding your comfort zone is necessary if you're to grow. And you must grow to use creative skills. And, in turn, you *will* grow by tapping your creativity. Expanding your comfort zone will improve your self-esteem and bring you much more satisfaction. Believe me, you can do it!

*M*an often becomes what he believes himself to be. If I keep on saying to myself that I cannot do a certain thing, it is possible that I may end by really becoming incapable of doing it. On the contrary, if I have the belief that I can do it, I shall surely acquire the capacity to do it even if I may not have it at the beginning.

—Indian spiritual and political leader and humanitarian
Mahatma Gandhi (1869–1948)

· 5 ·

Choosing Your Focus
and Setting Your Goals

BEHIND ALL CREATIVE endeavors is some form of expectation, often fame and fortune, sometimes simple satisfaction. Let's look at the fame thing first.

You know how it works: You hold your first exhibit, the critics come, and they proclaim you the next Picasso! Or you screen your first independent film at Sundance, and then Paramount, TriStar Entertainment, and Universal Studios all beg you to accept a megadollar deal! Or you send your first novel to a major publisher unsolicited, and it's not only enthusiastically accepted but nominated for the Pulitzer Prize! That's how it works, right?

I'm afraid if your expectations are similar to these, you're setting yourself up for disappointment. I won't rule out those possibilities, but I suggest you don't invest all your hope in them.

Do you know some "important" person who will help you break into the business? Have you met lots of gallery owners? Are you sure about what an art opening involves?

Have you been to the Sundance Film Festival and know what it takes to enter a film? Do you know where to get the cash you need to make that independent film?

Do you have plenty of writing experience? Do you know which publishers will even consider unsolicited manuscripts?

If your answer to any of these questions is yes, that's great. Go for it! You have a pretty fair chance of fulfilling your expectations.

If your answer is no, as it is with most of us, you may be expecting a bit too much. You'll have to expend more time and effort. You may need to:

- Find a mentor who can teach you about the business
- Talk with several gallery owners before one agrees to show your work
- Study the film industry in depth and find out the requirements to get that film into Sundance
- Learn that *unsolicited* means *unrequested* or *not submitted by a literary agent*, and that most publishers refuse unsolicited manuscripts because they're already inundated with other work

This chapter helps you examine your creative expectations, set goals and priorities, and find your focus. Then it helps you solidify your commitment to your art—whether you're seeking public recognition or wanting to express yourself privately.

Let's start by examining your expectations.

CREATIVE EXPECTATIONS

IT'S USEFUL TO examine what motivates you before committing to your art. What draws you to it? What do you hope to gain? What images come to mind when you think about your talents? What do you see yourself doing?

Maybe you like challenges and crave recognition. Maybe you want family, friends, and strangers to acknowledge your gifts. Maybe exploring your creativity helps you manage your illness. Maybe you're driven to express yourself, and your talent brings unparalleled joy. Maybe creativity is your greatest treasure. Maybe you expect to earn a bit of pocket change—or a lot of money. Maybe you believe that using your gift is what you're meant to do. That your creative focus is what you're meant to be. So take a moment to consider your expectations before you take the plunge.

Your motivations can relate to any area of life. You could:

- Dance to keep in shape
- Try your hand at watercolor
- Perform at a fund-raiser
- Act in plays to meet people
- Journal to examine your life and grow
- Sing to worship
- Do crafts for relaxation
- Film a documentary to bring a social problem to light
- Indulge in any creative outlet that helps you express or release your feelings in a constructive way

Perhaps you're thinking that if you learn woodcarving you can make toys for your children or grandchildren. Or you may want to clean your old flute and brush up enough to join the community orchestra. Or you may want to learn to operate your camera better so you can make dramatic photos to hang on your walls.

Or your expectations may be just as aggressive as those mentioned earlier in this chapter. In any case, considering both expectations and what you need to invest to fulfill them is very helpful.

CREATIVE INVESTMENTS

ALL CREATIVE ACTIVITIES require some amount of time, energy, and usually money. Just how much depends primarily on your motivations and expectations. Depression makes us think that such activities take way too much time, energy, and money. Such thoughts paralyze us, so we don't even start. Mania and hypomania make us think we can accomplish creative tasks in record time, with plenty of energy and money to spare. That's rarely realistic.

The following chart can help you address these motivations and expectations and determine how much time, energy, and money you wish to commit to your art. In a grid like the following, list five of your creative interests. The Creative Life Toolkit contains a blank form you can use. What motivates each interest, and how much you might need to invest to proceed? A key appears at the top of the chart.

Whether you have one or more than one creative interest, list it (or them) in the first column. Use the columns under "Expectations" to prioritize what you expect to get from that art. Use a 1 to indicate what motivates you most and a 3 for what motivates you least.

In the columns under "Investments" prioritize what you believe it will take to meet your expectations. Use a 1 for the highest investment and a 3 for the lowest.

In this example, I'd expect more satisfaction than money or fame to come from doing stained glass. And I'd expect to invest more time than energy and money in it.

SAMPLE EXPECTATIONS & INVESTMENTS

⭐ = Fame   ❤ = Satisfaction $ = Money   🕐 = Time   📈 = Energy

Creative Interest(s)	Expectations			Investments		
	⭐	❤	$	🕐	📈	$
Stained glass	3	1	2	1	2	3
Salsa dancing	2	1	3	2	1	3
Jewelry making	3	2	1	1	3	2
Theatre	2	1	3	1	2	3
Performing in coffee house	2	1	3	1	2	3

In writing my book *Bipolar Disorder Demystified: Mastering the Tightrope of Manic Depression*, I wanted to honor my sister's life, to help others understand why people sometimes have suicidal feelings, and to reduce the stigma of bipolar disorder. My underlying motivation was to create something positive out of my grief over losing her.

I expected that writing the book would help heal me and would potentially supplement my income. I didn't expect wide-reaching fame. As it turned out, the project greatly increased my knowledge about mood disorders and strengthened my sense of purpose.

I knew that writing *Bipolar Disorder Demystified* would push me well beyond my comfort zone because, until I decided to write it, I hadn't told people about my illness. I could have written a novel, but I was determined to write the truth and not dilute it. A novel clearly wouldn't do.

From previous experience, I knew the book would take lots of time and energy. And I knew I'd need to invest some money to promote it through printed materials for book signings, mailings, and Web site fees.

If you have trouble deciding on and prioritizing expectations and investments, you're not alone. These challenges often go hand-in-hand with a mood disorder. The next section will provide some ideas to help you make decisions and prioritize more easily.

MAKING DECISIONS AND SETTING PRIORITIES

WHEN YOU'RE DEPRESSED it takes a major effort to make any decision, then you're likely to doubt it once you do. When you're manic or hypomanic, creative inspirations flow into your brain rapidly. As much as you want to capture each and every one, it isn't possible. In hypomanic states, I've often longed to get back into stained glass, take salsa lessons, learn to make jewelry, return to the theatre, and play my guitar and sing in a coffee house. Immediately! Trying to do everything at once only fuels the depression that invariably follows.

 TEXAS ARTIST, MUSICIAN, *photographer, actor, and dancer RK, age twenty-three, started experiencing bipolar symptoms when she was sixteen. She says her illness brings passion to her art. "Often, when I am in a manic state, I have much more energy than seems to be humanly possible, and I am able to create much, much more than I would if I were in a 'normal' mood." Her senses, RK says, are heightened as well. "I feel more sensitive to everything. Colors are brighter, I can pick out more subtleties in sounds. My mind is like a shutter; I can capture a moment seemingly before it happens. I feel more connected to the human condition (thereby being able to pull out more resources to act better), and I have SOOO much energy. I could dance all night because my muscles have quicker response time."*

Not only does mania spark her passion, but depression does as well. "Even when depressed, I can create amazing works of art. Being able to feel that level of pain, that level of sadness enables me to move others and sort of helps me share my experience." RK channels her depression into music. "I can also play piano really, really well when depressed, for some reason."

One challenge in using creativity that RK is still working on is not giving up hope when things aren't going well. Her advice to others, as well as to herself, is: "Feel the emotions as they come, acknowledge them, but don't let them take over."

When manic or hypomanic, you may make so many snap decisions that most wash away before you can follow through. You might forget you decided anything! Getting your decisions and priorities down is crucial for moving forward with your art and your healing. Trust me.

When I was writing my first two books, my husband Ralph tried to get me to list the steps I'd need to take and set some priorities. But due to hypomanic impatience, I just wanted to sit down and write! I stubbornly resisted his efforts. To me, "prioritize" was the P-word. It made me want to turn and run! I didn't think I could handle it.

Not making those tough decisions and setting those pesky priorities backfired on me. Because I didn't handle them, I gave up part of what control I had over my life. I lost a lot of time, energy, and money. Don't let the same happen to you!

Eventually, you have to face decisions and priorities. Here are several ways that can help you do so, even if you're totally stumped. The methods below are by no means scientific, but they'll help you make decisions when you feel unfocused.

Method 1—The simplest way to make a decision is to flip a coin and go with your gut. If the coin lands heads up and you're tempted to try again, you probably subconsciously prefer the option that tails represents. If the coin lands tails up and you want another flip, you probably prefer the option represented by heads. If you simply can't decide based on one try, go for two out of three—but no more unless the coin lands on its side. If that happens, keep flipping until the coin lands once more on heads or on tails.

Method 2—Ask a relative or friend, or your doctor or therapist for advice. Even someone whose advice you usually discount can help. It can clarify what you really want.

Method 3—Write all the options you're considering on different colored pieces of paper and spread them out. Which option did you write on your favorite color? Go with that, as it will probably be the option you subconsciously prefer. If that doesn't work, rule out any options you wrote on colors you're not fond of. That at least narrows the field.

Method 4—Have someone else write your options on colored papers and spread them out while you're out of the room. When you return, see what color first jumps out at you and choose the option written on it. If you simply can't decide on a color, try Method 5.

Method 5—Prioritize your options by using a form like the following, adapted from John Crystal and Richard Bolles's book *Where Do I Go from Here with My Life?* The Creative Life Toolkit contains a blank form you can use.

SAMPLE OPTIONS & PRIORITIES

	Options	Winners & Losers				
1	Get back into stained glass.					
2	Take salsa lessons.	1	②			
3	Learn how to make jewelry.	1	②	3		
4	Return to theatre.	1	2	3	④	
5	Play my guitar and sing in a coffeehouse.	1	2	3	④	5

Start by listing your options on each line as you think of them. Don't worry about their order. You need not use every line. If you're depressed, you may not be up to more than one or two. That's perfectly fine. If you're manic or hypomanic, you may want to add others, but *restrain yourself*. Limit your list to no more than five options.

Now compare the first option to the second and circle the option that seems best (in this case, salsa lessons as opposed to stained glass). Next, compare the "winning" option to option 3 (salsa lessons instead of jewelry making). Circle that winning option and compare it to option 4 (returning to theatre versus salsa lessons). Compare that winning option (theatre) to option 5 (performing in a coffeehouse). The final winner (theatre) becomes your top priority.

We've won the P-word battle—and without excruciating pain! You can use a chart like this to make decisions and set priorities in many different circumstances.

FINDING YOUR FOCUS

ONCE YOU'VE CHOSEN your top priority, it's time to dive in even deeper. If your top priority is returning to theatre, what exactly does that mean? Will you focus on acting, on directing, or on a technical aspect like building sets or running lights? You may wish to try all these roles sometime, but which will you focus on *now*?

In *Flow*, Mihaly Csikszentmihalyi states the cost of not finding your focus: "The inevitable consequence of equally attractive choices is uncertainty of purpose; uncertainty, in turn, saps resolution, and lack of resolve ends up devaluing choice. Therefore freedom does not necessarily help develop meaning in life—on the contrary. If the rules of a game become too flexible, concentration fades, and it is more difficult to attain a flow experience. Commitment to a goal and to the rules it entails is much easier when the choices are few and clear. . . .

"Inner conflict is the result of competing claims on attention. Too many desires, too many incompatible goals struggle to marshal psychic energy toward their own ends. It follows that the only way to reduce conflict is by sorting out the essential claims from those that are not, and by arbitrating priorities among those that remain."

To move ahead with any creative endeavor, you need to focus, particularly when you're taking it to the public. Physician and author Jane Mountain, who also has bipolar disorder, says: "I feel as though I am always starting over. . . . Sustainability is a lifelong issue. I think I would be better off in many ways if I had focused on one thing."

For many years I, too, had trouble finding a focus because I feared being typecast. Specializing felt so confining. I thrive on variety.

Haunted by the saying "jack of all trades, master of none," I *tried* to find a focus, but there was so much I wanted to do! Each new experience influenced me so easily. I'd get overinspired each time I discovered a different creative outlet. I'd get so high about the possibilities that my husband would have to peel me off the ceiling!

I'd think, "What's so bad about being well-rounded? Why force myself into some box? Could I help it if I was multitalented? Did indecisiveness have to be some awful shortcoming? Couldn't my resistance to being squished into some box indicate something more than immaturity, more than irresponsibility? Couldn't it represent something good?"

I'd agonize over being told, "Just decide what you want from life and go for it." Fearing the consequences of following my desire to write, I jumped from one job to another. I got bored when I mastered a new skill and the struggle was gone. I needed a new challenge. I was driven to keep learning and growing.

Finally, I whittled down my interests and decided to focus on writing. Then the next question was: What type of writing would I do? Fiction or nonfiction? In what genre? Short stories or books? Articles or columns? About what subjects?

I toyed with different options for years. I did what I viewed as "prostitutional writing" as a technical writer, because it paid a decent wage. I wrote how-to articles and humor pieces for magazines and newsletters, on everything from aerobics to fresh-cut vegetables. I spent a couple of years writing children's picture books that went unpublished. And I wrote about not being able to decide what type of writer to become!

For years, when asked, "What kind of writing do you do?" I'd cringe. I'd mentally review my twelve "specialties," and then answer, "I specialize in such and such," and then just when the person began to show some interest, I'd say, "but I *also* write about blah-dee blah-dee blah." It was nerve-wracking.

I finally decided to write about publication style—writing standards tailored for different audiences, markets, mediums, organizations, publications, or products. The decision gave me some relief and helped boost my self-esteem.

I wrote monthly columns as the "Style Meister," becoming the "Ann Landers" of publication style. I began the column to set the stage for my self-published book, *Style Meister: The Quick-Reference Custom Style Guide*, but the column itself gave me some local recognition. Although the book was very well received and sold a fair number of copies, I lost interest a few months after it came out.

I'd learned a lot in my seven years as the Style Meister, but my heart was no longer in it. So I made a "slight" shift of genre and began writing about mental illness. As they always say, "Write what you know"!

Despite your experiences during hypomania and mania, you can't go twelve different directions at once! You'll burn yourself out. Focusing offers quite a few benefits:

- It reduces the learning curve and makes it easier to keep your skills sharp.
- It makes it easier to find and keep good contacts.
- It saves valuable energy and often money.

So save yourself some grief. Focus on one specialty at a time. You don't have to commit to one *forever*, just for a reasonable amount of time. If you simply can't do that, limit yourself to no more than three related specialties.

When freelance writer Kelly James-Enger started writing full time, she also used what she calls the "saturation bombing" technique: "I queried every magazine I could think of with a wide variety of ideas. At one point, I had fifty-four queries out. . . . Nearly every article concerned a subject new to me, so each time I wrote one, I spent hours researching and learning about the topic so I could write about it with authority."

While you don't have to limit yourself to a single specialty, it helps if your specialties are related. For instance, when James-Enger decided to focus on health, fitness, and nutrition, her income quadrupled: "[I] broke into high-paying markets like *Health, Redbook, Self,* and *Modern Maturity*, and hit the six-figure mark for the first time as a freelancer."

SETTING GOALS

THE BETTER YOU describe and visualize your goals, the easier they are to achieve. But they must be readily achievable—particularly when you have a mood disorder. It's unlikely critics will proclaim you the next Picasso at your first exhibit. It's unlikely studios will offer you mega-dollar deals when you screen your first independent film. It's unlikely your first book will win the Pulitzer. All these dreams are possible, but they're highly unlikely, so don't count on them. Most of the time, you must work yourself up to such accomplishments gradually.

Dancing to keep in shape, journaling to examine your life, and doing crafts for relaxation are reasonable places to start. So are learning to carve wood, brushing up on the flute, and learning to operate your camera better. Focusing on one of these options doesn't mean you must stop there. It's just a place to start. Starting, in itself, will help your recovery, and any of these options can grow into something larger as you strengthen your knowledge and skills.

If you've ever been to a goal-setting workshop, you probably learned what experts consider the three most important characteristics of a useful goal:

1. It must be specific.
2. It must have a deadline.
3. It must be measurable.

Without these characteristics, your goal will be too fuzzy and be too hard to envision. Following are a fuzzy and a focused goal for an artist starting out.

SAMPLE FUZZY GOAL & FOCUSED GOAL

FUZZY GOAL:	I'd like to have my art exhibited.
FOCUSED GOAL:	I'd like to have two dozen of my oil paintings of Rocky Mountain wildflowers exhibited next April at the Senior Center.
DEADLINE:	Next April
MEASURE:	Two dozen paintings

The first goal is fuzzy because it isn't specific, doesn't have a deadline, and isn't measurable. It doesn't answer, What type of art? What subject? How many pieces? Where? or When?

The following goal paints a clearer picture: "I'd like to have two dozen of my oil paintings of Rocky Mountain wildflowers exhibited next April at the Senior Center."

Understanding the creative process can affect the strategies you develop to achieve your goal. So let's take a look at it now.

THE CREATIVE PROCESS

THE CREATIVE PROCESS consists of more than just getting inspired, producing a product or delivering a performance, and then waiting for the applause.

Although many people expect inspirations to "come alive" once they've learned a role, composed a melody, or shot a photo, that's not quite how the process works. Creativity comes in phases, some of which you may never have explored.

No one describes the creative process exactly the same, but I see it as seven major phases:

1. Identification
2. Preparation
3. Implementation
4. Evaluation
5. Incubation
6. Modification
7. Completion

The phases aren't always sequential. Often, their order depends on your choice of art or the project itself. Some phases may overlap, interact, or repeat. If you're immediately thrilled with your work, or you're facing a tight deadline, you might skip a few phases. But normally, you'll move through each one at some point.

■ PHASE ONE: IDENTIFICATION

This phase involves choosing something to do. Whether your Muse has inspired you or you have only a vague notion of what to do, you brainstorm and toy with ideas. You mull things over and consider what you want to convey.

Researchers discuss the creative process in terms of "problems" and "solutions." When I first learned this, these terms bothered me. I could see how they applied to inventing and science, but not to the arts. What changed my mind about the terms was something Robert and Michele Root-Bernstein wrote in *Sparks of Genius*. They said all creative people use common "tools for thinking," which include "emotional feelings, visual images, bodily sensations, reproducible patterns, and analogies."

The "problem" and "solution" then become how to express your emotions, images, sensations, patterns, and analogies in a way that others will "get" them. What do you want your audience to think, see, or feel? How do you want your message to come across?

Your "solution" is what makes your creations unique. So, first you identify the "problem." Don't worry if you don't know how to solve it yet. Work through the process, and the answer will come.

Texas artist WR paints professionally, creating both realistic and stained-glass-like murals. "When I talk to someone about a mural I'm going to paint, the only way they can trust me is if I show them pictures of other works I've completed, and they say, 'Oh, wow! That's really great.'" WR may have an image in his mind when he starts a piece, but he never knows quite how the final result will look. "I enjoy that process," he says. "I enjoy finding out how it's going to go myself."

If you simply can't identify a "problem," just choose a mode of expression (sketchpad or clay, musical recording or instrument, camera or journal) and move on any way you can.

▪ Phase Two: Preparation

Next, you get ready to work and settle in. You prepare both physically and mentally. You gather tools and materials. You psych yourself up.

Most creatives follow set routines or rituals: Checking lights and sets. Tuning instruments and playing scales. Warming up muscles. Changing voices, adjusting bodies, and trying to "get inside" characters.

Perform whatever rituals you need to turn on your creative flow, but don't spend too much time or get obsessive about them.

▪ Phase Three: Implementation

This is the most obvious, active phase of the process—the one during which you "do" your art. You may not know where to aim your camera. You may face a blank music staff or a blinking cursor on a screen, but it's time to get going! It's okay if you don't know your precise destination or exactly how you'll get there. Sometimes uncertainty is an advantage.

Don't be discouraged, just turn on your "faucet of creativity" and quench yourself with whatever comes out. Just as tap water doesn't immediately emerge at the ideal temperature, your creative flow needs a while to run.

Maintain a sense of playfulness during phase three, and stay open to new possibilities. Don't stick rigidly to an outline, storyboard, or plan. Lock up your inner critic.

Let your inner child loose. Leave the door ajar and lay out the welcome mat, in case your Muse drops by. Ask "What if's." Experiment. Have fun! Trust the process and use whatever comes.

What's most important during this phase is to get moving and keep moving, regardless of the direction you take or what emerges. Most likely, you make some wonderful discoveries.

If you experience a block, follow the advice of writer, poet, and playwright Gertrude Stein (1874–1946). John Hyde Preston once asked her what to do when "no words came and if they came at all they were wooden and without meaning." Stein laughed and replied, "The only way to resume is to resume. . . . If you feel this book deeply it will come as deep as your feeling is when it is running truest. . . .

But you do not yet know anything about your feeling because, although you may think it is all there, all crystallized, you have not let it run. So how can you know what it will be? What will be best in it is what you really do not know now. If you knew it all it would not be creation but dictation."

Even if you despise what you produce, don't destroy it. You may find value in it later, or a part of it may spur better ideas. Hang on to it and watch your creation evolve.

■ PHASE FOUR: EVALUATION

Now is the time to step back and examine the progress you've made toward your "solution." When possible, put some distance between phase three and this phase. Even a few days away from your project will provide a new perspective. Review what you've filmed, listen to what you've recorded, read your draft.

Let your inner critic out during this phase, but keep that sucker on a short chain! Whether you ask others for feedback at this point is entirely up to you, but I recommend it. You'll usually gain valuable insights from doing so.

How well does your work capture the feelings, images, sensations, patterns, and analogies you want to convey? Does your "solution" fit the "problem"? Does everything "click"? If not, consider another approach. Put another way, it's back to the drawing board. But, banish your inner critic before you start over so it won't get in the way.

■ PHASE FIVE: INCUBATION

During this phase, you let your subconscious ponder potential "solutions." You stop concentrating on the "problem" and go do something else. Incubation supplies the spark and magic for creation. This phase frequently occurs throughout the entire creative process. Don't try to start and stop incubating at a predetermined point.

Your subconscious will supply interesting observations, urge you to notice different patterns, and suggest new analogies. Your subconscious will work hand in hand with your Muse.

> *The* imagination needs moodling, long, inefficient, happy idling, dawdling and puttering. If good ideas do not come at once, or for a long time, do not be troubled at all.... Put down the little ideas however insignificant they are. But do not feel, anymore, guilty about idleness and solitude.
> —Brenda Ueland (1891-1986), American writer

When you've moodled as long as you want or can, return to your work. If you don't yet have a new "solution," it will come in time. The biggest mistake you can make is to wait for the "right" inspiration. That could keep you from ever starting! Your Muse will come when it's good and ready—usually sneaking up and surprising you while you're hard at work. Stick with the process and move on.

■ PHASE SIX: MODIFICATION

Now is the time to cut, shape, deepen, reorganize, or replace your most recent "solution." If a new inspiration surfaced during your moodling, see how well it works. Again, ask yourself how well your work captures the feelings, images, sensations, patterns, and analogies you're trying to communicate. Is this "solution" a better fit? Are you relatively satisfied?

When I wrote *Bipolar Disorder Demystified,* I wanted to put readers without the disorder in the shoes of those who have it. To experience the struggles and feel what we feel. I began writing knowing I wanted to start the book with an analogy, but nothing I came up with felt right.

I plowed on without the answer. Then, when waiting for a friend to show up for a lunch date one day, my Muse popped in the answer. It suggested using a tightrope walker to illustrate how difficult it can be to maintain balance, and the danger that untreated bipolar brings. This idea sped my momentum.

Try not to get discouraged when things don't turn out precisely as you'd like. Remember, your dissatisfaction might just be your disorder talking. Talk back to it!

Watch for perfectionism. Although you'll want to do the best you can, expecting "perfection" can stop you cold. If you listen to the "perfection police," you'll spend your remaining years in phase six! You'll never complete anything. Worse yet, you might give up your creative dreams entirely. Please don't let that happen!

■ PHASE SEVEN: COMPLETION

During this phase, you apply the final polish and declare your work complete. You frame that piece, hold that concert, send that baby to print. It may not be "perfect," but you must learn to let go. As you finish more and more projects, you'll keep honing skills, refining technique, and recognizing how your unique process works.

Learn to celebrate, set this "problem" behind you, and start thinking about the next project!

STAYING CONSCIOUS AND TAKING YOUR TIME

DON'T GET so wrapped up in creating that you forget to meet your basic needs. Set a timer (or two or three!) when you start to work to remind you when to stop for meals, exercise, or breaks—or to get yourself to bed. Do what you can during the time you've set aside for your art. Then, when you break away from it, let your subconscious take over.

 FIFTY-EIGHT-YEAR-OLD *Colorado physician, public speaker, writer, and musician Jane Mountain believes her disorder has helped her "synthesize and better understand many processes and to get the 'bigger picture' of how things relate." Mountain says she's good at understanding things intuitively. Here's what she enjoys most about the creative process: "Seeing things in new ways is something that gives me pleasure."*

Although she says her creativity doesn't get blocked, it ebbs and flows. Mountain has learned to take in information, brainstorm on it, and then let some time pass while it germinates. Only after that does she create her final product.

"Pace yourself and get outside of unrealistic expectations," Mountain recommends. "Don't let mania take you so far that you bounce down into a lower depression. Instead, try to even out the creative process. Long term, this will help you be more productive in achieving your dreams."

The creative process challenges people with mood disorders more than others because we harbor unrealistic expectations when we're ill. Often, when after months and months of depression, we feel better, we want to make up for lost time. If we get impatient and rush the process, we sabotage our efforts.

Having addressed the creative process, let's see what strategies you might use to achieve your goals.

BREAKING GOALS DOWN INTO STRATEGIES

ONE WAY TO check for reasonability is to explore the strategies and major steps you can foresee that will help you achieve your goal. You can ask others to brainstorm about strategies with you, or you can brainstorm on your own and then talk them through.

While brainstorming, record or "mind map" every idea that comes up. Move quickly. Don't stop to reorder ideas or to judge anything. Even ideas that seem silly or impossible at first may spur other, incredibly unique and doable ideas. Here's a completed mind map.

SAMPLE MIND MAP

Ask who's in charge of fundraising.
Check dates of other events.
Write a proposal with musicians.

Religious Community

Mental Health Association
Come up with funding proposal.
Meet with executive director.
Meet with board of directors.

Sing & play guitar at community fundraisers

PTA
Check school holidays.
Meet with president.
Write proposal.
Contact other musicians.

Scouts
Arrange with Scout leader.
Ask about sound equipment.
Practice 1 hour a day!

Musicians' Cooperative
Come up with program proposal.
Discuss who will choose performers.
Agree on program theme & format.

Mind mapping is especially good for showing how ideas and activities might relate, and structured lists and forms are good for prioritizing and scheduling.

OKLAHOMA *photographer and artist SF, age forty-six, has received treatment for unipolar disorder for nineteen years. She believes, however, that "a more accurate diagnosis would be Bipolar Type II, mixed."*

She says her severe depressive episodes "paralyze" her, and hypomania makes it difficult to focus and complete any projects. "This," SF says, "can lead to a sense of failure and subsequently, depression."

SF says she overcomes these challenges with "strict self-discipline. I make 'rules' for myself. I set limits on the number of projects I can begin to reduce my distractibility and narrow my focus."

Also, SF sets small goals when she's depressed, "ones that can be easily accomplished." She says that meeting a goal—no matter how small—provides an "emotional reward."

She advises others with mood disorders to recognize their limits and to carefully manage their time.

When you're ready for a more structured approach to planning, try a form like the following, to think everything through. The following example evolved from the previous mind map. The Creative Life Toolkit contains a blank form you can use.

SAMPLE GOAL, STRATEGIES, & STEPS

GOAL:	Sing and play guitar at community fundraisers.
DEADLINE:	Start this spring and do three fundraisers a year.
MEASURE:	End of spring – one fundraiser done; end of year – three fundraisers done
STRATEGY #1:	Perform at Scout fundraiser.
STEP #1:	Talk with Scout leader.
STEP #2:	Confirm schedule and logistics.
STEP #3:	Prepare for performance.
STEP #4:	Invite community leaders to performance.
STEP #5:	Perform show.
STRATEGY #2:	Perform at PTA fundraiser.
STEP #1-5:	(Same steps as above)
STRATEGY #3:	Perform at church fundraiser.
STEP #1-5:	(Same steps as above)

Chapter 11 addresses how to plan projects in more depth.

Once you have a clear vision of your major strategies and the steps you'll need to take to use them, you'll better understand how much time, energy, and money you'll need to move forward.

MAKING A COMMITMENT

YOU KNOW IN your heart what you truly want to do, whether you realize it or not. You may say you have no clue what you want and spend years in frustration, but you do. Just look inside and follow your heart.

I spent many confusing years, knowing in my heart what I wanted but avoiding it out of fear. Here's what happened.

My decision to finally become a writer made a *huge* difference in my recovery from my recurring depressions and has made my life *much* more fulfilling. I always knew I wanted to write, but I first had to banish a bunch of Terrible Too's.

I'd had many jobs over the preceding fifteen years, some of which involved other creative skills. But I returned to writing every time.

Although I studied all aspects of theatre in college, what I enjoyed most at that time was playwriting. And, later, when I majored in instructional design in grad school and focused on producing audiotapes, slide/sound shows, films, and videos, what I enjoyed most was scriptwriting.

Later, when designing and producing educational materials for high-tech companies and publishers, what I enjoyed most was, of course, writing them. I enjoyed it most because it's what I do best, but I kept circling around my target because of my Terrible Too's.

When I stopped all this circling around and committed to my writing, it greatly reduced the frequency and depths of my depressions. Life is much more rewarding when you follow your heart.

As a creative with a mood disorder, you may sometimes have difficulty making reasonable decisions, focusing, and prioritizing. But when you truly commit to your creativity, these activities will be simpler. You'll be better able to apply your energy in ways that move you closer to your goal. You'll learn to view setbacks as temporary. You'll learn to reject deceptive doubts. You'll blast through blocks and barricades. You'll find ways to manage conflicts.

Such challenges are part of the creative life, whether you have a mood disorder or not. They don't mean you won't reach your goals.

*W*hat you believe about yourself because you have a diagnosis of mental illness can often be more disabling than the illness itself.

—Ike Powell, South Carolina Department of Mental Health

MAKING YOUR COMMITMENT

WE'VE REACHED THE big moment: putting your creative commitment in writing. Remember, making a commitment doesn't mean spending *all* of your time on your art, as many people believe. If you feel ready to commit to your creativity, to embrace it and move forward, then make a contract with yourself. But do so only when you're ready. See the Creative Life Toolkit for a blank contract.

If you're not ready yet, read through the rest of the book. Then, return when you feel ready. Take whatever time you require.

SAMPLE CREATIVITY CONTRACT

I, _____ Sally Simms _____, commit to spend 6 hours/week

on my creative project(s) while carefully fulfilling my basic needs, managing my mood

disorder, and balancing the rest of my life.

_____ *Sally Simms* _____   _____ May 1, 2007 _____

Once you've truly committed to your creativity, the next step is to consider how you'll support that commitment. This requires a close examination of the rest of the factors in your life. Chapter 6 and 7 will lead the way.

*T*he relationship between commitment and doubt is by no means an antagonistic one. Commitment is healthiest when it is not without doubt but in spite of doubt.

—Existential psychologist and author of *The Courage to Create*
Rollo May (1909–1994)

· 6 ·

Supporting Creativity by Handling the Basics

EVERYONE MUST ATTEND to basic physical needs like sleep, nutrition, exercise, and stress reduction. But those of us with mood disorders must be extra vigilant. In spite of how you may feel during an episode, your physical needs matter tremendously. They must be a top priority. You simply can't reach your creative potential if you ignore what sustains your body through the day and night.

Once you get caught up in a creative project, your sense of time may shift. In *Flow*, Mihaly Csikszentmihalyi writes, "People become so involved in what they are doing that the activity becomes spontaneous, almost automatic; they stop being aware of themselves as separate from the actions they are performing. . . . Every flow activity . . . provided a sense of discovery, a creative feeling of transporting the person into a new reality. It pushed the person to higher levels of performance, and led to previously undreamed-of states of consciousness."

Due to the shifted sense of time and an altered sense of consciousness, you might forget or discount how much sleep, nutrition, exercise, and stress reduction you need to be able to function at your highest capacity. Stopping to handle these basics can be a hassle. But overlooking them complicates a mood disorder, and sometimes leads to disaster.

If you don't take care of your body, where will you live?

—Anonymous

This chapter suggests how to accommodate your physical needs so you can get the most out of your creative time. We'll start with the hottest issue.

MEDICATION

MEDICATION IS EXTREMELY controversial among creatives. For many creatives with mood disorders, it boils down to this essential question: Will taking psychotropic meds reduce my creativity? Fortunately, experts believe that's rarely the case.

Danish psychiatrist Mogens Schou did a groundbreaking clinical trial using lithium to help treat both bipolar mania and depression. His data on lithium's effect on twenty-four artists with bipolar disorder revealed increased productivity in twelve, unchanged productivity in six, and reduced productivity in six.

The subjects who showed the greatest improvement in quality of work and productivity when taking lithium were those who had the most severe disorders. Those who relied on inspirations and insights they got during manic highs experienced less creativity.

Because of the high risk of suicide, it's risky not to treat a mood disorder. Yes, medication may very well reduce the number and intensity of inspirations. On the other hand, not taking meds often makes it harder to complete projects or to do so in a way that other people "get" what you want to express. You need to weigh how one medication versus another affects your overall physical and emotional health, as well as how each enhances or dampens your creativity.

But medication is a personal choice. That decision is up to you and your doctor. We'll therefore look at both sides. Perhaps these stories will help you determine how medication might affect your creativity.

■ **THE NEGATIVES**

One Star's Perspective

*A*CTOR AND WRITER Carrie Fisher resisted medication because she treasured the elevated confidence, quick wit, and adventurousness that accompanied her mania. She thought it made her special and set her apart from others. In The Best Awful, Fisher says, rather than medicate mania, "Send a thank-you note and enjoy it while it lasts; save your medicine for someone who has something bad—like pneumonia."

Fisher did, however, eventually accept medication.

FORTY-YEAR-OLD *dancer, artist, musician, and writer LS of Coventry, England, made and sold earrings before going on meds, she believes they dulled her creativity. "I might think about making some earrings, but then another voice kicks in that says, 'I can't be bothered and it's too much effort,' which is strange when the condition has made me be creative in the start." Still, she plans to start selling earrings again soon at crafts fairs.*

WRITER AND ARTIST *AMC says her illness is "heaven and hell combined." But, so far, she's passed on medication because she cherishes her highs. Because her "writing is fluid and ideas are unending," she says, "I will push it down to the wire for creative sake." AMC does admit she can imagine the possibility of needing medication at some point but she doesn't take it now.*

INDIANA WRITER CT, *age thirty-one, reports that she used to be hypomanic most of the time. She describes her thoughts as being like a computer trying to work with one or two applications while others started running in the background. "If you get . . . more than your computer can handle, your computer will crash," she says. "I'm on top of the world going along at my own pace—anything is possible and there is a solution for everything. Then suddenly reality hits— right upside the head with a two-by-four—and I crash."*

> *Before her diagnosis, CT says, "I was creative as hell at work. I was always coming up with solutions to problems." After a particularly bad depression, she started taking medications. Her thoughts cleared, but she misses her quick solutions. "I feel as if I have lost my 'special powers.'"*
>
> *CT now takes an antidepressant and a mood stabilizer. "I am learning to change my lifestyle (no caffeine after 5 p.m., plenty of sleep, less workload at work, selling the house for less financial stress, verbal therapy, no shopping unless it is necessary). I have just started on my path, so I am still a work in progress."*

In a 2002 article in the *New York Times*, psychiatrist Richard Friedman shared his experience in treating a thirty-six-year-old photographer he calls Sheryl.

Sheryl, who had suffered lifelong depression, was not only skeptical that medication would work but afraid it would dry up her creativity. Even when severe depression "artistically paralyzed" her, she thought depression had a positive effect on her work. She believed that artists must suffer to produce great work. Friedman assured her he had successfully treated several highly creative people and predicted there would be no problem.

Prior to starting treatment, Sheryl shared her photography portfolio with Friedman so they could see how the meds might affect her work. He says, "In stark black-and-white photos, she had captured the homeless and poor. Her kinship with the dispossessed was obvious, and the images were sad and moving."

Within two months of starting antidepressants, Sheryl's depression lifted. However, Friedman was surprised by Sheryl's response to medication. Her photographic style had changed. Instead of black-and-white shots of dispossessed people, she was producing color photos "of raucous boys and amorous couples." Her new photos sold well, but Sheryl viewed them as inferior to her previous work.

She stopped taking meds but continued therapy. Within three months, Friedman said, Sheryl relapsed into depression but resisted going back on antidepressants until she'd been depressed for several months. "A little depression probably was good for her art," Friedman concluded. But because of the suffering her depression brought, Sheryl opted for medication.

Although most of the preceding people took medication only reluctantly, other creatives are grateful for meds.

■ **THE POSITIVES**

Another Star's Perspective

ACTOR AND WRITER Patty Duke (Anna Marie Duke) was relieved to get a diagnosis that explained her symptoms, and to start taking lithium. In *Call Me Anna: The Autobiography of Patty Duke,* she writes, "I've found that my creativity has been enhanced by the treatment, that the comfort I now feel with myself allows me to take much bigger risks than I ever would have before. The downside of the drug Is so small compared to the release of my power over myself, why mess around!"

OKLAHOMA ARTIST DP, *age thirty-three, made and sold jewelry in stores and at art shows, both before starting on meds and while first taking them. When manic, she says, "I could stay up all night and design and make jewelry and get a tremendous amount done." She believes that mania also helped her take more creative photographs.*

DP decided to go off meds, hoping to get that energy back. But it backfired. "I had to completely stop my jewelry business and haven't taken a single picture in months," she says. DP resumed both medication and psychotherapy. She thinks she's making great progress. "I am very proactive in my health care. I read books to also learn to help myself cope." DP expects to return to jewelry making soon.

"MEDICATION IS A *wonderful thing," says actor, writer, artist, and filmmaker BLA of California. "I am so happy to live in the twenty-first century. That, and I see my therapist once a week." Her advice to others is: "Medication, therapy. Medication, therapy. Medication, therapy. . . . Don't do one and not the other." She reports that she tried going without but that it didn't work. "Forget the myth of the melancholy artist," BLA adds. "Allow your brain some time to heal. It's amazing to see life from an entirely new perspective. I am so, so grateful."*

FORTY-FIVE-YEAR-OLD *musician, writer, photographer, and public speaker JB says her medications lessen the performance anxiety she sometimes gets when playing one of several instruments or singing. She advises others to "Give the meds a chance. Keep at what you love to do. . . . It is better to be stable than a freaked-out 'genius'—which might be a big delusion anyway."*

 CONNECTICUT ACTOR AND *writer PM, age thirty-six, says, "When first diagnosed, I was in denial. My second episode was acutely psychotic and my life was forever altered." PM says she had to start at square one. "I was barely able to bathe, eat, and think for myself."*

She overcame her challenges, she says, "through the support of great doctors, good medication, an awesome therapist, an amazing husband, {and} some family who were healthy enough to be supportive."

PM managed to return to college for a second degree, earn her master's, become a mother, and write a book manuscript. "I overcame my challenges by taking small steps forward, a couple back, then a few more forward, and so on. It seems everything I have done has taken longer than it should have, but I have accomplished so much."

 ALABAMA POET KO, *age forty, says, when manic, she writes poetry for four to five hours at a clip. "I'm awakened from sleep compelled to write. I quickly get a pen and paper and write as fast as my pen will move. I don't know what I am writing until I see it printed on a page." When not manic, KO says she "can only write poetry for a specific occasion, and I have to 'think' about what rhymes and {ensure} that it flows well."*

She believes that people who are taking meds can still be creative; it just takes longer to get inspired. She cautions others not to stop medication or to change their dosage just to access creativity. "That path," she warns, "leads to self-destruction."

Psychologist and author Dean Keith Simonton says, "Creators should have no fear that therapeutic treatment for disabling mental or emotional disorders would undermine their creative potential."

■ THE ADJUSTERS

Other people find that adjusting dosages—with their psychiatrist's support—helps them better access their creativity. This has been the case for me. We have lowered one medication and increased another to improve my concentration and energy, and we still tweak my meds from time to time.

 FORTY-NINE-YEAR-OLD political newspaper columnist SL of New Jersey says medication reduced his creativity and productivity. "I find it harder to write. I feel less creative, less witty, and certainly my output of writing has dropped significantly." Although medication calmed his mania, SL says it brought a dullness. "Most people cannot see it, but I can tell."

Hard work and intense concentration help SL meet his deadlines, but he finds it hard to generate unique topics and ideas. He says he enjoys work less than before—but not enough to abandon medication. "Try to balance the meds . . . with the need and desire for creative thinking," he says. "I have complained to my doctor and we have made several adjustments to try to reduce the dose. I know better than to stop taking the medication, because of the horrible consequences I faced when untreated."

■ MY PERSPECTIVE

I, too, miss the creative rush of hypomania. The thrill of those late-night inspirations when I'd pop out of bed and record my thoughts for hours. Eventually my husband would wake up, track me down, and force me back to bed. I resented my personal "police force," certain that I'd lose some brilliant idea forever.

But I was so scattered and unfocused that my "brilliant" inspirations never went anywhere. Frequently, I couldn't make any sense of what I'd written, and even when I could, others couldn't or wouldn't even try.

I've stayed on medication religiously despite my misgivings and the fact that it took *years* to pin down the right "cocktail." My doctor and I still adjust the dosage on occasion. I've managed to publish three books, as well as to complete many other creative projects, but I doubt I could have done so without meds.

Ultimately, whether you decide to take medication or not is a personal decision to make based on the severity of your symptoms and your doctor's advice. If you decide to reduce or go off your meds, please keep others informed. *It's extremely dangerous to stop many psychotropic medications "cold turkey"!* Many must be gradually reduced. Make certain your doctor and your loved ones know about your decision so they're equipped to deal with an emergency, should one arise.

Taking medications as prescribed and working closely with your psychiatrist, psychopharmacologist, or physician is, I believe, quite important. But attending to basic physical needs is crucial as well. Of particular importance to those of us with mood disorders is getting enough restorative sleep.

GET ADEQUATE SLEEP

GETTING THE AMOUNT of sleep you need is challenging, especially if your art interferes with your normal sleep patterns. If you perform at night, you may get too psyched up to sleep. If you rebel against your biorhythms in the effort to keep up with fellow performers and enjoy their company, you may be courting long-term trouble from the ill effects of too little rest.

It's tempting to go with the flow and listen to your inspirations while they're driving you to produce, but doing so puts you at great risk. It takes an awful lot of discipline to ignore the Muse and force yourself to sleep—but it's necessary. Sooner or later, sleep deprivation will catch up with you. Regardless of what your brain claims, the rest of your body requires sleep. Going without is tough on anyone, but when you have a mood disorder, sleep deprivation can dangerously deepen depression or trigger a hypomanic or manic episode. Plus, sleeplessness threatens creativity.

 NORTH CAROLINA WRITER *and language arts teacher HG, age forty-one, has been getting treatment for bipolar disorder for twenty-one years. The energy that accompanies her illness, she says, helps keep her going but makes it difficult to keep up with all of her ideas without jumbling her thoughts. "I keep spinning and spinning so that I can't think straight or stay with one aspect long enough to follow through."*

Creative tasks tend to consume her. Although she doesn't want to stop until she thinks her work is perfect, she's letting go more and taking better care of herself. "I am learning that if I leave something for tomorrow, I will still be able to do it, that I will not stop breathing and die."

HG especially stresses the importance of sleep: "A good night's sleep drives {my creativity}; lack of sleep blocks {it} in a major way." Her advice to others is to "stay on meds, report truthfully to doctors, hire a talk therapist you really dig, take care of your looks, exercise, treat any and all comorbid {concurrent} conditions, drink water, don't drink too many beers, learn how to get in touch with your center so you can trust yourself and relax." Several other techniques help HG control her symptoms— verbal self-monitoring, conscious breathing, and meditation. She says her mantra helps her feel safe and trust that it's okay to stop and go to sleep, or to eat a meal.

How much sleep a person needs varies with the individual, but on average, adults need between seven and nine hours a night. Don't expect to get by on two or three. Because of your mood disorder, you may require more.

Seven Tips for Sweeter Slumber

- Stick to a regular bedtime and wake-up time as much as possible.
- Stop consuming caffeine, drinking alcohol, and smoking several hours before bedtime. Better still, give up all three of these habits.
- Stop any vigorous exercise at least three hours before bedtime and do relaxation exercises right before bedtime.
- Turn down the lights and lower the noise level.
- Relax, unwind, and keep troublesome discussions out of the bedroom.
- If you eat a late-night snack, choose carbohydrates or dairy products. Turkey eaten with a carbohydrate is also an excellent choice.
- If you can't drop off within an hour, do something else until you tire. I find that moving to the living room and reading something that's not too engrossing helps me drift off.

Trying to force sleep nearly always makes things worse. It's a bit like the challenge to not think about a white elephant, which almost always makes you think of nothing but white elephants! If your insomnia relates to being bombarded by great ideas for projects—or to worries in other areas of your life—keep a pad and pencil at the side of your bed. (And a flashlight, if you'll need it.) Once you've captured what's on your mind, it's easier to get to sleep.

Many people with mood disorders also have trouble getting up. For me, it's a constant battle. Sometimes this is a depressive or bipolar symptom; other times it's a medication side effect. I've known people who require one medication to get to sleep and another to wake up. If you continue to have problems getting to sleep, staying asleep, or waking up, talk to your doctor.

Fifty-four-year-old New York writer, public speaker, and craftsperson DK says bipolar disorder allows her to concentrate on projects "to the exclusion of all else." When immersed in a project, she has difficulty remembering to eat and sleep. I'm the same way. Unfortunately, for many of us who are bipolar, that intense focus can make us forget it's time to go to bed.

Know how much time you need for nightly rest—and make sure to reserve time for adequate sleep. Remember, sleep is essential to your health and well-being, and as such, is essential to your creative life.

Let's move on to nutrition, which is as important as sleep.

EAT NUTRITIONAL MEALS AND SNACKS

PROPER NUTRITION IS a very basic need. Your body can't function long on creative fumes alone! What and how often we eat affects the development of neurotransmitters in our brains.

■ HELP BALANCE YOUR NEUROTRANSMITTERS

Neurotransmitters regulate behavior and are closely linked to mood. *Serotonin*, *dopamine*, and *norepinephrine* (also called noradrenalin) have the most significant impact. Another important neurotransmitter is *acetylcholine*.

Serotonin eases anxiety and depression. Low levels can contribute to sleep disorders. Serotonin also:

- Boosts mood
- Brings calmness
- Decreases inflexibility and irritability
- Increases tolerance for pain
- Reduces food cravings

Dopamine and norepinephrine:

- Increase alertness
- Increase energy
- Help us think and act more quickly
- Help us cope with stress

Acetylcholine aids memory and general mental functioning.

Maintaining a balance of complex carbohydrates and proteins, and consuming the right amount of vitamins and minerals helps keep neurotransmitters balanced. Our bodies need foods containing the amino acid *tryptophan* to form serotonin, dopamine, and norepinephrine, and foods with *choline* to make acetylcholine.

■ **EAT THE RIGHT FOODS**

CAUTION! Certain nutrients and substances are dangerous when you're taking an MAOI. Doctors rarely prescribe MAOI (monoamine oxidase inhibiting) antidepressants because of the difficult dietary restrictions they bring.

MAOIs build up tyramine, an amino acid present in some foods, beverages, and medications. This can elevate blood pressure significantly, cause a stroke, or even kill you. If your doctor prescribes an MAOI, make certain you understand exactly what substances you must avoid!

Essential fats are also important. Omega-3 fatty acids help treat mood disorders, as well as other diseases. Fish is one of the best sources of omega-3s, but if you don't get enough in your diet, you can take flaxseed oil or a fish-oil supplement. Ask your doctor about recommended doses if you use supplements.

Fresh foods are always best, but dried or frozen

foods are often good choices, too. As much as possible, avoid prepared foods, which are usually full of hidden sugars, sodium, and harmful fats. Because they're free of harmful chemicals, organic foods are an even a better choice.

Hidden Sugars

Acesulfame potassium	Lactose
Cane juice	Maltose and Malts
Dextrose	Saccharides
Glucose	Sorghum
High-fructose corn syrup	Sucrose

Spikes and drops in blood sugar can trigger dramatic mood shifts, cause irritability, lower energy, and increase food cravings later. During depression, we may become insulin-resistant, and during mania, more insulin sensitive. Complex carbohydrates and regular meals provide a steady level of glucose, the type of sugar that fuels our cells.

This chart lists some foods and beverages that affect brain function, mood, and energy levels. Note the foods and nutrients you must avoid if taking an MAOI antidepressant.

FOODS/NUTRIENTS	REASONS TO EAT OR AVOID
Complex Carbohydrates • Cereals (preferably sugarless) • Dried beans • Potatoes • Wheat germ • Whole Grains: brown rice, oatmeal, rye bread, whole wheat bread	• All increase serotonin • Wheat germ also contains omega-3 fatty acids • **If taking an MAOI, avoid breads, cereals and other products containing soy flour or yeast, as well as soybeans**
Simple Carbohydrates (Sugar and white-flour products) • Breads not made from whole grain flours • Cakes, candy, cookies • Crackers • Doughnuts, pies • Sweetened soft drinks • White rice	• All quickly spike blood sugar and drop it later, depleting energy

FOODS/NUTRIENTS	REASONS TO EAT OR AVOID
Dairy Products • Cheeses • Eggs • Milk • Sour cream • Yogurt	• All raise dopamine and nor-epinephrine levels • Eggs also contain choline, which aids brain function and improves memory • **If taking an MAOI, avoid aged cheeses, sour cream, soy-based dairy products, and yogurt**
Fish • Anchovies, sardines • Crab • Halibut, herring, mackerel • Salmon, tuna	• All raise dopamine and nor-epinephrine levels
Fruits and Vegetables (preferably dried, fresh, or frozen) • Apricots • Avocados • Bananas • Broccoli (raw), carrots • Cantaloupe • Dark green leafy vegetables—collard greens, kale, dark green lettuce, spinach, turnip greens • Eggplant • Figs (dried) • Legumes • Mangoes, oranges, plums • Sauerkraut, tomatoes	• All increase serotonin • **If taking an MAOI, avoid avocados, eggplant, legumes, sauerkraut, tomatoes, and overripe fruits—especially bananas and plums**
Meats • Beef • Pork • Poultry • Veal	• All raise dopamine and nor-epinephrine levels • Turkey contains tryptophan • **If taking an MAOI, avoid canned or dried and fatty meats like duck, liver, and sausage, as well as soy-based meat substitutes, like tofu**

FOODS/NUTRIENTS	REASONS TO EAT OR AVOID
Nuts and Seeds (raw) • Almonds, sesame seeds, sunflower seeds • Flaxseeds, pumpkin seeds, walnuts • Soy nuts	• All contain omega-3 and omega-6 fatty acids, which help brain function • Flaxseeds, pumpkin seeds, and walnuts have the most fatty acids • If taking an MAOI, avoid soy nuts
Oils • Canola oil, flaxseed oil, soybean oil, walnut oil	• All contain omega-3 fatty acids
Beverages and Products Containing Caffeine • Alcohol • Caffeinated coffees, soft drinks, and teas • Chocolate • Some antidepressants, anti-seizure medications, appetite suppressants, beta-blockers (for high blood pressure and heart disease), thyroid hormone replacements, allergy and cold remedies	• All can interfere with medications, cause insomnia, lead to irritability, and lower energy later

How much of the recommended foods is enough? The answer varies with your age, sex, and activity level. Check out the U.S. Department of Agriculture's updated dietary guidelines and food pyramid at www.healthierus.gov/dietaryguidelines and www.mypyramid.gov. These sites offer extensive information and tools to help you calculate your nutritional needs.

■ TAKE TIME OUT FOR MEALS AND SNACKS

Whatever it takes, try to avoid missing meals. Not only will eating nourish your body, but also taking time for a meal will give you a chance to replenish your creative juices. Jot a note to remind yourself where you stopped, take a break to eat, and then resume where you left off. You'll usually return with better perspective.

Actors and singers need breaks to rest their voices. Artists need to step back from their work from time to time. Dancers and musicians need breaks to rest their bodies. Writers need to review what they've written to maintain a consistent tone. Look at nutrition this way: your body relies on food to create new tissues, build bones, and help your brain function. Eating therefore *supports* your creativity rather than hinders it.

Give yourself more than just a few minutes for meals and snacks. Rushing will only increase your stress. Trust me. I've wolfed down way too many meals while speeding on my way to an appointment. That's not only stressful but also highly risky! Allow yourself time to reach your destination a few minutes early, then use those minutes to relax.

Allow at least a half an hour to calmly sit and eat. Set an alarm (or two or three). Lunch with a friend. Or eat in a park or on the porch, enjoying nature.

Hand-in-hand with food comes exercise, which helps optimize the way your body processes all those nutrients you consume. Exercise can also energize or relax you, as well as help you manage your mood disorder.

EXERCISE REGULARLY

NO DOUBT SOMEONE has suggested exercise to treat your depression or bipolar disorder. While exercise can't cure a mood disorder, it sure can help. Elizabeth Somer and Nancy Snyderman, authors of *Food & Mood,* say, "People who stick with an exercise program consistently report they feel good, physically and mentally. Even those who are despondent rave about their better moods once they start exercising."

Exercise increases oxygen and blood flow to the brain as well as norepinephrine and dopamine levels. This improves alertness, concentration, and energy. It's a good way to de-stress.

*J*ogging is very beneficial. It's good for your legs and your feet. It's also very good for the ground. It makes it feel needed.

—American cartoonist Charles Schultz (1922–2000),
creator of *Peanuts*

It's often difficult to pull away from a creative project to go exercise. At times, I want to skip a session, and I resent the time it takes to travel to and from the gym. I want to keep working until I reach a project-determined goal, like finishing a chapter. However, I always feel better after exercise and return to my work refreshed.

A team of researchers at Middlesex University's School of Psychology, in London, say exercise enhances both creativity and mood. Quite a bit of anecdotal evidence suggests that exercise can also help people break through creative blocks.

The Middlesex study compared sixty-three participants' responses both after exercising (with aerobics or dance) and after viewing a "neutral" video. The researchers measured participants' moods using an adjective list, and measured creative thinking using three measures on the Torrance test, a popular divergent-thinking test that includes verbal and figural responses, and creative activities.

Participants' moods increased significantly after exercising and decreased significantly after watching the video, and their creative thinking increased as well. The researchers concluded that physical exercise improved mood and creativity independently of each other.

Exercising regularly can be a tough habit to develop. It's particularly difficult when you're depressed, and may even seem impossible. But studies have shown that even a single aerobic workout helps reduce depression and anxiety and improve self-esteem.

Aerobic exercise increases heart rate and oxygen flow and helps burn off excess manic energy. Non-aerobic exercise strengthens muscles, increases flexibility, and reduces tension. The following chart lists examples of both aerobic and nonaerobic exercises.

AEROBIC EXERCISE	NONAEROBIC EXERCISE
Aquatics	Pilates
Bicycling	Weight-lifting
Walking briskly	Going for a stroll
Running or jogging	Stretching
Swimming	Yoga

If you're uncomfortable exercising in public, work out at home. Exercise programs are readily available on videotape or DVD. A sturdy

standing bicycle, treadmill, or rowing machine can be a good investment. You can often obtain inexpensive exercise equipment at garage
sales. Hand weights, Pilates balls, and stretchy bands are also good.

Sports that make your heart beat faster for a continuous time period
(basketball, racquetball, soc-
cer, etc.) provide an aerobic
workout, but those with frequent starts and stops (foot-
ball, golf, softball, etc.)
usually do not.

CAUTION! If you take lithium,
drink lots of water when exercising. Excessive sweating can lead
to dehydration, which can create
lithium toxicity.

One benefit of exercising
is, it lets your subconscious
mull over creative ideas. I get
some of my best inspirations when walking around my neighborhood
or swimming laps.

Exercising for even as little as ten minutes a day will get your blood
flowing. You can also try to incorporate simple exercise like walking
(rather than driving or riding the bus) into your daily routine. Forty-
four-year-old North Carolina artist, musician, and writer JT lifts weights
three days a week to maintain his muscle tone and walks on alternate
days to increase his endorphins.

To prevent boredom, choose a variety of exercises and approaches:
Take a class that will get you moving, or exercise with a friend. Like anything, exercise is easiest to stick with when you do something you enjoy.

Oregon artist FD says, "I just got into dance because I was looking
to do something to get into shape again. I took up belly dancing. I love
it! . . . Sometimes [during a depression] I just need to get a little fresh
air or exercise."

Forty-year-old English dancer, artist, musician, and writer LS enjoys
taking Qi Gong classes. She says they both relax her and increase her self-
awareness.

Talk with your doctor before beginning any exercise program. When
you start (or restart after a period of inactivity), go slowly. If you overdo
it, you'll have trouble sticking to it, plus you'll risk injuring yourself.

This brings us to some ways that professionals can help support your
creative efforts.

THERAPY

Studies have shown that "talk therapy" with a professional can be just as effective as taking medication for *mild* mood disorders. They've also found cognitive-behavioral therapy particularly helpful for those of us with mood disorders. Cognitive-behavioral therapy helps you change the way you habitually think and behave. Many of the suggestions in this book, especially in chapters 4, 5, and 13, are based on this approach.

Adding therapy along with medication makes your treatment more effective, and adding support groups to that combination helps even more.

Arkansas writer and artist KB, age fifty-three, teaches school, and writes and paints for her own satisfaction. "I gain a certain peace from these activities," she says. KB uses medication and positive self-talk to manage her disorder: "I also have a wonderful therapist who has given me strategies to deal with the different feelings. My biggest problem is dealing with coworkers who put me down. [My therapist] has taught me how to respond to these people and protect my dignity."

Thirty-something Louisiana actor, writer, artist, and filmmaker BA is working with her therapist to recover long-repressed talents. "I have learned how to breathe a lot easier throughout my day," she says. "When things get crazy, I'm not as quick to decide the day is ruined, I'm a failure, my kids will end up in therapy, and the dog will shit in my shoes all because I am such a horrible person. It's really great to catch myself in a stressful situation and realize, 'Hey, I'm not freaking out!' And sometimes I'm even laughing if the situation is idiotic enough," adds BA.

A good therapist can also provide useful feedback about your creative work and help you sort out problems as they arise.

Aside from physicians and therapists, there may already be other people in your immediate life and your community who can provide support, constructive feedback, and a sense of balance. Reach out to them.

EMOTIONAL SUPPORT

Emotional support is crucial when managing a mood disorder. Most of us isolate ourselves when we're depressed; and irritate, offend, or hurt others when we're manic. We may be embarrassed by our episodes or rejected due to the social stigma surrounding mental illness.

It helps tremendously to talk with someone who understands and empathizes.

Twenty-three-year-old artist, writer, photographer, actor, and dancer RA says her younger sister keeps her going when she's severely depressed and suicidal. "I think of how much she always looked up to me (she even chose to play the same instrument as me in band)," RA says. "She suffers from depression, so I often find that we help each other through things." When RA feels especially bad, she says, "I can talk to her and she gives me strength."

You might obtain emotional support through any or all of the following:

- Individual or group therapy with a professional
- Peer-to-peer support groups
- One-on-one talks with someone else who has a mood disorder
- Family
- Friends
- Your religious community
- Internet support groups or chat groups

"When I was a young man, I used to be in a fairly successful band," says musician and writer AT, age forty-one. "[During that time], the illness struck for the first time. . . . My partner and my friends helped me through, and encouraged me to carry on, even though I felt that I was not worth it at times."

Surrounding yourself with other creatives is not only a way to learn or network, but a way to obtain emotional support and perspective.

COGNITIVE SUPPORT

As a CREATIVE person, you also need cognitive support. I don't mean cognitive behavioral therapy (though that is valuable in itself). I mean interacting with other artists who share your creative interests. Meeting with other actors, artists, dancers, filmmakers, musicians, photographers, or writers expands your knowledge of your art, generates new project and marketing ideas, as well as emotional support. If such a group doesn't exist in or near your community, try starting one yourself! Even if you think no one in the area shares your interest, post some flyers or run an announcement in the newspaper. You may be surprised who responds.

Over the years, when I've focused on my writing, I've actively participated in both "writing practice" groups and critique groups. My involvement has made my writing stronger, and I've enjoyed getting to know the other writers.

South Carolina decorator and writer YM, age fifty-five, says she functions well no matter what her mood is. "I do this with a lot of support from my family, friends, co-workers." Open communication with her doctor also helps. Because YM's supporters know her well, they notice when her mood is changing and steer her back on course. She says, "It helps my mood when I am doing things that I love and can feel a sense of accomplishment."

Besides getting enough sleep, eating right, and obtaining emotional support, you need to manage your stress, so it doesn't take a toll on you mentally or physically.

STRESS MANAGEMENT

HAVING A MOOD disorder is, of course, more stressful than living a "normal" life. Our minds sometimes release too much *noradrenalin, and we* get stuck in the "fight or flight" mode. But you *can* reduce your stress to some extent. In *Strong Imagination,* Daniel Nettle advises us to choose our surroundings, companions, and professional challenges carefully to lower our stress.

A positive outlook and solid support system helps. And, of course, we can apply stress-management techniques like aromatherapy, deep breathing, journaling, massage, physical activity, relaxation exercises, and warm baths. Using your creative talents can also reduce stress. But even creative acts produce stress if you don't take breaks and you go overboard.

Illinois musician and actor EK, age sixty-two, gets severe performance anxiety: "When I had to perform as a singer in front of an audience . . . I often felt that I would pass out from panic. . . . My feelings of duty forced me to perform even though the experience was torturous. Self-calming techniques, such as Autogenous Training [a form of self-hypnosis in which you consciously examine what underlies your anxiety], have helped me considerably over the years."

Simple Stress Relievers

Become a marionette—Sit on a chair and pretend you're a stringed puppet. Let your muscles go limp, and lower your head while you count to twenty-five. Then imagine a puppeteer pulling your strings up. Start from the wrist and raise each arm. Then raise your head and straighten your torso. Finally, get up slowly, knocking your knees in and out and waving your arms as your "strings" untangle.

Take "beach ball" breaths—Stand and inhale through your nose, breathing in as much air as you can and pretending your stomach is a beach ball being pumped up. When your lungs are completely full, exhale through your mouth and imagine that ball collapsing. Pull your stomach toward your spine and keep exhaling until completely out of breath.

Stretch like a cat—Stand and pretend you're a cat on its hind legs, trying to snag a toy mouse that's just out of reach. Stretch one arm and then the other as you imagine trying to get the mouse.

Some of the ways I deal with stress are to sing, play the piano or guitar, shoot photos, draw or color, cross stitch, swim laps, walk or sit outdoors, read in a hammock, watch my fish swim in the aquarium, play with my cats, cook and enjoy a healthy meal, or even straighten a closet, drawer, or cabinet!

Don't allow your stress to push you in a counterproductive direction.

■ AIM FOR BALANCE

Jane Mountain, author of *Bipolar Disorder: Insights for Recovery*, encourages those with bipolar disorder to "balance high energy with calming exercises. Curtail your activities [during mania]," she says, "by taking breaks throughout the day and avoiding overstimulation . . . such as loud music . . . Short breaks to relax or take a walk will help tame the energy of mania without decreasing your productivity. Be productive, but don't fuel the mania."

Because you may be making a major life change by focusing more on your creative goals, your stress might increase. It's therefore important to recognize signs of oncoming episodes and to have a plan in place, should a crisis arise.

■ LEARN YOUR EARLY WARNING SIGNS

Learn what warning signs you typically display before a depressive or manic episode hits, and share them with your loved ones. They can then bring them to your attention, or if necessary, intervene on your behalf. Knowing the thoughts, feelings, and behaviors that signal an impending episode will help you address problems before they get out of control.

Here are some of my early warning signs. The Creative Life Toolkit contains a form like the following for your use.

SAMPLE EARLY WARNING SIGNS

BEFORE DEPRESSION	BEFORE MANIA/HYPOMANIA
Excessive sleep	Insomnia
Compulsive eating	Forgetting to eat
Low self-esteem	Euphoria—or sometimes anger
Withdrawal	Increased sexual activity
Trouble making phone calls	Impatience with others
Self-destructive thoughts	Increased spending

Some creatives experience blocks right before an episode. For instance, twenty-three-year-old Arizona artist, photographer, writer, and dancer SH says, "Since lack of creativity is one of my first signs of depression, I will mention it to my doc, who gets me on antidepressants until the bout is over."

Thirty-three-year-old Florida writer, actor, photographer, and artist RM says creative ideas come easily to her when she's hypomanic but that it's hard to focus and to follow through. "I do ten things at once, but nothing gets completed until I get 'normal.'" In addition to taking meds, RM monitors her moods. "I have to keep in tune with my feelings and get them in check before they get out of control." For her, this may mean changing medications, getting more sleep, or using aromatherapy.

One effective way to learn your warning signs is to monitor your moods by tracking them daily. Some sources where you can obtain tools for mood tracking appear in the Resources section.

Even with the best of precautions, however, an episode may occur.

DO SOME CRISIS PLANNING

BECAUSE MOOD DISORDERS cause recurrent episodes, it's good to have a crisis plan in place so your loved ones know precisely what to do—and not do—should an episode occur. Here are some issues a crisis plan should address:

- Symptoms that indicate the need for treatment but that you may not recognize during an episode
- Names of people you'll permit to confer with mental health providers
- Treatment facilities you prefer and those you find unacceptable and why
- Doctors you prefer and those you find unacceptable and why
- Medications you prefer and those you won't accept and why
- Other treatments you might accept, the circumstances in which to use them, and why
- Treatments you find unacceptable and why

Such plans guide those helping you through an episode and reassure you that your wishes will be considered.

 VIRGINIA MUSICIAN AC, *age fifty-one, teaches and performs music professionally. She says, "Being severely depressed, music was an escape from the world—didn't have to speak to a human being, or look at a human being. The downside, however, was the effort it took to get out of bed and get motivated to work."*

AC went on medications and says they helped even out her moods.

"I physically feel better than I have in a long time—my body and mind {are} more in sync; the down side is that I am not sensitive, or emotionally able to be as creative, come up with great ideas, feel in my gut and soul as I could. My imagination skills are more dull."

She says she misses that heightened sensitivity. "{I'm} still trying to adjust; trying to lower my expectations and allow myself to live in the day. I am angry, and continue to be angry at the loss of so much I had (perceived or real)."

AC suggests you "find someone who can be a better judge in determining what and how you are doing; write down the dreams, inspirations and ideas when they come. You can work on them when you're better focused and ready."

Daniel Nettle emphasizes the need for treatment when a person gets psychotic: "For successful creative performance, psychoticism must be combined with other qualities (and it rarely is, which is what makes outstanding people outstanding)." Among the qualities he cites are hard work, good organizational skills, commitment, and persistence. "It might not seem very romantic . . . but most professional writers get up pretty early in the morning and get to bed on time, most musicians put in six hours practice a day, and most visual artists work long weeks. All these people have to drive themselves on through years of relative tedium, frustration, and low return, which requires self-discipline, humor, and resilience."

Now that we've addressed the basics you must handle to manage your illness as well as support your creative efforts, let's see how you can squeeze more creative time into your schedule.

*I*deas come slowly, and . . . the more clear, tranquil and unstimulated you are, the slower the ideas come, but the better they are.

—American writer Brenda Ueland (1891-1985),
If You Want to Write

· 7 ·

Scheduling Creative Time

YOU CAN FIT more creativity into your life, even with a busy schedule. You do it by taking your commitment seriously and making it a top priority. That can mean anything from reserving a few hours a week for a hobby, to significantly altering your lifestyle. I suggest starting small and increasing your commitment gradually. I'll bet you can squeeze in more creative time than you think.

You usually need to change some aspects of your life so you can devote more time, energy, and money to your art. Will you spend less time watching TV, less time shopping, less time on the Internet or the phone? You might need to budget more carefully, or cut back on your work hours.

How much time, energy, and money are you willing to invest in your art? Notice that I said "are you willing" rather than "can you," because you probably have more power over your time, energy, and money than you think.

This chapter helps you examine the major areas of your life and adjust your schedule in a way that supports your creativity. Let's start by determining the percentage of time you want to spend in each area of your life.

THE WHOLE LIFE GRID

SUSAN JEFFERS, AUTHOR of *Feel the Fear and Do It Anyway*, uses a model she calls the Whole Life Grid to explore different areas of life. It looks something like the following figure, though I added arrows to indicate that these areas can all relate to your creativity.

SAMPLE WHOLE LIFE GRID

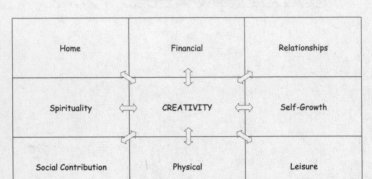

Here's what each part of the grid might involve:

- Home—the environment and surroundings in which you live
- Financial—career, job, living expenses, savings, investments
- Relationships—quality time with a significant other, family members, friends, colleagues
- Spirituality—religion, connection to the universe, meditation, developing your higher self
- Self-Growth—education, learning, new experiences
- Social contribution—charity, community involvement, volunteering, enhancing our society
- Physical—sleep, nutrition, exercise, medical treatment
- Leisure—hobbies, play, relaxation, sports, recreation

Visualizing these areas—and how your creativity relates to each one—can help you determine the percentage of time you want to devote to each part of your life. Working with such a grid can help you examine the relationships between different areas of life and further explore your motivations.

Since this book is about embracing your creativity to aid your recovery and to regain your life, I've placed Creativity in the center square and Physical directly beneath because it supports creativity. What you place in your grid and where, however, depends on what you value most. Your grid may look different from the previous example.

The Creative Life Toolkit contains a blank Whole Life Grid for you to work with. If some other aspect of your life takes precedence over your creativity or you want to change any areas, please do so. If I've omitted some area of your life, add it. Likewise, omit those areas you have no interest in or wish to set aside. Combine some areas if you wish.

I *do* suggest that you limit your grid to just nine squares to keep things simple. And don't feel pressured to use all nine. It's nice to save a square or two in case something interesting comes up.

How might your creative commitment relate to other areas of life? Can you draw on your talents to improve what you want in these areas? For instance, singing might strengthen a bond with a child, meet a spiritual need, or make a social contribution. Take a moment to think about that.

You don't have to decide precisely *when* you'll do everything. Don't schedule your time too tightly, or you'll add to your stress. We'll look at scheduling in more depth later on.

On multiple occasions I've created complicated schedules with activities planned down to every quarter-hour. Sticking to such schedules is impossible! My therapist says my elaborate schedules were probably attempts to control my disorder. Leave yourself some open time and flexibility.

■ HOME

How much time will you invest in keeping your home clean and tidy? This doesn't mean scrubbing the entire house until it's gleaming and you can eat off the floor! How long does it take to do laundry and other household chores? Might you get someone else to help or do low-priority tasks less frequently to squeeze in more creative time? Could you use a dry cleaner to launder and press clothes you now care for yourself?

Instead of preparing each meal separately, could you prepare multiple portions at one time to simply reheat later? Could you buy staple items, such as paper goods or canned goods, in bulk to save on trips to the store? Could you order some items online and have them sent as regularly scheduled deliveries?

■ Finances

If you have or plan to seek a job outside your home, how much time will you devote to it, including commuting time? Taking public transportation that bypasses traffic jams, or carpooling with someone to take advantage of designated faster lanes, might give you extra time to study or pursue certain kinds of arts. Does your job entail professional reading to do, courses to take, or other after-hours tasks that may cut into your creative time? Is it possible to work less than full-time, partially from home, or on a freelance basis? Is flex time an option? Could you lengthen your lunch hour or working hours to free up some time, or even a full day to work on your art? Could you cut back on "extracurricular" socializing with colleagues to create more time for your art?

Even if your job is to take care of your home and family, you probably have financial responsibilities like paying bills or meeting with an accountant. How much time do these take? Can another member of the household take over some of these duties? Can you take advantage of direct-payment and direct-deposit plans to handle your paychecks and regular household bills?

After depression had paralyzed me for more than six months, my psychiatrist suggested that more structure might help me get back on track. During that depression, my life consisted of going to appointments, reading self-help books, and barely managing to care for my husband and children.

I wasn't sure I could return to work, but I followed my doctor's advice. I contacted an acquaintance and asked if I could work at her desktop publishing company part-time. She enthusiastically hired me, asking me to work more hours than I thought I could manage. I ignored my gut feeling and took the job anyway. It was below my capabilities and paid less than I'd received before, but it got me out of the house and provided some much-needed structure.

My boss later assigned me more-stressful projects, which I did, though not all that confidently or successfully. When it got harder and harder to meet her expectations, the stress caught up with me. After she let me go, I turned to freelancing.

Freelancing was a better fit for me. I was less financially secure, but with a flexible schedule I could better manage the challenges my disorder brought. I could use my creativity and build a business while still taking care of my physical needs. I could work when I was stable enough to, and cut back when I was not.

■ RELATIONSHIPS

How much time will you reserve for a significant other, for family members and friends? If you have young children, is your partner willing to take over some tasks to allow you more time for creative pursuits? Can you afford daycare or a babysitter? How much time will you leave open for seeking and developing new relationships? Don't try to go it alone! It's crucial to get emotional support when you have a mood disorder. Even creatives without mood disorders may find it hard to balance their need for privacy or productivity with the demands of their closest relationships.

Especially if you don't have a significant other or if family and friends don't understand you, try joining a support group. An excellent place to find one is the Depression and Bipolar Support Alliance (www.dbsalliance.org or 1-800-826-3632). DBSA's affiliated chapters sponsor in-person peer-to-peer groups, and the organization also offers several types of online groups.

Other groups can be helpful to people with mood disorders and to those with creative talents as well. The Resources section has further information.

Sixty-four-year-old writer, artist, photographer, and communicator JMR says he benefits from his Recovery, Inc. support group. He writes books, articles, and newsletters. JMR also gives sermons and seminars, does radio and TV productions, and makes audiotapes.

Forty-four-year-old North Carolina artist, musician, and writer JT has found Arts Anonymous helpful. The group, based on a twelve-step model, focuses on creative recovery.

Whether you're first learning about an art or already know a lot about it, you may want to counteract family

CAUTION! If you attend Alcoholics Anonymous or a similar twelve-step group, keep in mind that it's important to continue taking medications your doctor prescribes. They're not the same as the addictive, illegal drugs these groups advise people not to use.

disinterest by developing friendships with those who share or encourage your creative interest. Read the community calendar section of your newspaper; look at events postings at your library and community center, and in stores. A knitting shop, for example, may hold regular sessions that aren't classes per se, but simply times for knitters to work on their craft together. Don't discount non-health-related groups as holding the potential for being a support group.

■ SELF-GROWTH

What about classes, workshops, reading, and other mind-expanding experiences? Even with a mood disorder, you can learn and grow. Doing so will help speed your recovery. And it's also fun!

Don't just assume that the only way to increase your creativity is to use hands-on skills directly in the art. Let's say you wish to take up oil painting. Apart from perhaps taking an oil-painting course, you could also learn about it by reading biographies/monographs of painters who have worked in oil and reading about its history. You could visit museums to examine brush strokes, the effects of underpainting, and the like. And you could also study color theory and the history of color. All of these facets of painting will enrich your final product or maybe even inspire new applications for your creative knowledge. For example, you may learn so much about the paintings at a particular museum that you could apply to become a docent or tour guide there, and share your knowledge with others. Open yourself to new experiences related to your actual goal.

■ SPIRITUALITY

Do you participate in religious services or a faith community? Do you connect with your spirituality in other ways (not counting religious delusions that sometimes accompany manic episodes)?

Do you follow or wish to learn more about New Age philosophies and pursuits such as yoga? Do you find being outdoors spiritually fulfilling? How much time can you devote to these activities? Are you part of a regular group that uses such an activity either as therapy or a form of recreation? This could be great if others in the group are also creatives who invigorate and inspire you; however, if you meet with them regularly simply out of habit, it may be a time to reevaluate how much you benefit from the group. If it's merely become rote, and you don't really *enjoy* doing it, maybe it's time to find a more meaningful way to connect with your spirit, and enhance or support your new direction.

■ LEISURE

Be sure to build in breaks and leisure time—time away from your chosen art. Relaxation provides perspective. How much time will you spend on hobbies, play, and sports? How much to celebrate holidays and vacation? It's a mistake to work twelve hours a day, seven days a week. Trust me, I've done that. Taking time off keeps you energized and focused.

If necessary, actually schedule time-outs. They're just as important to keeping up your creative flow as is working at your craft.

■ SOCIAL CONTRIBUTION

How much time will you spend doing community or volunteer work? Be careful not to overcommit. I've done that as well. When hypomanic, I once was active in fourteen different organizations, served on the board of directors for one, chaired a committee for another, and was president of a third. I struggled to keep on top of my business and wondered why I was so stressed. Duh! Don't do the same.

Sometimes you can "multitask." For instance, through my involvement in DBSA, I gain emotional support and form close relationships, as well as make a social contribution. Be careful, however, not to multitask when one of the tasks requires direct concentration.

Whether you're doing an activity for fun or out of a sense of social consciousness, consider your involvement in terms of whether it offers (a) avenues for advancement of your creativity or (b) outlets for it. If you come away from volunteer work exhausted or frustrated, or feel the hours you give to it interfere with what you really want to do in your spare time, consider delaying or maybe even permanently shelving that activity.

On the other hand, if you have not been involved with community or volunteer work, this may be the time to look into it. Which organizations might help you hone your creative skills, provide valuable contacts, or perhaps even enhance your résumé. Let's say you are trying to get a free-lance design business off the ground. Volunteering to be the brochure or poster designer for a well-regarded community group could be time well spent if it helps you expand your portfolio, exposes you to the public, or brings potential clients. It might even bring a tax deduction!

CALCULATING YOUR TIME

WE ALL HAVE only twenty-four hours a day (much to my disappoint-ment!). We can't stop the earth's rotation just to catch up. We have to work with what we've got. Value that time.

If you're depressed, watch out for negative self-talk that says your time isn't worth as much as other people's. That's just the lowered self-esteem of depression talking, not the truth. *Everyone's* time is extremely valuable, mood disorder or not!

If you're hypomanic or manic, rein in those grandiose demands that other people follow your schedule. Be patient with them, despite the perception that they're so t-e-r-r-i-b-l-y s—l—o—w! Remember, their time is valuable as well, and they must move at their own pace.

Now we'll look at how you'll spend your time in relation to your Whole Life Grid.

Start by determining how much time you spend—or want to spend—on taking care of your physical needs. Answer this when you're relatively stable rather than depressed or manic/hypomanic! If you can, get feed-back from others or ask them to help you. In the Creative Life Toolkit, you'll find a Weekly Time Allotments Form and a Time and Schedule Form similar to the following, which will help you organize your day in blocks of time for all your needs—physical, emotional, and creative. Here are some categories to consider when filling out your forms.

■ **PHYSICAL NEEDS**

Sleep—How much sleep do you need to feel refreshed? Base this on how many hours you sleep when stable as opposed to when you're depressed or manic.

Meals and snacks—How much time will you take to eat three balanced meals a day and any planned snacks, at a leisurely pace? How much time to shop for groceries? To prepare food? To eat and clean up after?

Bathing and dressing—How long will you allow for grooming? Even if you work at home alone, you'll need to bathe and dress sometime!

Exercise—Experts now recommend a minimum of half an hour of aerobic activity each day. You don't have to do it all at once. Exercising for ten minutes, three to six times a day, will do as well. How much will you do?

Destressing and preparing for bed—Allow time for bedtime preparations, if you haven't already included that in time for sleep.

Attending to the Basics

REMEMBER, YOUR PHYSICAL needs are *extremely important*! Ignoring them *always* backfires. Although everyone must sleep, eat, and get some exercise, meeting these needs is more crucial when you have a mood disorder. *You simply can't afford to ignore your physical needs!*

Pay attention to treatment issues, too. Visit your doctor and therapist regularly. Attend to medications and lab tests as needed. Participate in a day program or support group that helps you better manage your disease. Your creativity will surely suffer if you ignore physical and treatment needs!

Treatment and support—How often will you see your doctor and/or therapist? Meet with a support group or talk openly with an understanding friend or family member?

Commuting and errands—Don't forget how much time it takes to get from one place to another. Allot some time for even short errands, too, as these can quickly add up.

■ TIME FOR CREATIVITY

Here are two ways to examine how much time to devote to your creativity. One is mathematical, and one is visual. The mathematical method is for folks who aren't calculator-dependent like me.

Start with the total number of hours in a week (168). In the following examples, I've allotted eight hours of sleep a night, an hour and a half for breakfast and starting the day (bathing, dressing, and so on), and a half an hour in both the morning and the evening for commuting and errands. There's also time each day for a one-hour lunch, half an hour of exercise, a two-hour dinner, and half an hour for stress-reduction activities and preparing for bed.

You may spend (or plan to spend) more or less time on any activity. For instance, I need nine to ten hours of sleep a night, usually take a shorter lunch, and average an hour a day for exercise (including getting to and from the gym). The following examples are just guesstimates. The Creative Life Toolkit has a blank form for your use.

The mathematical method—Record whatever time you'll spend on each activity in the right-hand column of the Weekly Time Allotments form, as in the sample below. Your balance will help you determine the time available for your creative activities.

You're probably wondering why this sample doesn't show the time that work, school, caring for a family, and other activities take. The reason it doesn't is that people often think of those commitments as inflexible, but they rarely are. When you use your imagination (and as a creative, you surely have one), you can come with all sorts of possibilities.

SAMPLE WEEKLY TIME ALLOTMENTS

HOURS PER WEEK = 168	TIME ALLOTMENTS
Sleep:	56.0
De-stressing & preparing for bed:	3.5
Meals & snacks:	28.0
Bathing & dressing:	3.5
Exercise:	3.5
Commuting, errands, etc.:	7.0
Subtotal:	101.5
BALANCE FOR CREATIVE ACTIVITIES:	66.5

The Visual Method—If you prefer a visual approach, check out the following example. *Don't consider this a schedule.* Use it to determine how much time you have available for creative activities. The Creative Life Toolkit has a blank form for your use.

SAMPLE TIME & SCHEDULE FORM

TIME	MON	TUES	WED	THURS	FRI	SAT	SUN
MIDNIGHT							
1–2 AM							
2–3 AM				Sleep			
3–4 AM							
4–5 AM							
5–6 AM							
6–7 AM			Bathe & dress; cook, eat breakfast, & clean up (or eat out)				
7–8 AM			Commuting time				
8–9 AM							
9–10 AM							
10–11 AM							
11 AM– NOON							
Noon			Cook, eat, & clean up lunch (or eat lunch out)				
1–2 PM							
2–3 PM							
3–4 PM							
4–5 PM							
5–6 PM			Commute & Exercise				
6–7 PM			Cook, eat, & clean up dinner (or eat dinner out)				
7–8 PM							
8–9 PM							
9–10 PM			Stress reduction activities				
10–11 PM							
11 PM – MIDNIGHT			Sleep				

Notice that the preceding examples leave 66.5 hours a week open. If you don't require as much time for any of these activities, you'll have that much more time to work with.

Naturally, you may perform these activities at different times. For instance, if you perform at night, you might sleep well into the afternoon and work into the wee hours of the morning. For now, don't worry about specific times. Just estimate how much time an activity takes each day or each week.

If you do something every other week or even monthly, include it in your estimate. For instance, I see my therapist every other week, and each trip takes an hour and a half, but I reserve the time as if I saw her every week. This approach reserves a bit of time for emergencies and surprises, which always come up.

Estimate time for maintaining your health. For instance, it takes me nearly half an hour a week to sort medications into daily pillboxes.

■ SCHEDULING SPECIFIC TIMES

Write activities you want or need to do at a specific time directly on the Time and Schedule form, or shade in the corresponding boxes.

Once you've determined how much time you have available, you can schedule creative time during those hours when you tend to be most energetic. (For me, that's *not* the first thing in the morning!) If you don't yet feel ready to do that, do it after completing this chapter.

■ BUILD IN SOME FLEXIBILITY

As you consider each part of your schedule, estimate how much time each commitment will take. You don't have to decide when you'll do everything. Don't schedule your time too tightly.

Use pieces of paper you can move around to experiment with different activities and different times.

How much time will you allot for leisure? Caring for your home and handling finances? How much time will you invest in relationships and in self-growth? Spirituality and social contributions?

Use your Whole Life Grid and Time and Schedule Form as you answer each question.

 FIFTY-SOMETHING OREGON *artist FD says routine and structure help her keep things stable, but one continuing challenge is getting overbooked when she's sliding into mania and doesn't take time to*

get recharged. "If {free time} happens once a week, I am okay," she says. "I try to keep a few free-time windows open each week. I like at least four hours of time, but a full day and evening of time is heavenly. And I like to have this free time at home."

During her depressions, FD moves forward a step at a time. "I put one foot in front of the other . . . to do small things that eventually lead to getting the big things done." Her advice is, "Frame yourself in as much structure as you can take. . . . Accept when your resources aren't what your mind wants to create. It is actually very rewarding to learn to live within the confines of your life while being creative."

If a written schedule seems "anal," remember, it's only a way to realistically estimate the time available for creative work. You don't have to follow it exactly. This approach is meant to be flexible. Keep in mind that a written schedule will help you focus and manage both your creativity and your mood disorder, for a positive impact on both. At the very least, it makes you aware of how much time you're actually spending on various aspects of your life. That way, you can work on reducing unwanted or unnecessary activities that consume your days . . . or applying your discovered "free" time toward your creative goal.

As you build your schedule, question each habit and assumption carefully. Don't assume you must keep the same commitments or do things at the same time as you do now. Consider varying your routine. Keep asking, *What if? What can I do about this responsibility? How can I arrange more creative time?*

Once you've handled the basics, you're ready to add the other stuff.

THE CONSEQUENCES OF COMMITMENT

THE MAJORITY OF creatives don't spend all of their time on their art. Most have day jobs that may or may not be especially creative. Some attend high school or college. Many have family responsibilities. Others have community commitments. You don't have to devote *every minute* to your art.

If your interest lies in doing rather than being and you want to make a solid commitment, where do you begin? By understanding the potential consequences of that commitment.

Both positive and negative things take place when you make a commitment. On the positive side, you become more conscious of connections related to your talents and opportunities to use them than you were before. On the negative side, once you've made a commitment, doubts, blocks, and barriers instantly arise. That doesn't mean you've made the wrong decision or that it's time to quit. Just consider them opportunities to confirm your commitment.

■ The Positive Side

The part of your brain that makes you more aware of connections and opportunities is called the *reticular activating system*. This system relegates the stimuli that constantly bombard you to one of two places: your conscious mind or your subconscious. Acting as a filter, the reticular activating system alerts you to whatever you might find important and files the rest in your subconscious.

Without this system, you'd be aware of all the sights, sounds, and other sensations you're exposed to simultaneously. It would be like performing onstage fully conscious of everything inside you and everything around you every second. You'd see the ushers escorting latecomers to their seats, the individual slats of the wooden stage floor, the other performers waiting in the wings. You'd hear the audience members' whispers, the humming of the air conditioner, the flush of a toilet in a nearby dressing room. You'd smell your own body odor as well as that of your fellow performers. You'd taste the lingering remnant of your last meal on your tongue. You'd feel the heat from the spotlights on your skin, the silkiness of your costume, the pressure between your feet and the stage floor. It would be overwhelming!

Instead, your reticular activating system watches out for your current needs. What's important to you as the performer in this example is connecting with your audience, hearing the cue to start your part, and concentrating on delivering the best performance you can. The rest is unimportant at that point.

When you wholeheartedly commit to your art, your reticular activating system will consider it a top priority and help you move toward your artistic goals. You'll notice new sights, sounds, and other sensations that relate to your goals. You'll discover useful information in newspapers, books, and magazines. You'll catch related programs on the radio or TV. You'll overhear conversations about your art and meet people whose interests mesh with yours. It's really magical! At the risk of sounding "airy-fairy," the universe will flood you with everything you need. And you'll simultaneously tune out distractions when you need to concentrate to give creativity your all.

This doesn't mean you can commit to your art and then just sit back and watch things fall in place. You must pay attention to the incoming information and use it to move forward. Just as with anything, reaching your goals requires a lot of work.

■ THE NEGATIVE SIDE

When you make such a commitment, doubts, blocks, and barricades also crop up. Major conflicts and fears emerge, frequently the very moment you make that commitment.

You may doubt that you're talented enough. Or cringe at anything short of a spectacular reception. You could have trouble starting or finishing a project or find it hard to concentrate. A friend or family member's illness may require your attention. You might lose the income you're counting on to fulfill your dreams. You might wonder what on earth you were thinking and be tempted to turn and run.

Your conflicts and fears may paralyze you for a while. But that doesn't mean it's time to quit. All these challenges are perfectly normal, for any kind of artist.

Committing to creativity can require a few sacrifices. If you schedule creative time on a day off, you may have to stop sleeping late or spending so much time shopping. If you decide to work on your art during lunch breaks, you'll have to turn down offers to eat lunch out. You may have to cut back on TV viewing, e-mailing jokes, or talking on the phone. You may need to encourage or arrange other activities for your partner or kids to pursue while you spend some time alone; or hire a babysitter during your creative time. Once you and your family get used to making such sacrifices, you'll be surprised how much time is left.

Changing long-established habits takes a while. Some experts say it takes three weeks or more to ease a new habit into your routine. If you start making exceptions, those exceptions will snowball: your creative time will dwindle and your creative "faucet" may go dry. That in itself can trigger a depression. Unless a life-threatening emergency arises, follow a "no exceptions" policy.

But if your illness gets so severe that that's not possible, don't beat yourself up. If a major depression drains your energy and keeps you in bed, resume your creative work as soon as you can. If a manic episode makes you unfocused or scattered, get treated and then move on. Your commitment to use your talents is important, but you must deal with your mood disorder first.

PROTECTING YOUR CREATIVE TIME

ONCE YOU'VE RESERVED your creative time, make it sacred. It takes a lot of discipline, but it's extremely important. Avoid the trap of thinking, "I'm not inspired enough today; I'll do twice as much tomorrow." Those tomorrows quickly snowball. It gets harder and harder to regain that creative time once you've let it slip away.

This doesn't apply when you're in severe depression or so manic that you lose control. But the rest of the time, do your best to protect the time you've set aside for creative work.

It's all right letting yourself go as long as you can get yourself back.

—Mick Jagger, member of the Rolling Stones

Protecting creative time often requires developing new habits, like not answering the phone or the door. Or telling the kids to solve arguments on their own. Protecting creative time may require learning to say no without apology or guilt. That's no easy task when your confidence has bottomed out from depression or when you're oh-so-certain you can do it all. Creative time is precious no matter how inexperienced or accomplished you are. No matter whether you plan to make it big or to use your gifts for your own enjoyment, demand respect for your artistic needs.

Don't think your time isn't worth much if you're not earning money. Using creativity to heal is just as meaningful—perhaps more so—than making big bucks. Show others you're serious about your commitment and do whatever you can to use that time well.

KANSAN SK, AGE *twenty-six, says she loves "art, creating using oil pastels, soft pastels, watercolor, clay, jewelry-making, costuming, and lots of arts and crafts. I can go from being able to see something in my head and creating that exact thing on paper." However, her mood shifts challenge her ability to use her talents. At those times, she says, "I can't grasp the basics of drawing. Which makes it frustrating."*

Deep breathing and writing in a journal help SK cope. She communicates how she feels when a mood shift starts, and describes her thoughts to understand them better. "I can pull out something I have done or written and I can look back at what I was going through at the time and reconnect with that emotion."

"Find that something that brings you a sense of inner peace because that is what matters. Once you have that peace and calm inside yourself you can apply it to everything in your life," SK says. "It's a way to let go without a stigma. Mood disorders come with a stigma for some people, when you let go of that and realize it doesn't mean you're crazy, it doesn't mean you are a bad person, it means you have something extra to offer when you harness it in a good way. You come to peace within yourself, still have bad days, but are able to share. And you know you will make it."

EXERCISING YOUR MUSE

NUMEROUS EXERCISES EXIST to help you expand creative thinking. Rather than detail them here, I'll mention some general approaches.

■ CREATIVITY WORKOUTS

In *The Creating Brain,* Nancy Andreasen suggests a daily "creativity workout." Here are its major components:

- Explore a new, unfamiliar subject area in depth.
- Imagine yourself as anyone or anything else and in any other place.
- Observe what's happening around you and improve your ability to describe it.
- Think without censoring your thoughts and in a way that disconnects you from the outside world.

Andreasen recommends you devote at least a half an hour a day to your creativity workout.

■ Journaling

Many authors suggest variants of journaling. Journaling involves more than relaying what's happened to you each day. It includes expressing thoughts and feelings and working things out on paper. Two examples include freewriting and morning pages.

When freewriting, guru Natalie Goldberg says, you must allow yourself "to write the worst junk in the world." She stresses the importance of not giving in to self-censorship. Instead, she suggests you keep your hand moving and don't stop to make corrections or cross anything out. In *Writing Down the Bones*, Goldberg offers many helpful exercises to get you started.

Best-selling author Anne Lamott notes the importance of moving forward even when you don't know where you're going. She relays a story about her brother when he was ten and overwhelmed about writing a report about birds. Their father's advice was, "Bird by bird, buddy. Just take it bird by bird."

This advice applies to any kind of art. So get started and keep moving step by step, or image by image, sound by sound, or word by word.

In *The Artist's Way,* Julia Cameron suggests starting each day by writing three handwritten stream-of-consciousness pages that she calls "morning pages." Techniques like these are particularly helpful when you have a mood disorder. They help drain the "gunk" out your brain each morning and clear obsessive thoughts and worries. You can then more easily concentrate on your passion and open the creative flow.

Kansas writer CG, age eighteen, says, "I make myself write a little every day. It's never going to be like I was when I was up [manic], but I can still try."

Aim to journal as frequently as your illness allows. If you miss some days, be easy on yourself and just pick up again as soon as possible. Your days go much smoother when you journal or write morning pages.

■ Nurturing Your Inner Child

Julia Cameron also suggests going on weekly "artist dates." During an artist date, you explore new places, new experiences, new ideas, or view ordinary things in different ways. You use the time to connect with your inner artist—or inner child.

You might ride a bus or bicycle around town to explore alternative routes. You might go to a foreign restaurant and taste foods you've never heard of. You might lie back on a blanket in the park, close your eyes, and absorb the surrounding sounds. You might indulge in an unfamiliar art. Reserve quality time for your inner artist just as you would for a child.

Rather than think of creativity workouts, journaling, and artist dates as demands to cram into a crowded schedule, consider them vital (and fun!) activities to summon your Muse. They will improve both your creativity and your mental health.

Now that you have reserved time for them, you're ready to build and/or enhance your creative skills.

> '[Write] every day for a little while,' my father kept saying.
> . . . 'Do it by prearrangement with yourself. Do it as a debt
> of honor.'
>
> —Anne Lamott (1954-), *Bird by Bird*

· 8 ·
Shoring Up Your Skills

IF YOU ARE interested or talented in any type of creative art, you're meant to *do* something with it. It's part of your identity. Part of who you are. Not expressing that part will likely worsen your mood disorder and surely limit your self-actualization. Please don't do this to yourself!

So where do you start? You can obtain or improve creative skills in a number of ways:

- Conventional schooling
- Informal classes or workshops
- Independent study
- Private lessons
- Rehearsals and practice
- Conferences
- Interactions with others who share your interests
- Mentors

In any kind of learning situation, criticism will likely rear its head. Criticism simply surrounds the creative territory. It's something you must simply learn to deal with. Nobody can please *everybody*. Not even some who's perpetually hypomanic.

It's also crucial to learn and work your creative process. Don't expect miracles!

This chapter presents a variety of options for learning and strengthening creative skills.

DEALING WITH CRITICISM—YOUR OWN AND OTHERS'

IF YOU GET bitter and defensive about someone's not liking your idea, you may feel as if the person is attacking you directly. Sometimes you'll feel like attacking back. But if you allow your mind to fool you that way, the one you hurt will be you. Remember, it's just one person's opinion. Listen to his or her comments, then just say, "Thank you for your feedback."

Later, when you're calmer, consider whether any part of that person's message feels valid. Think about what seems to be on target and what seems to be way off. Most often, you'll feel these answers in your gut. If you have trouble deciding, get a second opinion—or third or fourth. Don't mention the first person's comments when asking for additional opinions. Once you've determined which comments to accept and which to ignore, put the incident behind you.

If you're afraid your work isn't good enough to show to others, remember this is a *learning* opportunity and others taking a course or attending a conference are learning too. Creative works don't have to be perfect. In fact, they're often more intriguing when they're not.

The biggest obstacle for most creatives afraid of showing their work is their inner critic. This is especially true of people who suffer depressive episodes. The unrealistic thoughts that accompany depression often lead to "clogs" like this:

- People will laugh at me if my work isn't perfect.
- If another student doesn't like my work, I can't make it as a creative.
- If the teacher or other students praise someone else's work, it means mine is no good.
- They don't really like my work; they are just pretending to because they're afraid to upset me.

GEORGIA WRITER MM, *age thirty-six, says when she's up, she's written as many as "fifteen to twenty pages in a day or two. . . . When I am depressed I force myself to write in my diary, but when I'm up, I have to write, something, anything, I just have to put words on paper."*

But she throws those pages out when her mood becomes more stable. "I think anyone else would think they were stupid," MM says. "I don't have the confidence in myself to let others read my stuff."

Instead of lashing out at those she's angry with, she writes about her feelings to keep from hurting theirs. She says she usually trashes what she writes or stores it "in one of my many boxes and chests I seem to collect."

Don't listen to that inner critic. It's lying to you! No creative is consistently outstanding. Don't expect that of yourself, especially while you're honing your skills!

Daniel Nettle says imaginative people must be "abnormally, almost irrationally, buoyant," and that they must produce a lot if they're to be successful. He points to psychologist Dean Keith Simonton's work, which indicates that "what distinguishes the most eminent producers from the rest . . . is not that their work is consistently excellent. It is mainly that they produce a lot, and, the more they produce, the more likely it is that some of it will be excellent."

Don't, however, feel pressured to produce too much too soon. Allow time to absorb new ideas and to go through the entire creative process. Remember that creative works need time to grow.

And finally, especially if you opt for formal education, watch out if you get into a manic or hypomanic state, as you may be inclined to express your own viewpoint too forcefully or insist that others adopt your ideas. Challenging your instructor or arguing with classmates usually isn't constructive, even if you do have a "better" idea.

CONVENTIONAL SCHOOLING

MANY PEOPLE WANTING to develop a new interest or tap a talent they've submerged for years assume the best way (or only way) to do so is to return to school. Some assume school isn't an option because they're afraid they won't get in.

Twenty-something, bipolar Florida writer, artist, photographer, actor, and dancer YU is a Ford scholar. She uses creativity to help her stand out, for instance, she included a comic book with her college application. "I have gotten accepted to higher classes," she says, "because I am creative and I try different things."

While it's important to learn the basics of an art, it's rarely necessary to obtain a formal degree. Much depends on what you want to do with that knowledge. Certainly, if you want to use your art for your own enjoyment, you won't require a lot of training. If, on the other hand, you wish to teach that art, you'll need a solid grounding and most likely an advanced degree.

If you're hypomanic or manic, formal education will help you discover there's more to your art than you imagine. New information you pick up will slow you down a bit, enhance your skills, and bring you closer to reality.

If you frequently experience the loss of self-confidence that depression brings, you may feel more secure about your skills if you get formal training. You'll be less obsessed and worried about what you don't know. You won't become defensive about not knowing everything you think you "should"—and would know—if only you'd gone to a conventional school. Defensiveness about a perceived lack of knowledge can make you unreceptive to new information.

■ CHOOSING A SUITABLE LEARNING ENVIRONMENT

People react differently to the same learning environment. The situation that stimulates one person will be much too stressful for another. Stay clear of high-stress, competitive programs until you've been stable at least a couple of years. Talk over your plans with your doctor and therapist before applying.

If you choose to attend such a program, make certain you have solid support. You may need to go slower or take fewer classes due to concentration or memory problems. If you need special accommodations, get advice from your state disability or rehabilitation office or from a similar office on the school campus. You might also inform your teacher that you have an illness or are taking medications that affect your concentration and memory. Sometimes, a teacher will work with you to reduce your stress.

■ ONE DOWNSIDE OF FORMAL EDUCATION

Conventional schooling does however bring a potential disadvantage, especially in creative fields. Out of a concern to do things the "right" way, you may actually jeopardize your creativity. This is particularly true if your instructors are sticklers about tradition. If you get too absorbed in tradition and try to force your work into a rigid mold, you're less likely to have original ideas. If you feel that an instructor is leading you in the wrong direction, try taking a different class in the subject, taught by someone else, to see if it's just a personality issue with that instructor, or a broader problem.

There's many a bestseller that could have been prevented by a good teacher.

—Short-story writer Flannery O'Connor (1925-64)

One of Georgia O'Keeffe's biographers, Roxana Robinson, relays how formal education affected O'Keeffe's work.

WISCONSIN-BORN ABSTRACT *painter Georgia O'Keeffe (1887–1986) was best known for her series of magnified flowers. Two of these paintings are Red Poppy and Black Iris III. After a severe "nervous breakdown" in 1933, O'Keeffe began painting stark animal-bone pieces in the desert. Black Cross, New Mexico is one example.*

Although her vision faded during her last few years, O'Keeffe worked on her art until her death, just a few weeks short of her ninety-ninth birthday.

At Chicago's Art Institute and New York City's Art Student League, O'Keeffe's artistic training had focused on imitating classical and European art produced primarily by men. This approach discouraged O'Keeffe. "I began to realize that a lot of people had done this same kind of painting before I came along," she said. "I didn't think I could do it any better." Although formal classes helped her master techniques in several different media, O'Keeffe was unfulfilled because these styles squelched her creativity.

When O'Keeffe later studied at New York's Columbia University, her instructor, Arthur Wesley Dow, encouraged students to rely more on their own ideas rather than imitate traditional styles. He introduced his students to Eastern artists' use of minimalism and open space.

According to Robinson, Dow's instructional approach inspired the "powerful, confident, feminine . . . highly personal" works O'Keeffe became known for. O'Keeffe introduced warmer, brighter colors than those traditional painters had used.

Here's Frank Barron's take on traditional approaches: "If the society we live in puts too much emphasis on an established 'right' way of doing things, it may cause a loss of adventuresomeness and willingness to experiment. The creative is often the unconventional. To be original means to be different in some important way, and often it takes courage and daring to be different from those around us."

Formal education can stifle creativity, but it still has its place. If you opt for formal education, you may qualify for financial aid, based on your diagnosis. A number of grants, scholarships, and government programs help people with disabilities, and because mental illnesses are disabilities, we can get assistance unavailable to "normal" folks. Finally, our disorders bring some perks!

■ The PASS Program

One government resource is PASS (Plan for Achieving Self-Support). PASS is a work-incentive program developed to help people with disabilities obtain the schooling they need to get a job or start a business. The Social Security Administration oversees the PASS program. A mental illness becomes a disability officially when you are unable "to engage in substantial gainful activity by reason of any medically determinable physical or mental impairment or combination of impairments that has lasted or can be expected to last for a continuous period of not less than twelve months or result in death."

The PASS program helps with such expenses as tuition, books, and supplies while you're in school, work-related tools and equipment for a job, and start-up costs for a business. You can get help with additional expenses, depending on your PASS and your circumstances.

You can even use a PASS for jobs and businesses in the creative arts. The job or business you choose for a PASS must have a strong possibility of meeting your financial needs well enough to eliminate your need for government assistance.

If you're currently receiving SSI (Supplemental Security Income), a PASS will allow you to collect and set aside more money without jeopardizing your SSI income. If you aren't receiving SSI because your income is too high, a PASS will allow you to set aside enough money that you may qualify for SSI. You'll find information on contacting PASS in the Resources section.

■ OTHER FUNDING SOURCES

Many other scholarships, grants, and fellowships are available for education. Some places to start searching for them are the College Board, FastWeb, the Foundation Center, and Sallie Mae College Answer. Contact information appears in the Resources section.

One type of aid that many low-income people obtain is the federal Pell grant. Pell grants are helpful if your income has decreased because of your mood disorder. Provided you attend classes and meet other obligations, you don't have to pay back a Pell grant. The College Board offers complete information on Pell grants.

Some arts organizations and arts commissions also award scholarships and grants. Most require you to submit samples of your work. One starting point for finding arts organizations is Arts Resource Network. Another is the book *Putting Creativity to Work: Careers in the Arts for People with Disabilities,* edited by Paul Scribner—even if you're not disabled.

The Resources section has provides more information about these options.

Long-term conventional study may not appeal to you if you're unable or reluctant to leave home when depressed, or if you get impatient with teachers and classmates when you're manic or hypomanic. But you have many other options.

INFORMAL CLASSES AND WORKSHOPS

IF YOU DON'T want to invest the time it requires to return to school and obtain a degree or don't feel you need an in-depth education to enjoy your art, you can look into informal classes and workshops. These are often offered by arts organizations, art museums, colleges and universities, community schools, crafts stores, and senior centers. Some are half-day or evening sessions; some run several weeks. Frequently, class and workshop schedules mesh with school semesters or sessions. Informal classes and workshops are often much less expensive than traditional education. Some programs may be free or require minimum financial outlay; others may be quite costly. If you aren't sure you wish to pursue a particular art, opt for free or less expensive programs until you're fairly certain it's worth it to invest more. A higher price does not necessarily indicate that an instructor has more expertise.

As an adult, I've taken ballet, graphic design, guitar, and Web site design through The University of Texas's informal class program. I've taken life drawing and page design at local art museums. And, after deciding to focus on writing, I've taken so many classes and workshops through the Writers' League of Texas that I may very well hold the record!

Informal classes offer great opportunities to network with other attendees about other courses or educational options that may be available in your area that aren't well advertised.

Whatever your preferred mode of learning, you can supplement it by studying on your own.

INDEPENDENT STUDY

IN THE PAST, independent study consisted primarily of college correspondence courses and reading whatever you could find about your art. Today we have many more options. Organizations offer courses on all kinds of things on the Internet, and many of these courses are free. Some sponsors offer a limited number of free classes and then sell you additional classes, on a time-limited subscription basis or a one-time payment.

Creativity is a type of learning process where the teacher and pupil are located in the same individual.

—British children's book author and illustrator Beatrix Potter (1866–1943), best known for *The Tale of Peter Rabbit*

On the Web are many free complete or sample classes on audio editing, design, desktop publishing, digital photography, guitar and piano, music theory, painting, Web site design, and all types of writing. Some links on the Internet lead to dead ends, such as advertisements for arts schools, colleges, and universities, or for off-line events, products, or people looking for creative work. Two good sources for free classes are About.com University and Barnes & Noble University. Internet (or distance learning) courses take advantage of technology by having you submit assignments by e-mail or post work on Web sites. Some have you scan artwork or display photos by uploading them to the Web for grading or critique.

You could also design your own coursework by picking up reading requirements for college courses (which may be available on the college's Web listings for the courses) and then reading the books on your own. Other terrific resources are the bibliography and resource sections at the back of books, which can point you toward even more about the subject that has been published or posted on the Web. Or plug appropriate keywords into an online book dealer's Search function to see what's available, and then check out the books at your library if you don't want or can't afford to buy them.

Still another avenue is to study the art or craft itself. If you'd love to take up quilting, for instance, take every opportunity you can to examine both historic and recently made quilts to see how they're stitched together, and what patterns and colors have been used. Let the art itself speak to you about how to proceed.

 CANADIAN ARTIST AND *writer JS, age thirty-three, says her illness allows her to "see the world with a very broad perspective" and that her problem-solving and analyzing abilities help her pick up many creative skills on her own.*

She taught herself how to create "jewelry, kids' books, poetry, dream-catchers," and many other things "with very little instruction, and no manuals." Once someone taught her how to make single- and double-crochet stitches, she made "an almost professional-looking set" of booties and a sweater with a pocket by merely analyzing another set and using "creative commonsense."

JS rarely starts something, she says, until she's "really in the mood to make it," because she gets so obsessed she doesn't want to stop until it's done.

JS uses her gifts primarily for herself but sometimes teaches her new skills to friends and family. "It can be very therapeutic to be able to use your creative talents to express yourself so that you can either help heal yourself . . . or cope with day-to-day stuff," she explains. "It also helps you keep busy in a healthy way."

MANUFACTURER-SPONSORED PROGRAMS

IF YOUR ART involves computer software or hardware (audio editing, design, desktop publishing, digital photography, Web site design, and so on), check with their manufacturers. Some offer free face-to-face classes or helpful information within communities, over the Internet, or through e-mail newsletters.

I've found informal classes offered by Adobe Systems particularly helpful for learning new design and publishing software. I once attended a free two-day training for which I paid only the cost of my hotel and travel. Most software comes with online help, a full user manual, and/or a demo to get you started. You may wish to expand that knowledge by participating in a user group or reading other books that describe features in more depth.

LIBRARIES AND INTERLIBRARY LOANS

OTHER SELF-STUDY options may be available at your public library or from other libraries through interlibrary loans. Some libraries charge shipping costs when you borrow materials from these other libraries. When not enrolled, I've gained access to all the libraries at The University of Texas by purchasing a visitor's card for a small annual fee. I've devoured a wealth of information from the Austin Public Library.

One further source of information is specialty book clubs. One such club, Writer's Digest Book Club, sells annually updated books not only on writing but on other arts as well, for example:

- *Artists & Graphic Designers Market*
- *Children's Writer's & Illustrator's Market*
- *Photographer's Market*
- *Songwriter's Market*

Although focused toward marketing your work, these guides contain other helpful guidance. You can find other information in trade magazines or in the arts sections of bookstores.

Remember that, in addition to books, libraries often offer audio and video recordings. If you're a dance fan who wants to dip a toe into performing, look in the library's catalog for dance videos and CDs of music to dance to. If you're interested in theatre, look for videotaped plays. Also available on video are many documentaries and how-to demonstrations concerning crafts or fine arts. As for music, in addition to current albums, library collections may contain a treasure trove of LPs and CDs of recordings no longer commercially available. As with books, you can often borrow these amazing resources absolutely free! Explore whether public libraries or universities have special collections that you can use on-site.

Museums may have a private library they permit people to use on the premises. Often, these include rare books or videotapes or historic materials that could be very instructive. Ask at their information desk if such a collection is available, and what you must do to access it. Simply taking an interest in the art or signing up for a lecture may be enough to gain access to the institution's private holdings.

PRIVATE LESSONS

MANY OF US associate independent study in the arts with childhood dance or music lessons. Although one-on-one attention is less prevalent for adults, it still has its place. Some good places to locate instructors who will work with you privately are the same places that offer informal classes and workshops. You can often locate a potential instructor by contacting an arts organization or a nearby college or university department devoted to your art. Sometimes advanced students will provide private instruction.

REHEARSALS AND PRACTICE

OF COURSE, ACTORS, dancers, and musicians are well aware of the importance of practice and rehearsal. What may escape other types of creatives, though, is the importance of practicing (and sometimes rehearsing) their art. For example, sculptors may practice with less expensive materials than those used in their final piece. Filmmakers may practice by taking multiple shots of the same scenes or by producing very short films. Photographers might practice by shooting a subject until they obtain the perfect shot.

Watching creatives at work or in rehearsal is another way to learn. If you want to become an instrumentalist or conductor, see if your local orchestra permits outsiders to attend rehearsals. If you want to learn more about creating costumes for the theatre, ask to take a backstage tour of a professional company's costume rooms. These experiences can provide a taste of a professional working environment and the creative process, in a way that is far more real than any classroom environment.

CONFERENCES AND CONVENTIONS

CONFERENCES AND CONVENTIONS also provide great opportunities for creative growth. They're not just for academics, businesspeople, and Shriners. They're excellent places to learn more about your art, to make contacts, and to find other helpful information.

Don't rule out a conference just because of cost. Many conferences offer scholarships, and others allow those who volunteer to attend free or at a reduced price. Just a few hours stuffing conference packets or helping at the registration table may be enough to get you in the door.

If you're unfamiliar with organizations that sponsor such events in your art, try searching with terms such as "photography conference," "photographers association," or "photography group." The book *Putting Creativity to Work*, listed the Resources section, also contains information on many types of arts organizations.

INTERACTIONS WITH OTHER CREATIVES

AT SOME POINT you need to step beyond the safe bounds of your own space and out into the world. This can involve interacting with other creatives in a class or critique group, or collaborating on projects.

If your self-confidence is down or you're feeling isolated because of depression, challenge yourself to speak to at least one person before things get going in a class or group and/or after things wrap up.

Good starting points for such conversations are:

- Asking if they've taken a class (or been to a group) like this before, or what interested them in coming.
- Asking them about their work before sharing information about yours, particularly if you're hypomanic or manic. This will usually open a person up as well as help you calm yourself.
- Actively focusing on what the other person is saying rather than what you plan to say yourself.
- Not rushing when you talk. If you don't feel you have anything valuable enough to say, or think you're too much of a newbie, just say you're there to learn all you can.

Again, if you're on the hypomanic or manic side, watch out for coming on too strong. Slow yourself down and let others talk about their interests before you share those great ideas you have.

Don't volunteer to collaborate with everyone on everything that comes up, or on a project that might be over your head. It's easy to get overstimulated when you're among fellow creatives because it's exciting to hear about new projects and ideas. Remind yourself that you can head in only one direction at once. Don't abandon your own priorities because you're so enthused about everything you hear.

If working with another person sounds exciting, at least sleep on it a night or two before making a commitment. First, get to know your potential collaborator over at least a few days. Chapter 13 contains more information about collaborating and communicating effectively.

■ MORE ABOUT HANDLING CRITICISM, REJECTION, AND DISAPPOINTMENT

All creatives must learn how to deal with criticism, rejection, and disappointment. That's especially hard for many of us with mood disorders, particularly during depression. If your self-esteem is down to begin with, it's hard not to take criticism and rejection personally. And disappointments feel like the end of the world. But they're not.

I handed in a script last year and the studio didn't change one word. The word they didn't change was on page eighty-seven.

—Actor, comic, director, and screenwriter Steve Martin, introducing the Best Adapted Screenplay award at the 2003 Oscars

Remember, criticism is just someone's *opinion*. As a rule, most people are judging the suitability of *your work* to see if it matches their own interests or meets their foreseeable needs—not judging *you* personally. And often they base their opinions entirely on their own taste.

Frequently, a critic is way off base. Other people may have completely different opinions. Whenever possible, gather feedback from several sources rather than taking one person's, or one group's, to heart.

We don't like their sound, and guitar music is on the way out.

—Decca Recording Company, rejecting the Beatles, 1962

Having authorities judge or reject your work is difficult. If you've set your sights on a leading role, a solo, or a published work, it may break your heart when the director, conductor, agent, or publisher chooses someone else. But other chances will come along.

TWENTY-ONE-YEAR-OLD *Nevada writer, actor, artist, dancer, and photographer VM says her illness has challenged her creative talents by making her paranoid about sharing her work with others. She'll think, "it won't be up to par, when it always is."*

VM currently views her writing as "an exercise to get my emotions out in the open." She hopes to break into freelance writing soon. Her advice to others is, "If you've been diagnosed with bipolar, try not to let it get you down. . . . You probably have a hidden talent just like I do, and many other people with this ailment. Although it takes satisfaction from your life that others get to experience, it also gives you something nobody else has. In a way we are lucky, as bad as it sounds."

If you get rejected when you're manic or hypomanic, you might be offended that you weren't chosen. Shouting at the person or firing off a nasty letter only sets you back, but calmly asking what you can do to get chosen the next time could help. You may not always have a chance to get such feedback, but when you can, ask. Constructive criticism can tell you where you might improve. Don't tune out completely if you don't like what you're being told, and don't presume the person doesn't know what he or she is talking about. You may miss what you really do need to know. Plus, you may be beating yourself or your critic up over something different than what the person actually meant. Maybe your work was indeed very, very good, but someone else's just happened to be better or that person fit the need better than you did.

*R*esentment is like drinking poison and then hoping it will kill your enemies.

—Nelson Mandella (1918–), former president of South Africa, civil rights leader, and winner of the 1993 Nobel Peace Prize

Likewise, avoid retaliating against the person who was chosen for that role or solo. Don't resent someone who has just obtained an agent or publishing contract. Instead, extend your congratulations and ask that person for advice.

Don't just give up when your work gets criticized or rejected. Try to learn something from the experience. If you're angry, express your anger appropriately and privately at home (say, by beating on a pillow or working out frustrations by exercising), and then keep moving forward.

■ CRITIQUE GROUPS

As a writer, I get a lot of value out of attending manuscript critique groups and writing groups. Although that idea may be intimidating, remember that critique group members are there for the same purpose. Some may have years of experience; others may be total newbies. But each work being critiqued is a newbie, too.

Critique groups are either "open" or "closed." Open groups regularly welcome new members. Closed groups limit the number who can participate.

If they turn you away, it's not because of who you are. They're simply ensuring that each member gets enough time to receive a useful critique, and going over their maximum membership could jeopardize that.

In the groups I've attended—all open critique groups—members bring multiple copies of their current manuscript for others to review. We distribute one copy to each member to read silently during the meeting. Then we discuss each person's work as a group.

Each member offers a different perspective. Some help you clarify your message. Others generate ideas that never occurred to you. Still others provide the exact tip you need to make your work shine. In addition to commenting on what you've produced, such groups brainstorm together, share marketing ideas, and exchange leads for projects. Group members' comments may conflict, but you weigh the information and decide if you agree. Use whatever comments seem helpful and discard the rest.

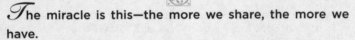

The miracle is this—the more we share, the more we have.

—Actor, film director, photographer, and poet Leonard Nimoy (1931-), best known for portraying Spock in *Star Trek*

Occasionally someone in a critique group will offer only negative comments. Negative criticism is hurtful but it's usually based on self-protective snobbery. If negative behavior occurs in a group, don't take it personally. Rather than argue with that critic, say you'll consider his or her point of view, or mention that the purpose of the group is to provide constructive feedback. In any case, try to stay calm. Remind yourself that the people in the critique group are commenting (or should be) only on your current creation, not on you or your artistry as a whole.

Learn to distinguish between negative and constructive criticism. Constructive criticism aids creative growth. When we critique constructively, we "sandwich" gentle constructive suggestions in-between statements about what we liked best. Expect this for yourself and model it when you critique others.

Some critique groups rave about your work but offer no useful feedback. It's flattering to hear how much someone loves your work, but that doesn't help you polish it. If you join a group that only bickers *or* provides only flattering critiques, move on. If you think the group might be helpful but you're not certain, go at least three times before deciding whether to join. As a rule, different people show up from meeting to meeting. You just might click with someone who shows up the second or third time.

COMPETITION

MANY PEOPLE WHO enter creative fields are concerned about their competition or about others stealing their ideas. Competition certainly exists, but it doesn't have to do you in. No one is the same or taps their talent in the same way that you do.

I know it's very difficult to lose out to a rival. It takes a lot of practice to learn how to keep from shutting down. The person who rejects your work usually has a specific need in mind—a different body type to fill a performance role, a film of a different genre or length, a different type of instrument or vocal range. Don't let losing out to someone else damage your self-worth.

Do your best to realize that you and your rivals have different things to offer, even if those differences seem slight to you. Sometimes your work or talents will fit the situation best; other times, your competitors' will. The same person who chooses the other person today may choose you tomorrow.

Some creatives pass along opportunities they're too busy to tackle or opportunities that might fit you better. I've received a few jobs that way and have passed along many others. So treat your fellow creatives well!

Be nice to people on your way up because you meet them on your way down.

—Singer, pianist, comedian, and actor Jimmy Durante (1893–1980)

Just like depression and mania, competition comes and goes. Thank goodness competition isn't nearly as severe as mood disorders!

MENTORS

BACK IN THE old days, people learned their craft by working as an apprentice for a master in the art. These days, you have to seek a mentor on your own. This more-experienced person can show you the ropes and suggest ways to meet challenges and resolve problems.

Someone you meet through an arts organization, at a class or workshop, in a critique group, or at a conference may have interests similar to yours but considerably more experience. Such a person is an excellent candidate to mentor you.

It's sometimes intimidating to approach a new person, especially an authority. If you know someone who'll introduce you that's great. But often you won't. In such a case, stand where the person can see you and signal that he or she is ready to talk. Don't interrupt the person's current conversation or "get in his or her face."

When the person turns to you, say you're new to the field and eager to learn as much as you can. Ask if the person has ever mentored someone, and if he or she would be willing to mentor you. See if you can meet occasionally for lunch or coffee so you can pick the other person's brain. Most people are happy to share what they know.

 AWARD-WINNING INDIANA *novelist, short-story author, and professor Frances Sherwood's bipolar disorder went undiagnosed and untreated for thirty-five years. Her disorder made it difficult to sit still long enough to concentrate and write. Depression blocked her creativity and mania "frittered" it away. Although she started writing professionally in 1986, she admits, "It took me a long time to gain confidence."*

When asked whether she had a mentor, Sherwood recalled a psychiatrist who offered hope during a 1990 hospitalization. The doctor "took my pain seriously," she says, and "believed in me."

Sherwood has found cognitive therapy particularly valuable. Medication, willpower, writing a daily to-do list, and remarrying at the age of fifty-five also helped, she says. For other creatives with mood disorders, Sherwood urges, "Don't be afraid of professionally prescribed medicine. Have hope."

If someone isn't receptive to your request to mentor you, it doesn't mean no one will be. Politely ask for a referral to another person in the field. Ask, but don't beg or press the issue. Provide a business card or a note with your name and contact information so the person can reach you later. Sometimes no one comes to mind at the time you're asking, but the person thinks of someone later on.

Well-established studio artists—like painters, potters, or photographers sometimes take on assistants to do studio chores (preparing clay, washing out brushes, sweeping) in exchange for informal lessons and critiques.

No matter what your level of skill is, you can always learn more and improve. Keep your work from becoming stagnant by doing something to expand your knowledge every year.

As you learn, retain work for a portfolio or a demo. Keep a list of trainings, credits, or information you may need to show others what you can do. Many times, you'll be surprised how little evidence you need to prove your talent. One of my greatest regrets is not shooting a video— or even photos—when my plays were produced, because I was living on Cloud Nine. All I have are scripts, memories, and paper programs.

YOUR IDEAL LEARNING ENVIRONMENT

NOW LET'S EXAMINE the ways you prefer to learn and how your mood disorder influences them. Consider the following questions in relation to the ways you tend to feel and act during depressive or manic/hypomanic episodes.

- Does being with other people overstimulate or scare you?
- When manic, do you tend to offend or scare others?
- Do you tend to isolate during depressive episodes?
- Is it hard for you to sit still and listen?
- Do you dominate conversations or argue with others when you're manic/hypomanic?
- Do you have trouble concentrating during an episode?
- Is it hard to learn new information when you're depressed?
- Does it bug you when others require more time or more explanation than you do?
- Are you nearly always late when you go someplace?
- Do appointments and commitments often slip your mind?

If you answered yes to most of these questions and you tend to have frequent episodes, you may want to focus on independent study, private lessons, or working with a mentor rather than other, more formal or group-related learning options. In any case, research the options available in your community or one you'd consider relocating to.

Read the business pages in phone books and the back pages of trade magazines. Look for brochures, flyers, and business cards posted on bulletin boards at theatres, museums, crafts stores, dance studios, performance halls, camera shops, and libraries. If you have Internet access, search for the type of art you want to learn or improve, plus the words learn and classes. For example: search for filmmaking+learn+classes.

A chart like the following can help you record the details. This example is for someone who wants to learn how to make videos with professional studio equipment. The Creative Life Toolkit contains a blank form for your use.

SAMPLE LEARNING OPTIONS & INVESTMENTS

LEARNING OPTIONS			INVESTMENTS
Name, Place, & Teacher	Phone & Address	Day, Time, & Dates	Cost (include Books, Tools, & Supplies)
Television Production I, Radio-TV-Film Program, Community College	979-123-4567 13579 Outskirts Road Yourtown, ST	Lectures: Tues. & Thurs. 8–11 a.m. Labs: Tu/Th — 2 hrs between 1 & 7 p.m. Jan. 16–May 17	$240/class (includes lab) Books $200 Blank tapes $6
Television Production I Community Access TV	979-345-6789 6789 Central Yourtown, ST	Sat. 9-12, 2-5 Feb. 16	Class $200 Blank tapes $4
Film Society Conference/Workshop	898-123-4567 Outoftown, ST	March 16-18 Register by Jan. 5	Conference $300 Workshop $100 Gas $75 Hotel $128 Parking $21 Extra meals $36 Blank tapes $2

Once you've done your research, you can make an informed decision. There are, of course, other factors to consider than days, times, dates, and costs. For instance, the person using this sample chart might choose a semester-long class to obtain hands-on experience or a degree. Or, he or she might choose to join the community access workshop because the station allows those who take it to produce their own shows. Or, the person might choose the conference and its associated workshop to make out-of-town contacts and see what's going on in the industry.

It is the nature of an idea to be communicated, written, spoken, done. The idea is like grass. It craves light, likes crowds, thrives on crossbreeding, grows better for having been stepped on.

—American writer Ursula K. Le Guin (1929–), *The Dispossessed*

· 9 ·

Finding and Organizing
Your Creative Space

ONCE YOU'VE COMMITTED to spending more time on your talents, you'll need a place to work on them. The type of surroundings you need for creative work varies with the phase of the creative process that you're in, says Mihaly Csikszentmihalyi. During the planning and preparation phase, you need an orderly, familiar environment, where you can concentrate without distraction.

When allowing your subconscious to "moodle" over creative ideas, you need more stimulating environments—places where you can make new connections and gain new insights. During the implementation and evaluation phases, you need to return to more familiar environments, ideally, the space where you'll spend most of your creative time.

Sketchbook drawings, story ideas, and haunting melodies aside, you'll need a place to work in. For most creative pursuits, you need not rent an office or studio—particularly at first.

For example, a jeweler or a stained-glass artist might need only a table or workbench for assembling pieces and an area in which to store a soldering iron, some small tools, or materials like metals, glass, beads, and stones.

A musician might need only an instrument and a cabinet to hold sheet music. A dancer may need only a clear floor and some closet or drawer space in which to store dance shoes, leotards, and such.

The amount of room you need for creative work could be insignificant and involve little reconfiguration, or it could be large and substantially different than it is now.

This chapter shares what to consider when claiming creative space, including ways to set it up, organize it, and make it a nurturing environment. This is important for all creatives, but in particular for those of us with mood disorders. The chapter also explores the art of filing—something I've struggled with for years. I can't *begin* to say how many hours (or was it years?) of therapy focused on this topic! In my ongoing quest for a workable system, I've discovered some great tips to share with you.

FINDING WORKSPACE

A SEPARATE BUILDING or room is ideal to help you maintain privacy, screen out noise, concentrate intensely, and protect equipment and supplies. It also helps separate creative work from other parts of your life. Some creatives work in guesthouses, garage apartments, or toolsheds. Some work in an area of their house that has a separate entrance, such as a basement.

But many of us don't have such options. We may have to get by with a corner of the kitchen or living room, or an alcove or closet. Or, your workspace might be mobile. Some artists manage quite well with a sketchpad and many writers use a laptop computer in a bookstore, coffee shop, or library. Other creative artists use a picnic table, porch, or garage.

■ DOORS AND SIGNS

If your workspace has a door, shutting it will reinforce your commitment—both for yourself and for those who would otherwise interrupt you. If a door is out of the question, a tall bookcase, a partition, a curtain or bedsheet, or a folding screen may do. Just use your imagination.

Some creatives post "office hours," during which they're not to be disturbed, unless it's a life or death emergency. Of course, what constitutes a "life or death" emergency is subject to individual interpretation, especially in kids' minds. Both doors and office-hour signs help train family, friends, and coworkers to respect your commitments.

■ Sharing Space

Some creatives share a studio, storefront, or sales booth. Performers will likely need both rehearsal space and performance venues. Some will be free, others will ask you to share entry fees or tips, and others will charge you full price. But you can share costs with other creatives, rent space only when necessary, or barter to cut costs. Often, you can rent a work-space from educational centers or institutions that offer classes in the arts. Many of these places offer reduced rental rates for their students.

If you must share an area, you'll need a way to easily stash away your projects. You can scoop materials into large boxes or use a cart that you can roll into closet or corner. Moving your work away from other activities will prevent damaging your efforts. Or, something as simple as a sheet tossed over your table or easel will protect and conceal your work when you are not around. If you share a computer, or even if you have your own computer in a shared space, you may wish to password-protect your work to keep it private from curious eyes.

Ask others using shared space not to disturb or remove anything from your work site, even if it's just a pen or a pair of scissors. Have your own set of tools and ask others not to borrow them without your permission, so you won't have to waste precious time tracking down your supplies. (It should go without saying that you will respect others' work areas and pos-scssions as well.)

PHYSICAL STORAGE SPACE

Nearly any creative endeavor presents physical storage needs:

- A bookcase for reference books, scripts, or completed manuscripts
- A flat file for drawings
- A single drawer or cabinet for craft supplies, paints, or film reels
- A corner for easels or lighting equipment
- Closet space for art supplies, camera lenses, costumes, or a stage makeup kit

If you have a creative business, such as a T-shirt silk-screening company, you might also need appropriate places to store your finished products and any related packaging/shipping materials.

ELECTRONIC SPACE

IN ADDITION TO physical space, many creatives need a computer for creating products and marketing materials. Digital photographers, filmmakers, and musicians often use computers extensively and require specialized software. Look for special package deals and rebates on such equipment, especially around December, when the manufacturers offer deep discounts to maximize sales during the holiday season.

Any time you rely on computers, you need a way to make reliable backups. You don't want to lose your work if the system goes down. Also, get a good surge protection for your hardware. My current preferred backup device is a small "thumb drive" that functions like an additional hard drive. I just plug into my computer's USB port and back up my files. Thumb drives fit in pockets or purse, or attach to a keychain, so you can take your files wherever you go.

Be sure to keep an extra ink cartridge, blank CDs or disks, and extra paper or film on hand, so that if you run short at night or on a weekend, your work won't grind to a halt until the stores open. But don't overstock, as some items have limited shelf life.

Think about both the appearance and efficiency of the setting where your computer will be. If you use a public space, you have little control over your surroundings' noise level, light, and so on. Try to find the quietest, least hectic place in which to use your laptop—someplace where you won't be interrupted by friends or even curious passersby. If you are a filmmaker or musician, check out the noise level of your intended space at various times of day to be sure you won't be competing with sounds from an adjacent area or producing high-volume sounds of your own that may disturb others.

Make sure the keyboard height and your chair are ergonomically correct for your body. Select good lighting for the space and perhaps even tone down your computer screen, to minimize glare. Is the view from a window inspiring or distracting? Face your machinery in a direction that will best support your concentration, and use draperies, shades, or blinds accordingly. And be mindful of sound. If the computer's beeping is annoying, turn off or disconnect its speakers; if traffic or other sounds intrude, a low-level volume of soothing music or public radio discussion could counteract the problem as "white noise."

A telephone could be a useful part of your business or a distraction. If incoming calls frequently interrupt your creative time, remove the phone entirely from that area (using the connection only for e-mail, if necessary), or turn off the ringer in that room and let an answering machine record your calls from an extension in another room. Likewise, you might try leaving your cell phone outside the space and letting your voice mail handle incoming calls. At the very least, place an answering machine within your workspace and screen incoming calls, so that you need not pick up unless a matter is urgent. You may need to tell some people a better time to reach you if they customarily phone while you are working.

VIRTUAL SPACE

YOU'LL MOST LIKELY also want an e-mail account. However, if you're using creativity exclusively to release your feelings or plan to share it only with close family members and friends, it's not a necessity.

Take care not to waste your creative time on the computer sending e-mails and photos to friends and family, playing software games, surfing the Web, or visiting chat rooms. Don't even get started seeking or visiting sites that you know will only become a distraction, a reason to postpone your creative work. Think of the Internet as another work tool, not a toy. Just as you are creating a special space for your creativity, reserve your computer use for what will advance your art.

If you plan to advertise your performances, or to sell products or services, you'll probably need a Web site—even if it's just one page. Chapter 12 provides more specific suggestions on how to go about designing and setting one up.

WORKSPACE INVESTMENTS

TO SERIOUSLY PURSUE your art usually means investing in equipment, tools, supplies, and sometimes furniture. You may be able to borrow or rent some things you need. You can often find inexpensive furniture, equipment, and tools at garage sales or secondhand stores. You also might find bargains at "scratch and dent" sales or at auctions sponsored by government entities.

Think creatively about storage pieces, work surfaces, chairs, lamps, and even small tools. Kitchen or closet ware, or colorful pieces really meant for kids, might be just right for your needs. For example, art students and needleworkers often use a fishing tackle box to sort small supplies. "Dollar" stores usually sell a multitude of plastic storage boxes and bins for a fraction of the price that the very same items command in a hardware or home goods store. Objects you already have at home could serve a new life as workspace units—an old dresser might serve your storage needs better than an open set of shelves, if you need to keep your materials dust free.

You might purchase supplies that you'll use in large quantities at wholesale outlets or warehouse stores like Costco or Sam's, but sometimes regular retail or online stores offer even better deals. If others ask what you'd like for gifts, ask for items you need for creative work. I've received many reference books and some software programs as gifts.

You might also need special equipment to practice your art, such as a drafting table, potter's wheel and kiln, ballet barre and mirrors, a laser scanner, sound equipment, or lighting equipment. The costs can quickly add up. Most of us acquire furniture and equipment over time, which is probably a good thing. When things break or wear out over time, replacing them will drain less money than buying everything at once.

Before investing in anything, it's best to carefully consider what you need, why you need (or don't need) it, when you need it, and how much it costs. This is particularly important when you're manic or hypomanic. It's too fun to shop for things when you're in that state!

A form like the following can help you decide what's most important.

SAMPLE CREATIVE SPACE NEEDS

WHAT?	WHY/WHY NOT?	WHEN?	COST
Furniture			
Desk chair	Need new; old chair is shot	This week	225
File cabinet	For records & promo stuff	This month	75
Equipment			
Computer with 21" monitor	To see full pages better	Next fall?	5,000
Better color printer	Could use outside printer	———	5,000
Tools			
Design software upgrade	New version has new stuff	Next spring?	800
11"X17" tray for printer	Can print jobs at copy shop	Next year?	150

Once you've determined where you'll work and where you'll store tools and supplies, you'll probably need to adjust that space before you can use it. This often means clearing out clutter.

CLEARING CLUTTER AND GETTING ORGANIZED

LET'S FACE IT: Creatives, especially creatives with mood disorders, are rarely "poster children" for order and organization. More often, we practice our art on overflowing desks and tables, surrounded by bulging bookcases, crammed cabinets, and precarious piles. It's also common to let things pile up when you're depressed. Often, so much stuff accumulates that it's hard to walk through a room!

Clutter is a *major* drain of energy and wastes lots of potentially productive time. How much time have you lost trying to locate that great sketch you made last month, that picture that inspired a new poem, that scrap of paper where you jotted down that new band member's phone number? Wouldn't you rather be working on your art?

Common "wisdom" says a messy desk is a sign of a creative mind at work. To some extent, that's true, but messes also mess with creative minds. No matter how hard I try, everything becomes disheveled when I'm on a roll. I may begin with a pristine surface, but within an hour or so it's overflowing with mounds of articles, books, and scraps of envelopes and napkins on which I've scribbled inspirations and notes. It's as if a volcanic island of clutter has risen from the sea!

Jane Mountain says, "When you experience this feature of mania [snowballing disorganization], you could end up with a whirlwind of clutter strewn from one end of your workspace to the other. . . . You may have difficulty doing simple planning because of your decreased ability to organize. While a feature of mania is increased energy that sometimes leads to high levels of productivity, your focus can be so intense that it creates a stream of cast-off, unfinished activities meandering through your workspace. It's as though organization is held captive by activity."

Throughout my work life, I've spent more time than not floundering in a sea of stuff. I've hung onto files I haven't used for decades, magazines and newsletters I've never read. I had drawers full of clippings I "might" use as resource materials someday. I've had duplicate lists and calendars all over the place.

In my paranoia about losing data, I've made copy after copy and disk after disk of the very same computer files. My books and files have migrated from room to room. I've taken over the guest room, the TV room, and frequently, the kitchen table.

I've somehow managed to get things done, but not without lots of anger and frustration. I can't begin to account for the time I've lost hunting for things that were "around here somewhere."

Don't fall into the same trap that I did! Deal with clutter early and regularly. It's so much easier to resume a project when you don't have to bail the muck out first.

Disorganization, clutter, indecision, and feeling overwhelmed tend to accompany mood disorders—both in our minds and in our surroundings. Rather than having a place for everything and putting everything in its place, we're more likely to shuffle stuff around and around, and then resign ourselves to working in constant chaos.

Here's what two creatives with mood disorders say:

"I often cannot collect my thoughts enough to structure a coherent story. I start one way and slide off in another direction, winding up with four or five themes mixed in inappropriately. I also have long periods of writer's block."

"I found myself unable to write series because I would get off the track and get completely disorganized. I have written some short fiction which came out all right, but I am having difficulty finishing a novel because of the weird changes of themes, names, etc."

Clearing out the clutter and becoming organized can reduce stress and frustration and free up energy for creative work. Jane Mountain recommends having someone help you get organized so you can function efficiently, or confining your work to one manageable area rather than allowing it to take over an entire apartment or house.

If at all possible, I recommend you start the cleanup process on a weekend or holiday when you'll have several hours (or days!) of uninterrupted time.

If you don't have time to finish within a few days, just do as much as soon and as often as you can. You'll make considerable dents even if you work in half-hour increments. Keep in mind that organizing your workspace and keeping it free of unnecessary objects will help you keep your focus on the projects at hand.

■ **MY CLUTTER-CLEARING AND SORTING PROCESS**

For years, I've used this two-stage process to reorganize all aspects of my life. I try to separate decisions from emotions as I go through these steps as quickly as I can. Maybe my process will work for you.

Stage 1: Gather Your Supplies — The first step is to gather what you need for sorting your stuff.

1. Get a large trash can or garbage bag (or several).
2. If you recycle, get your recycling container.
3. If you need to destroy sensitive papers, pull out the paper shredder and grab some bags for excess shreddings. If you don't have a shredder, use bags or boxes that you can label "to shred."
4. Next, grab a stapler, scissors, tape, paper clips, and any other supplies you think you'll need. If you expect to store completed projects and inactive files away from your workspace, get plastic file boxes or heavy-duty file boxes (often called bankers' boxes), too.
5. Finally, locate at least a dozen large empty boxes. Label them with whatever categories you need. I suggest starting with some or all of the following:

   - Non-paper items
   - Urgent
   - Action
   - Bills
   - Medical
   - Taxes
   - Family papers
   - Sell
   - Give away
   - File

If you also have items that relate to specific projects, label as many "project" boxes as you need.

You might want to gather file folders and labels at this point. It might help for you to quickly review and then prelabel every possible category, so you can swiftly sort your papers directly into prepared files. Time management experts and professional organizers usually recommend handling each piece of paper only once. (Though some of them admit that's not always possible.)

However, that technique doesn't work for me. If it does for you, that's great! If I stop to label folders while I'm sorting, I get indecisive and overwhelmed. I find it easier to sort through everything first and then file it. I sometimes pencil a note to remind me why I'm keeping a paper or where I'll put it, but I don't actually file it yet.

If *you* can label files before or during sorting, it will save you time. I wish I could, but I haven't mastered that. Choose whatever method works best for you.

Stage 2: Move the Clutter—The second stage involves moving everything except heavy furniture and equipment out of your workspace and spreading it out in another room. Not permanently, just until it's sorted.

1. Haul those books, magazines, disks, CDs, DVDs, and videos, decorative items, tools, supplies, and whatever other clutter you may have into another room altogether. When I'm clearing clutter, I spread most everything out on a table or the living room floor.
2. Set small equipment and tools in one corner. Place supplies in another. Stack magazines in another. Stash decorative items in the last. Line books, journals, sketch pads, and canvases along the wall.

When you've placed everything in logical piles, take a well-deserved break—but not for long. You don't want to lose momentum. Maintain your determination to go on. After all, you're working toward your creative space here. You're reinforcing your commitment to your art!

After you've refreshed yourself, it's time to sort.

Stage 3: Sort the Stuff—During this stage, you'll sort on a finer level. Do as much as possible standing up. As you sort, try to make decisions quickly. Don't stop to admire your creations or to read materials as you go. As you pick up each item, do one of the following:

1. Toss or recycle everything possible. Some recycling centers want you to separate paper, cardboard, aluminum, cans, and glass. Others let you toss everything into the same bin.
2. Shred materials with sensitive information, such as bank account or credit-card numbers, and unneeded medical records.

3. Pop stray shoes and socks, disks, CDs, DVDs, videos, toys, and any other items not related to your art in a "sell," "give away," or "non-paper items" box.
4. Place other papers in a box you labeled during Stage One:

- Papers you must deal with today or before the week ends—*including bills*—go in the "urgent" box.
- Put papers with less immediate deadlines—other than bills—in the "action" box.
- Bills you *don't* need to pay within a week (or two) go into the "bills" box.
- Prescriptions, medical receipts, and health insurance claims go in the "medical" box.
- Receipts, statements, and financial papers you'll need for filing taxes and to support deductions go in the "taxes" box.
- Put papers like the kids' homework or grade cards in the "family papers" box. You can also use this box for things you'll delegate to others.
- Place things you don't need but that others might want in a "sell" or "give away" box.
- Put materials related to specific projects in individual "project" boxes, making sure you label them with the project and/or client's names and dates.
- If a paper doesn't belong in any other box and you'll need it soon or use it regularly, put it in the "file" box, whether you have an existing place for it or not.
- Finally, if you *must* keep information because you're *sure* you'll need it in the future and won't be able to obtain it easily, store it in a plastic or banker's file box. Predict a date by which you'll no longer need it—say a year or more out—then write that date on the box. Then when that date arrives, toss the box without opening it. No fair peeking!

If you're interrupted while you're sorting (as I usually am), just stack and set aside the boxes *temporarily* until you can resume. Don't combine anything you've already sorted! Keep unsorted items separate from sorted ones. Box up loose tools and supplies and move them to a *temporary* holding place. Make certain, however, that your "urgent" and "bills" boxes are easily accessible! Then work with one of the other boxes whenever you can squeeze it in.

PLANNING A LAYOUT

WHEN YOU'VE FINISHED sorting all the clutter, you need map out your workspace and decide where everything will go. It's ideal to make a floor plan, using pieces of paper cut to scale representing furniture and equipment, before moving anything. If you don't have the patience to do so, at least measure everything before you move it.

As you make your floor plan (or visualize the space), consider access to electrical outlets, phone jacks, and Internet cables. Limit the use of extension cords. Position items and equipment you use frequently within easy reach of where you'll use them. Make certain work surfaces and drawers won't collide and that nothing obstructs traffic patterns. You'll need:

- *A surface for a computer,* like a desk or a table. Try to keep most of this surface clear so you have adequate space to work. Printers, scanners, and other devices can sit on furniture nearby.
- *Project areas*, where you'll work on active projects. Avoid using your project space to store other items and completed projects, which are best kept elsewhere. I stack project-related items in separate piles on a bookcase and affix labels to the edges of the shelves.
- *Inventory space*, if you sell products like books, CDs, videos, or T-shirts.
- *A mailing and shipping area,* if you mail lots of letters or promotional materials or ship your own products. Aim for a space where you can store business- and catalog-size envelopes, stamps or a postage meter, a scale, shipping boxes and bags, and packing/strapping tape nearby.
- *An administrative area,* for paperwork, phone calls, and day-to-day business tasks.
- *A meeting space,* if you have clients in for meetings. A meeting space need not be permanent. I often meet with clients at a

restaurant, or at my kitchen table. For a more professional setting, you can sometimes rent or borrow a room. Local libraries, community centers, churches, and hotels often have meeting areas you can use free or for a small fee. If you use your home for business, you may need to adjust your liability insurance to be sure business guests are covered. (In fact, it's a good idea to ask if your insurer has a special policy to cover home business properties, so your equipment and workspace will specifically be insured against loss or damage.)

Once you've determined where furniture and equipment will go, you can start moving everything in (but bring paper materials in last). If you want to paint first, this is time to do so!

COLOR YOUR WORLD

THE COLORS YOU use in your creative space will affect your moods as you work. Colors can calm or energize you and even reduce physical pain! Scientists have studied the effects of different colors for years, and the Chinese consider the use of colors in feng shui (the art of arranging the environment to direct energy where you want it). Here are some findings:

- *Blue* helps calm and relax us, and has a peaceful effect.
- *Green* surroundings help reduce depression and anxiety, and sooth our nerves. Green also reduces exhaustion.
- *Orange* helps lessen fatigue and stimulates the appetite.
- *Pink* helps us relax and soothes our anxiety. Pink can also be tranquilizing.
- *Red* excites us, stimulates brain waves, and increases our heart rate.
- *Violet* creates a peaceful atmosphere and suppresses the appetite.
- *Yellow* energizes us and helps improve our depression and memory.

So, if you have frequent depressive episodes, your best choices are probably blue, green, orange (unless you binge when depressed), red, violet (unless you have a poor appetite), or yellow.

If your episodes are more often manic or hypomanic, your best choices are probably blue, pink, or violet (unless you have a poor appetite), limit the yellow, and definitely avoid red!

Also consider how colors in your creative products affect you, as this bipolar person with anger issues did: "I like to paint using several shades of blue, violet, and white to soothe my angry side. Someone suggested using brighter colors such as orange and red, and I said that would just make my anger simmer."

WORKING IN STYLE

FABRICS AND OTHER materials also play a part in creating a comfortable workspace. If you like things cozy or sensuous, choose wood over metal for furnishings, and select draperies and upholstery you'll enjoy seeing and touching. Just because it's a workspace doesn't mean it has to look like an office or factory.)

Don't fill your space with furniture or equipment that doesn't work for you or that you honestly hate. You'll be spending too much time there to live with something that annoys you. Make sure you'll feel comfortable working there.

> **CAUTION!** Don't get so involved in setting up and organizing that you never focus on your art! Move through this process as quickly as possible.

ORGANIZING YOUR SPACE

ONCE YOU'VE CLEARED clutter, drawn up a floor plan, and painted (or at least cleaned), it's finally time to move into your space. Position the furniture and equipment first, making sure you get help with any heavy items. Hang or stash your tools, and store your supplies. Then, one at a time, bring each box of papers in.

■ THE F-WORD

It's time to face the F-word: Filing. Can't put it off anymore. Most creatives would rather lick the kitchen floor clean than file! Filing is a left-brained, linear task, and we creatives tend to be visual people. It therefore intimidates us—*especially* when we have a mood disorder!

If you file something, it's out of sight and it might as well not exist, right? That thought alone can make you a "piler." Piling isn't bad in itself, but over time, piles can pile too high and tip over. So let's face the fear of filing head-on.

Filing Containers — You don't have to store papers in file cabinets. There are many other options: expandable pockets, accordion files, portable cases, or binders; open shelves, stretchable or stationary compartmentalized desktop holders, rolling bins, even just a chest of drawers of the right depth.

For instance, I use accordion files for resource articles and photocopies I need for current projects. I use three-ring binders for the following:

- Magazine and newspaper clippings
- Newsgroup user names, passwords, and cancellation instructions
- Technical notes and registration and serial numbers for computer hardware and software

Some papers are better off on clipboards or in plastic trays hung on walls. Whatever works for you is fine.

File Names and Labels — Naming files so you can quickly retrieve them is an art in itself. Make file names short so they'll fit easily on a tab or label, but avoid abbreviations you might forget later. Third-cut files allow more room for names than fifth-cut files. If you use hanging files, use clear tabs rather than colored. Colored tabs are more aesthetic, but you can't read the names through darker colors, and being able to read them is the whole point! If you simply must have colored tabs, affix labels on the outside of the tab rather than inserting them.

Sticks and stones may break your bones, but file names can never hurt you—unless you use different names for the same type of file! "Did I file those book reviews under 'marketing,' 'promotion,' 'publicity,' or 'PR'?" I've encountered such quandaries *repeatedly*, and I'm sure it's one reason I hate to file. Be straightforward in the way you name your files (and this goes double for naming computer document files!). Pick a system and use it consistently. You may want to keep an easy-to-access master list for reference.

These days, most of us need to find not only paper files but computer files as well. To keep stress down, use the same names for related paper and computer files. But which name do you use?

Rather than allow such decisions to stop you, try one of the following techniques.

Filing Techniques — Most people use one or a combination of alphabetical, numerical, or categorical files. Many people also maintain some type of index or cross-reference system to locate what they've filed. These consist of paper or electronic lists that you can skim visually or sort electronically.

You can organize files by color. I use different colors for major categories and then file alphabetically within the category. For instance:

- Green represents income (book sales, contracts, paid invoices, and such).
- Yellow represents expenses (charge card statements, receipts, payments to freelancers, and so on).
- Red represents crucial business information (sales, self-employment, and income taxes; business and Web site registrations; copyright papers, inventory records, and so forth).

Decluttering Tip

*B*ROAD CATEGORIES WORK best. Too many categories lead to chaos. As Mike Nelson, founder of Clutterless Recovery Groups, says, "Too much 'organization' is complication."

If unaligned files bother you, check out the following technique.

Pat Dorff, Edith Fine, and Judith Josephson, authors of *File . . . Don't Pile! For People Who Write,* have a method that keeps files aligned perfectly. They assign each broad subject area a code, such as MKT for marketing. Then they assign each file folder a number and description, such as, "MKT 101 Biz Card" "MKT 102 Flier," "MKT 103 Résumé," and so on.

They list the code and entire name of each file on a "Paperdex"—an 8½ × 11-inch form with each item in numerical order. If they later insert a "Headshots" file, they'll label it "MKT 104 Headshots." They can then store the files in either alphabetical or numeric order and still find them easily.

The files won't be alphabetical anymore, but you can find them by referring to your Paperdex. The following drawing illustrates this approach.

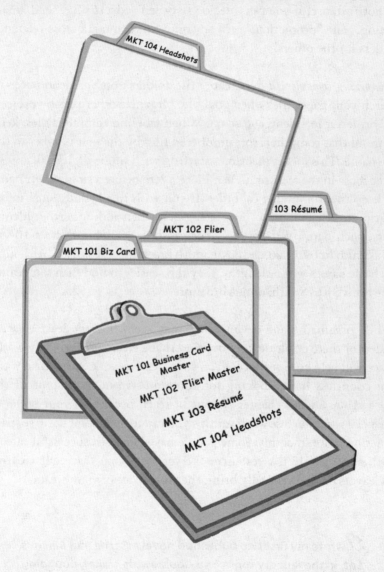

In *Clutter-Proof Your Business: Turn Your Mess into Success,* Mike Nelson suggests another technique that's great for fearful filers. Insert cross-reference folders wherever you might look for the same information.

For instance, if you can't decide between "advertising," and "marketing," and "promotion," pick any one and then mark cross-reference folders for the others.

Organizing computer files—Create "file folders" on your computer to match your paper files when possible. Organize other files by project, client, letter recipient, and so on. When labeling computer files, keep in mind that computers sort numbered files by the first number in the file name. This means file names starting with single digits will appear after those in the teens or higher. Place a zero before a single-digit name to keep them in numerical order. If you wish to add additional information to a name, use a "dot" or hyphen when adding further identifiers, such dates, versions, etc. For example, JohnSmith.ltr.9-10-06, JohnSmith.ltr.09.15.06, and SusanSmith.brochure.v2.10.01.06. Although such file names will be lengthy, they'll be easier to find than something like Smith ltr., Smith, or newbrochure.

While organizing and decluttering may seem like the least creative endeavor there is, please keep in mind that a clean, user-friendly workspace will help keep you focused on your creative work, rather than wasting countless hours looking for some elusive note. If some of the suggestions in this chapter are out of reach because of your home or financial situation, use whatever tips you can to make your creative space function more smoothly. Some people have launched successful careers with surprisingly few resources. Never lose hope that your creative endeavors could eventually bring the workspace of your dreams!

I wrote my first two published novels, *Carrie* and *Salem's Lot*, in the laundry room of a doublewide trailer, pounding away on my wife's portable Olivetti typewriter and balancing a child's desk on my thighs.

—Horror writer Stephen King (1947–)

· 10 ·

Staying Afloat Financially

$\mathcal{T}$HOSE OF US with mood disorders often face overwhelming financial challenges. Our gleeful hypomanic or manic overspending may have wrecked our credit or resulted in extraordinary debts. Our depressive episodes might have completely consumed our sick leave and vacation hours. Frequently, we'll have lost job after job due to our symptoms or to discrimination. We often fear we'll never be employable or that we'll only be able to find boring, low-paying jobs.

We face high medical expenses, even if we're lucky enough to have decent health insurance. We may have been told we're "not sick enough" or "poor enough" to get treatment from downsized community mental health services. We may be on disability and struggling to make ends meet—or worse, be unable to obtain disability at all.

Clearly, ours is not an easy road to travel. That's the bad news. Yet we must keep putting one foot in front of another and looking for ways to get by.

The good news is, you *can* find ways to make ends meet. You can often live more simply. Share a place, rent out a room, grow a garden. Unbelievable as it may seem, you can also apply your creativity to solve financial problems.

This chapter provides a number of suggestions to help you do just that, and to earn a living while pursing your creative interests. I'll share strategies for obtaining a day job, working part-time to gain more creative time, start freelancing, or simply earn a little extra money through your art.

JOINING OR REJOINING THE WORKFORCE

When we express interest in using our creativity more fully, the standard advice we get is, "Don't quit your day job!" The term "day job" refers to conventional employment, whether it means working days, nights, or weekends.

When you have a mood disorder, though, you might not have a day job in the first place. Typical knee-jerk reactions many of us with mood disorders have when thinking about day jobs are:

- I can't afford a job. *How could I get enough time off* to continue seeing my psychiatrist and therapist, and go to group therapy?
- I can't handle a job. *It's too stressful!* I'd end up in the hospital again.
- I can't even *apply* for a job. *How would I explain all those gaps on my résumé?*
- If I go back to work, *I'll lose my disability benefits.* If things don't work out, how will I survive?
- What about the *disclosure* issue? *No one* will hire me if they know I have a mental illness!

Right? These *are* legitimate concerns but may not be as crippling as they seem. Before you throw in the towel and walk away, please finish reading this chapter. You'll learn how to apply your creative skills to find or create work that's truly fulfilling or at least helps you "keep on truckin'."

 NEW YORK WRITER *Andrew Solomon, age forty-two, always wanted to be a writer and has written professionally since he was twenty. He has written for newspapers and magazines, including* The New Yorker.

Solomon's depression surfaced in his late twenties, following his mother's death. He spiraled downward into a severe major depression

*during his early thirties. He became "so incapacitated and so fright-
ened," that taking the twelve steps from his bed to the shower seemed
totally unmanageable. He wept, he recalls, "not only because of what
I could not do, but because the fact that I could not do it seemed so idiotic to me."*

*Despite his many accomplishments, Solomon says that during
severe depressions, "I believe I have no skills or talents." This experience is common to even the most gifted creative artists struggling
with mood disorders.*

*Solomon has authored several books, including the New York
Times bestseller,* The Noonday Demon: An Atlas of Depression.
*Solomon devoted five years to researching this masterful book, and
in the process, learned a wealth of information about his illness.
Solomon advises others with depression to learn about their disorder
and to get it under control. He manages his own depression with a
combination of medications and psychoanalysis.*

*Solomon's writing also helps him through depressive episodes. He
feels "a sense of urgency" to write. "When you're depressed, you're isolated. Writing gives me a sense of connectedness. It makes me feel part
of the web of humanity." Even when he feels lazy or not in the mood,
he says he forces himself to write.*

*Solomon isn't bitter about his illness, as he believes depression
teaches valuable lessons. He says it increased the depth of his emotions,
strengthened his relationships, and taught him "the value of every day."
Solomon now believes he has "a richer appreciation of day-to-day life."*

■ STEADY JOBS = FINANCIAL SECURITY?

One reason people take day jobs is for financial security—for that
steady income, those benefits, that pension plan. But I've got news for
you: *Job security does not exist!* Once, the entire department I was working in got laid off and asked to pack our belongings and leave within
two hours. So much for job security!

Even if your pay seems secure, a day job may become so time-
demanding (due to cutbacks or layoffs of other employees, for instance)
that you may be pressured to work extra hard or work extra hours just
to earn your current salary. Such situations are likely to drain your creative juices, or the time you have available for your private life.

Many creatives take boring jobs with little opportunity to use their talents because it seems the only way to support themselves and their families. Then they squeeze creative projects in during their free time. Their creative dreams inspire them enough to somehow make time for creative work, regardless. Here are some ways to swing that scenario if that applies to you.

CONVENTIONAL EMPLOYMENT

IF YOU DECIDE on conventional employment, at least while learning your art, I don't blame you. I did the same for many years.

But what's the best way to find a full- or part-time job that will cover your basic living expenses? Well, first you need to clearly define what you're looking for.

All too many of us start job hunting with no specific type of job in mind. We say we'll take *anything* we're qualified for, *anything* that pays a decent wage. Then if we find a job, we wind up dissatisfied and terribly unhappy. That doesn't help our mental health!

So get a clear picture of what type of job you'd like. Although you may dream of creative independence, free from concerns about a day job, some types of conventional positions are worth a look.

■ CONVENTIONAL CREATIVE JOBS

Jobs that relate to your creative interests are great ways to hone your craft. You might, for instance, become a ballroom dance instructor, stage manager, or photo framer, even as you dream of becoming a choreographer, playwright, or photographer. If you're just getting started in your art, consider applying for such positions as a box office manager, lighting technician, or publicity assistant in an arts business that interests you. Don't think of such jobs as menial if they place you in the center of an environment where you can absorb the creative flow.

Some creatives take jobs that directly further other creatives' careers. Twenty-eight-year-old Pennsylvania musician, writer, artist, actor, photographer, dancer, and filmmaker RB is one example.

RB works in entertainment sales, selling lyrics, music, photos, and art for CD labels to other musicians. It's sometimes frustrating to watch others "get all the breaks," and he feels left behind. But RB believes someday he'll get his chance to be a star and that his job offers some good perks. "I know one day I will meet the right person who will get me in the spotlight," he says, "but until then, I live for the thrill of seeing others benefit off of my talents."

The right conventional job can help you move closer to your dreams. Illinois writer LH uses her writing skills and expresses her creativity in a job she find very fulfilling. "I had the incredible luck of finding a job writing mental health education materials," she says.

An excellent resource for creatives with disabilities—which, incidentally, include mood disorders—is a free book, *Putting Creativity to Work*. It offers a wealth of information about jobs in creative fields, as well as sources for funding. See the Resources section for details about this book.

■ ACADEMIC POSSIBILITIES

Teaching is another option, and many creatives teach either full- or part-time. Teaching at formal institutions offers the advantage of semester breaks and often summers off.

Twenty-five-year-old Virginia writer, photographer, and musician JG enjoys using her talents in her fourth-grade classroom. As a teacher, she plans creative activities, draws on the board, and makes up and illustrates stories.

JG says bipolar disorder has helped stimulate her creativity and think outside the box. She manages, she says, with "self-discipline . . . and my husband's help."

Teaching at colleges and universities sometimes provides a way to integrate creative interests into your job. It also improves your chances of receiving grants and fellowships. However, grading and preparing for classes can consume lots of time when school is in session. And at the college or university level, you may run into additional demands on your time, such as committee meetings, and pressures to research and publish. Think carefully about whether you're up to the challenge and that you have good medical and emotional support.

It's not necessary to limit yourself to a conventional school or college. Twenty-three-year-old SH of Arizona says she enjoys "all sorts of crafts"—mixed media collages, microscope slide art, working with polymer clay, cardmaking, rubberstamping, and scrapbooking. SH enjoys crafts so much that she now teaches at the chain store, Michael's Arts & Crafts.

Other creatives teach their craft on their own, offering private lessons, online classes, or live workshops and presentations. Explore whether giving private lessons or group workshops might be lucrative in your area.

■ Creative Jobs within Noncreative Environments

If you can't find an arts-related job right away, you might find a creative job in a less creative environment, as artist SF has: "I am responsible for educating staff in a comprehensive behavioral medicine center. I develop curriculum using computer graphics, Print Artist, Print Shop, and PowerPoint."

Many commercial creative jobs may not feel creative or artistic, and you may even find the products you are writing about, illustrating, or photographing less than inspirational, but they may still enable you to hone your skills. Designing ads for a car dealership may sound like a boring way to spend each day, but it gives you an opportunity to develop your skills in the application of typography, graphic composition, and color.

IF CONVENTIONALITY IS INCONVENIENT

You might not be able to find a creative job right away, or might fear that any conventional full-time job will be too stressful. That's the way Texas writer DC, age fifty-three, feels: "When I'm high [hypomanic/manic] I think better and faster and can stay up late to work. But if I get too high I can't focus on one thought at a time."

"I want to get a job," DC says, "but I have no idea how I will feel when I wake up every morning so I can't be a reliable employee."

DC says she's had to quit several jobs over the years because of her disorder. "I don't want that to happen again." She has concluded, "It might be best for us to find some way to earn a living that does not require an eight-to-five job."

If you feel the same, consider a low-stress or part-time job.

■ Low-Stress Jobs

Frequently, low-stress positions are well below our capabilities. Even if they're boring at times, they could be worth exploring.

Oregon artist FD says that during menopause her symptoms worsened. "When I am down, I question who I am and what my abilities are, and usually I tell myself that I have very little going . . . and very little to give in a job."

FD was relieved to find a job that required less "brain power." Although her current job offers few opportunities to apply her talents, FD says, "at least I can do the job when I am depressed." When she's better stabilized, she hopes to find something more fulfilling.

■ Part-Time Possibilities

The right part-time job can be ideal to balance financial, creative, and psychological needs. By part-time, I mean half-time, three-quarter-time, or other positions with flexible hours.

For a while, I had a three-quarter-time position at a desktop publishing bureau. Working thirty hours a week rather than forty made the job less stressful than jobs I'd held before, but not a lot. I didn't have to use sick leave for the time I spent seeing my psychiatrist and therapist. And the additional nonworking time allowed me to get a bit more sleep (which I definitely needed!).

Another advantage was that my knowledge of desktop publishing and graphic design solidified, and I learned a lot about different customers' preferences. But the job didn't help me complete my own creative projects.

A better situation for me was working just under twenty hours a week for the textbook publishing company, Holt Rinehart Winston. I began as a proofreader, and within a year, joined the electronic publishing crew.

Once I learned to operate their layout software, the job brought very little stress. I came into work later than the rest of the staff and stayed later as well. Occasionally, I felt self-conscious about coming in late. But I got the sleep I required, and my schedule shielded me from stressful rush-hour traffic.

At Holt Rinehart Winston, I usually worked a three-day week, but when faced by a tight deadline, I put in extra time and then took off later. Over lunch hours, I either did a bit of research or some writing. I stayed at Holt Rinehart Winston for nearly five years. Working for a publisher tied in very well with my writing aspirations.

Forty-four-year-old North Carolina artist, musician, and writer JT owns his own pewter art business. "I create a variety of decorative and artistic cast pewter designs," he says. He supplements his income with a part-time day job.

Be aware that working less than thirty hours a week may mean not qualifying for health benefits, paid vacation, sick days, and other perks offered to full-time employees. Speak with the organization's human resource person to learn whether it could at least provide health insurance, if you're not covered another way.

Part-time jobs do come with another big potential trap: Some tend to expand well beyond part-time hours. Employers may pressure you to stay "just a little while longer" to complete a project. And often, that extra work sometimes becomes a regular part of the job. Be very clear about your boundaries if you take a part-time job.

Most of my freelancing career, I've pursued my creative interests *and* worked part-time for other people. For nearly two years, I worked for a nonprofit out of my home office. Not only did board members and officers call at all hours, but I also answered their toll-free line, which some callers used for genuine emergencies. How could I ignore their calls? Although the steady income relieved a lot of financial anxiety, the job seriously disrupted my writing. Sometimes the financial security of such a job isn't worth it because it consumes too much creative time.

Another possibility is having a second career to support your creative career.

"BACKUP SKILLS"

IN *HOW TO DANCE FOREVER*, Daniel Nagrin suggests that creatives find a flexible "backup skill" to support their creative work. This backup skill, he says, should:

- Pay enough to meet basic needs while working twenty hours or less per week
- Interest, excite, and challenge you

- Tap one of your talents (creative or not)
- Be something you can learn part-time in two years or less
- Be in demand where you live or plan to live to use your art professionally
- Earn at least three or four times the minimum wage

That's not exactly *easy* to do, but if you use your imagination, it may not be as difficult as it seems.

Here are some of Nagrin's suggestions: auto mechanic, bicycle mechanic, bartender, waiter or waitress (only in very expensive restaurants), beautician, massage therapist, housecleaner, driving instructor, bookkeeper, secretary, legal proofreader, translator, and computer programmer.

With today's throng of aging baby boomers, jobs in health care and elder care are also possibilities—provided they're not too stressful. North Carolina artist, musician, and writer JT works as a dental laboratory technician. He makes dental appliances (crowns, bridges, dentures), which allows him to apply his sculpting skills.

SCOUTING OUT OPPORTUNITIES

THE BEST WAY to search for jobs is *not* to check the classified ads in print and online newspapers, to call places and ask if they're hiring anyone, or to fill out applications at employment agencies and human resource departments. But that's what most people do.

You *can* find jobs using these methods, but they aren't the way most jobs get filled. Decide what type of job you'd like, then tell everyone you know what you have in mind. The best jobs come from personal recommendations and word-of-mouth—or by directly contacting the person you'd like to work for. This can provide an opportunity to explain how you could help the person or company reach important goals.

Using *all* of your connections is especially important when you have a mood disorder. If someone will recommend you, or agree that it's okay to say he or she suggested you contact the employer, it helps get your foot in the door.

The specifics of job hunting could take several books, books that already exist. One of the best is *What Color is Your Parachute?*, a bestseller by Richard Bolles.

Bolles explains in detail how to decide exactly what you'd like to do, where you'd like to work, and how to obtain—or create—the job of your dreams. His advice applies both to conventional and unconventional employment.

Assuming you do find an interesting job opportunity, how do you get around your mood disorder? Let's examine both traditional and non-traditional approaches.

■ TRADITIONAL RÉSUMÉS AND JOB APPLICATIONS

Conventional employers usually ask for the following information on résumés and applications:

Employment Background
- Organizations you've worked for, their locations, and the dates you were employed (including long-term freelance or contract jobs)
- Job titles and responsibilities
- Special skills and knowledge you gained on your jobs

Educational Background
- Degrees and certifications you've earned, along with schools, locations, dates, and sometimes your grade point average (GPA)
- Continuing education, such as seminars, workshops, and professional conferences, and their sponsors and dates

Nonwork Activities
- Professional associations, community groups, and charities you're active in
- Sometimes, extracurricular activities you engaged in while in school

Unless you're applying for a performance-related job, you need not include such information as height, weight, and eye color. Legally, employers cannot ask about age, marital status, or health-related matters.

For many of us with mental illnesses, the very idea of this type of résumé or application makes our blood run cold. It may feel like an interrogation meant to uncover your illness and screen you out. This is where concerns about gaps in employment rear their vicious heads. You might have a spotty work history, due to long depressive or manic episodes or to hospitalizations. You may have encountered discrimination, found it difficult to stick with a job, or even been fired a few times.

■ SKILL-BASED RÉSUMÉS

Rather than a traditional format that indicates previous job titles and the exact places and dates you worked, I recommend using a skill-based résumé. You can indicate years rather than dates, focus on special knowledge and strong points, and demonstrate your enthusiasm— even if you have limited experience. And, you can even emphasize volunteer work. Here's an example.

SAMPLE SKILLS-BASED RÉSUMÉ

SAM SNEED

345 S. Cedar   Home Phone: 246-345-6789
Yourtown, ST 24680   Cell Phone: 246-987-6543
USA   Email: ssneed@hotmail.com

JOB OBJECTIVE

Entry-level graphic design position with opportunities for learning and growth

SKILLS: Solid design and illustration skills, and experience with Adobe Illustrator, PhotoShop, QuarkXPress, Microsoft Word

EXPERIENCE: Brochure & newsletter design & production — Yourstate Community College Bilingual Education Center

                 Poster design & production — Yourstate Community College Theatre Department; Yourtown, ST

                 Art & layout — Yourstate Community College News

                 Staff artist — Southpark High News (Jr. & Sr. years); Yourtown, ST

EDUCATION: Attending Yourtown Community College Graphic Design Program; GPA 3.5 — (Certification expected next spring)

                 Southpark High — GPA 3.0 — Design I, II, & III;

                 Desktop Publishing; Spanish I & II

A good skill-based résumé can often get you hired without having to fill out a standard application that asks questions you'd rather not face. If the organization hires you and then has you complete an application after the fact, your foot will already be in the door.

Whichever kind of résumé you use, be sure to line up a few nonrelatives to use for references, should a potential employer request them. Ask people you've done your best work for if they'll be a reference, so they can think about what they'll say if a potential employer calls.

You may be wondering what else you might need to obtain a more creative job. Most often, you'll need a portfolio, headshots, a credit list, and/or a demo.

■ PORTFOLIO

Artists, photographers, and writers often need portfolios. You don't have to wait until you have tons of samples. Often, even half a dozen pieces will do. Employers rarely take the time to scrutinize portfolios extensively. Most just want to get a general sense of your style and what you can do. Also keep in mind:

- If you haven't done professional work, use pieces that you've done as a volunteer or even work you've done for your own pleasure.
- Make certain everything in your portfolio is clean and crisp.
- Rather than leave your portfolio behind, bring photocopies or duplicates for potential employers to review.
- Don't turn cartwheels to show your versatility. Include for each business opportunity the pieces that are most relevant to the position you seek.

■ HEADSHOTS, CREDITS, AND DEMOS

Actors and other performers usually need head shots (close-up pictures of themselves) and lists of credits that show roles they've played, places they've performed, and when. These creatives—as well as dancers, film-makers, and musicians—may also need demos (video or audio record-ings) of their work, but often, one or two will do.

Clearly mark any materials you supply. Adhere your name and con-tact information on the back.

INTERVIEWING FOR A JOB

I WON'T REPEAT standard interview advice because that's readily available in other books. In this section, I'll focus on concerns specific to those of us with mood disorders. Other than gaps in employment records, the most difficult problem we face is whether and when to disclose our mental illness. This issue alone keeps many of us from seeking jobs.

The following table lists both reasons to inform others about your illness and reasons to keep it to yourself. If you choose to inform your employer and/or co-workers about your illness, consider the timeframe. Will you disclose it during the interview? After you've been employed there a few months? The following table will help you consider some determining factors.

REASONS TO DISCLOSE	REASONS NOT TO DISCLOSE
You need some accommodation to do your job, such as coming to work later or taking time off to handle medical needs. The Americans with Disabilities Act requires employers to accommodate reasonable requests, but they can't do so if they don't know what you need.	You think your co-workers will make things difficult for you, or that your boss may not be compliant if you request accommodation of your medical needs.
Your co-workers may have become friends, and you think they'll be supportive.	You don't want co-workers to think you're getting special treatment and resent you.
You want to demonstrate to others that you're as capable as they are and that you have no need to be ashamed.	Other employees in the organization crack jokes about "crazy" people and don't seem open to anyone who's "different."
	You're afraid your co-workers will think less of you, be afraid of you, or reject you.

You may have additional concerns about disclosure, such as fearing you'll get fired if anyone knows. Firing someone because of a disability is against the law. However, if employers really want to get rid of someone, they'll usually find some way to do it.

In such a case, you'd be in a better position than someone without a disability. You'd have easier access to those who can help overturn an unjustified firing. The Resources section lists a place to start.

Some people with a mental illness who don't need job accommodations decide to disclose, but not immediately. They may wait until they've completed a probationary period (if the employer has one) or until after they've established good rapport and recognition for their work. I've used this approach both with conventional employers and with freelance clients in the past.

> **CAUTION!** Disclosing a mental illness is a personal decision you have every right to make on your own. Whether and when you inform others about your illness is up to you. Don't let anyone—including me—persuade you to share this information before you're ready! Or ever, if you don't want to do so.

If you decide to disclose your illness, it's best to get prepared for it first.

Before disclosing a mental illness, Fawn Fitter and Beth Gulas, authors of *Working in the Dark, Keeping Your Job while Dealing with Depression,* advise that you:

- Talk with your job coach (if you have one), your therapist, and/or an employment law attorney—and/or
- Speak to someone in the organization's Human Resources Department, Employee Assistance Program, and/or to the Equal Employment Opportunity/Affirmative Action officer.

All of these people are required by law to keep diagnoses, psychiatric histories, and medical treatments confidential.

If you need some accommodation and must disclose when you're being interviewed, Fitter and Gulas suggest you speak to the recruiter, Human Resources representative, or job interviewer. You'll say you have a disability and be prepared to provide proof if the person requests it.

If employers ask about gaps in your employment record, Fitter and Gulas say you might say you were:

- Taking medical leave (without going into specifics)
- Taking a sabbatical
- Handling a family matter that's been resolved

Please give careful thought to the disclosure decision and prepare yourself thoroughly. Although people are becoming more knowledgeable about mood disorders and therefore more open-minded, it's best to study your options before sharing such information.

Speaking of options, you may want to look into the government's Ticket to Work program.

■ TICKET TO WORK

Ticket to Work is a program run by the Social Security Administration to help people with disabilities return to the workforce without losing their Medicare or Medicaid benefits. The rules differ for those receiving SSI versus SSDI, and of course, the rules are confusing. The gist of the program is, if participants can't find a job or a job doesn't work out, they can get benefits reinstated without a waiting period. This provides some security for those concerned about having to reapproach the Social Security Administration for help.

If you apply for a Ticket to Work, have someone who has received training about Ticket to Work explain the program to you and help with your application. United Cerebral Palsy may be able to help or refer you to someone else who can. The Resources section provides contact information.

But suppose you don't want *any* kind of conventional job. Suppose your dream is to freelance or to run your own creative business. What do you do then?

FREELANCE AND ARTS-RELATED BUSINESSES

PEOPLE OFTEN THINK of "freelancing" in three different ways:

1. Doing your own thing with your art, and not compromising to please a paying market, no matter what.
2. Tailoring your work to a more predictable paying market, providing what customers want or need.
3. "Loaning" yourself out to complete individual projects for other people or organizations (some also call this "contracting").

In any case, you're running your own small business. You can pick and choose among projects and clients (at least when you're not too strapped for cash).

If you choose the first option, you better have a lot of reliable funding and people who support your interests. If you choose the third, you're essentially a "contractor," hired to apply your talents to meet others' priorities. Most freelancers choose the second option, and many supplement their income with the third (and/or with a conventional job).

In the sense of the first and second options, Mihaly Csikszentmihalyi says, "Creative individuals usually are forced to invent the jobs they will be doing all through their lives. . . . So creative individuals don't *have* careers; they *create* them."

 NEW YORK PHOTOGRAPHER *Diane Arbus (1923–71), who suffered from depression, learned her craft from her husband Allan Arbus, a U.S. Army photographer at the time, and her mentor Lisette Model. Together, the Arbuses ran a successful fashion photography studio for twenty years, then separated. She then studied further with Alexey Brodovitch and Richard Avedon.*

After her first photo-essay appeared in Esquire in 1960, Arbus made her living as a freelance photographer and photography instructor. She is best known for her surreal yet sympathetic photographs of dwarves, giants, nudists, prostitutes, and transvestites.

The year 1967 marked her first show at the Museum of Modern Art in New York. Some of her more famous photos include "Child with Toy Hand Grenade in Central Park, New York City;" "Identical Twins;" and "Jewish Giant at Home with His Parents in The Bronx, NY."

If you choose to freelance or run an arts-related business to earn your living, *ease your way in slowly* or do a *lot* of preplanning and talking with experts before plunging in. Chapter 14 explains the basics of starting and running a small business.

Even if you start with low expectations—"This is only a hobby. I'll just see where it goes"—it's a good idea to track your expenses and whatever money you bring in. You just might have a hit on your hands due to word of mouth alone. But don't count on it! You can track your income and expenses by using the categories on the IRS Schedule C: Profit or Loss from Business. Chapter 14 explains this in more depth.

Here's what some freelancers with mood disorders are doing:

Forty-two-year-old Indiana artist, musician, and writer LNA and her fiancé both have bipolar disorder. Her current passion is singing karaoke. "With singing when I am manic," she explains, "I am less inhibited . . . I don't care about criticism." Her fiancé helped set up an audition with a local band and LNA plans to do weekend gigs with them. "It will be a hoot," she says.

Although LNA claims that, professionally, she "collects dust," she does help out her fiancé. She promotes the candles and lamps he makes and provides advice about fragrances and aesthetics. "We travel [out-of-state] and go to flea markets," LNA says. Her fiancé plans to start making wooden gifts soon.

You need not always have a lot of money to get started. Some creatives create and sell their work with barely any means. Take forty-four-year-old California artist, dancer, and photographer BN.

When homeless during the 1980s, he says, he made drawings on 18-inch cardboard. People would stand around on the street to watch him work. "I had the joy of seeing people's reactions," he says. When one woman hung his drawings at a local college, BN says, it brought a lot of attention to his work.

BN urges creative people to "draw, draw, draw," or take lots of pictures from every angle that they can. "Music, dance, snap your fingers, tap your foot (hard!), listen. You can feel, imagine, and hear that train, or that person that done ya' wrong, or just the rhythm of being on a dirt road somewhere."

BN encourages fellow creatives to look "left to right, behind you, in front of you, look up, look down." Such changes of perspective can make creative work shine.

In addition to her mood disorder, Virginian NP, age fifty-four, has to deal with fibromyalgia (a disorder characterized by widespread musculoskeletal pain and fatigue). "It makes it so hard to feel like doing anything but I make myself get going.

"I love to work and stay busy," NP says. She's into woodworking and chair-bottom restoration. "When I get started I don't know when to stop. I teach classes in anything that I find a demand for and I especially enjoy working with young people and teaching them to repair/restore old furniture. I would hate to see weaving chair bottoms be a dying art."

Forty-eight-year-old Tennessee artist and writer CC sells her work at art shows. "My mosaic art sells well," she says, ". . . and I enjoy the process of creating them immensely."

Look at what you love to do most from the perspective of someone else who might love to experience or own it or learn how to do it, too. There's, literally, your job in the making.

*C*reativity requires the courage to let go of certainties.

—Pianist, composer, author, comedian, and actor Oscar Levant (1906–72), best known for his quick wit

· 11 ·

Managing Creative Projects Productively

YOU MIGHT ASSOCIATE the term project management with left-brained Type-A people who work for large bureaucratic corporations. You might think all those forms and lists and flow charts that project managers make don't apply to creative projects—especially not yours.

To some extent these are valid views. Many project managers *are* Type-A folks. And nearly all of them rely on lots of forms and lists and flow charts. And many creative projects aren't complex enough to need all that and can more or less evolve on their own.

However, project management tips and tools can help you plan and successfully complete many creative projects, possibly including yours. These tools need not be complex. Frequently, the simpler the tool, the better it works.

Monitoring projects regularly will tell you if you're on track or way, way off. It can ensure people with depression that they're making progress and that they *can* achieve their goals. It can help bring the grandiose visions of mania and hypomania closer to reality. So set your doubts aside, consider how project management might help you reach your goals, and read on.

WHAT IS PROJECT MANAGEMENT?

PROJECT MANAGEMENT HELPS you plan, schedule, and monitor all types of creations—large or small. It helps you use resources optimally, including time, energy, and money; equipment, tools, supplies, and space; and services and people. Most projects, whether formally planned and mapped out on paper—or simply imagined in your head, involve about a dozen major steps:

1. Describing the end result you want as thoroughly as possible—your goal or project's purpose.
2. Knowing what steps you must take and how important each step is.
3. Deciding the sequence in which to take those steps.
4. Estimating how long each step will take and when you need to start it.
5. Determining how you'll know when each step is complete.
6. Setting priorities for the project: speed, quality, staying within the budget.
7. Estimating costs, including any equipment, tools, supplies, services, people, and space you may require.
8. Projecting the risks or obstacles that might get in the way of its completion—and thinking about ways you can prevent or handle them.
9. Keeping tabs on expenses regularly so to stay within the budget.
10. Communicating with collaborators, outside services, and assistants.
12. Checking progress often and monitoring the project's flow.
13. Debriefing and celebrating.

Let's take a closer look at each of these factors.

■ ENVISION THE END RESULT

The end result is your goal or vision for the project. Is your goal to promote yourself and your creative work? Is it to present a single performance? Is it to produce a line of products? Is it to start and run a business where you can use your talents? Carefully answer each of the following questions:

- What do I want to offer? Performances? Products? Creative services?
- Why do I want to offer them? What do I value most about my creative work? What's its purpose?
- Who do I want to offer them to? Who would be my primary audience or customers? Might I find other markets?
- When do I want to provide my performances, products or services? Days? Nights? Times? Seasons? Dates?
- Where do I want to offer these performances, products or services? My home? Through a Web site? In an outside office? A theatre or performance hall? A museum or gallery? A retail store?
- How I want to offer them? Alone? With a partner? With a group of collaborators? Within a conventional or creative organization?

This information will help you solidify the scope of the project. What you need to do—and *not* do—to reach your goal. Carol Martin, director of production for the textbook publisher Holt Rinehart Winston, says one of the most important parts of project management is to define what the project is *not*. You can save a lot of time, expense, and aggravation by answering this question carefully. If you have depression, this information may help assure you that an overwhelming project is managcable even if it's sometimes intimidating.

■ SET YOUR PRIORITIES

Most anyone can get carried away during the creative process, get sidetracked, and lose sight of what matters most. But this is especially true when you have a mood disorder. One challenge I've faced as a writer is a tendency to over-research. I get so caught up in my reading that I'm left with very little time to write!

In the printing business (and in many others), there are three priorities: time, cost, and quality. Printers say you can have your print job quickly, inexpensively, or at high quality, *but you can't have all three at once*. If you want it quick, it's likely to cost more. If you want it cheap, the quality will probably suffer. If you want top quality, it's going to cost more and probably take more time. In other words, you can rarely have it all!

Yet, we may not accept this reality if we're manic or hypomanic. Arguing the point rarely gets you what you want and often jeopardizes relationships you'll need to further your art. So be careful!

Ask someone else to step in and deal with the person. Step back from the situation, handle your basic physical needs, talk with your therapist, and adjust your medications—with your psychiatrist's help.

■ MAP OUT THE STEPS TO TAKE

You often need a road map so you'll get where you want to go. With creative projects, people often dream about the end result without much thought to what it will take to get there.

Also, some of us get so sidetracked and we forget entirely where we meant to go! Our journey toward our destination is like a road trip where we turn down every appealing road and wind up having no idea where we are.

> THIRTY-ONE-YEAR-OLD *PH, a Wisconsin writer and dancer, says she's highly creative during her manic states. "I have come up with out-of-this-world creative advertising for many organizations. I have also written many poems, and I seem to sound and act smarter than the average person."*
>
> *When she's depressed, of course, it's another story. "Projects that started out so well end up not getting done," PH says. "I sometimes forget or don't understand what my initial plan for the project was."*
>
> *PH has found that explaining her entire plan, step by step, to others helps. "They can later help me by relaying back to me what it is I forgot or don't understand after coming down from my manic state."*

This is particularly true when we're manic or hypomanic. Impulsiveness and overconfidence tend to make us jump right in before realistically thinking things through. When we're depressed, we may be so fearful and overwhelmed that we can't envision completing even a *small* project or imagine where to begin.

■ DECIDE THE SEQUENCE IN WHICH TO DO THOSE STEPS

Some creative projects are simple and straightforward; others are quite involved. For instance, printing simple greeting cards off your computer for friends and relatives may take just a few steps. Software programs offer greeting-card templates with colorful designs. Most any computer system offers a variety of fonts to choose from. Office supply stores often carry easily folded paper stock and matching envelopes specifically for this purpose.

For a small project, you can get by with a checklist. Using greeting cards as an example, the checklist might look like this:

1. Choose template or design your own.
2. Choose font or fonts.
3. Write greetings.
4. Purchase paper stock and envelopes.
5. Print cards.
6. Address, stamp, and mail cards.

Obviously, the list will need to be tailored to your particular project and goal.

■ Estimate the Time You Need and Set a Schedule

This is a tough one. Just how long a creative project will take is hard to guess, because creativity projects often bring surprises during their development. This challenges most creatives but none more than those of us with mood disorders. If you have a depressive episode, you may be unable to work on your art for days or months on end. If you have a manic episode, you may either finish in record time or become overly involved and forget the priorities. Because of this, you must learn to cushion your schedule generously in case such problems arise. Here's what one creative artist says about the problems this has caused him:

"I have several deposits for commissions which I've not completed. I've held these for several years now, promising to get the work done. Now I stress out over them, don't answer e-mails, phone calls. It would be so much easier to just finish them but I can't. I think people think the ability to paint or draw is like turning on a faucet, but it's not. I can't explain how I have to be in the right frame of mind. I used to come up with excuses and I had carpal tunnel surgery two years ago (which is the last time I was seriously in my studio) so I tell every one my hand is still screwed up and the surgery caused more damage than good. Even now if someone asked me to do a commission I find myself saying yes but I know in my heart I can't."

In *Bipolar Disorder, Insights for Recovery,* Jane Mountain explains why those of us with bipolar disorder have trouble planning and managing projects: "When you experience grandiosity, your opinion about yourself is inflated and you are convinced you can do impossible things. . . . Grandiosity makes goals seem more attainable than they actually are. For example, you may believe you can do a six-month project in three days."

Mountain says, "You may not attempt even the simplest project since you believe that a three-day project will take six months to finish." "Clearly, an individual with bipolar disorder faces challenges in setting and reaching realistic goals."

I usually start large projects with great confidence, but if I become depressed, I'll get incredibly hesitant about certain tasks. One is calling someone—*anyone*—on the phone. I'll worry about it all day—all month, even—before I do so. I'll rationalize that the person hates being called so early—before having a chance to settle in for the day, or it's too late because it's now lunchtime. *Then*, I'll call around 4:59 p.m., thinking he or she might have headed home early.

I was surprised to learn that award-winning television personality Jane Pauley shares my problem: "What I don't do well," she writes in *Skywriting*, ". . . are the off-camera parts. The chase, the hunt—the 'get.' I'd call it the heavy lifting stuff because it can be so hard for me to pick up a phone. Ironically, I might even have a talent for that—but it's anathema to me—so I come to it with heavy, heavy resistance. I'm not competitive enough."

If you have similar behavioral patterns, keep them in mind when setting your schedule (or get someone who can help you out).

Developing a careful project plan—and keeping on top of its implementation—can help you look at the project more realistically and can go a long way toward completing your goal.

A project plan need not be perfect. You can make adjustments as needed, and in fact, you'll nearly always have to do so. As, they often say, If you don't have some sort of plan, you have nothing from which to deviate.

■ DECIDE HOW YOU'LL KNOW WHEN THE PROJECT'S DONE

You may find it absurd to decide how you'll know when a project is completed. Isn't it done when it's done? Not always. Especially if you take deep pride in your art and have perfectionist tendencies, as many of us with mood disorders do, "done" isn't always done.

Perfectionism can relate to self-esteem or to professional standards. Sometimes, it also relates to obsessive-compulsive disorder, which frequently accompanies a mood disorder. As Texas artist WR says, "I have a hang-up of perfectionism and absolute thinking. If I can't do something exceedingly well, I don't want to do it. If I get criticized I want to quit. If I don't understand something I don't want to attempt it. If things don't fit neatly in categories, I don't like to deal with them or organize them. I need to allow myself to fail and do things imperfectly and think of things in terms of improvement not perfection."

But, sometimes, creative people use imperfection intentionally. For instance, due to spiritual beliefs, many Native American tribes built deliberate flaws and asymmetry in their baskets, blankets, and pottery. They thought nothing people made could be perfect because only gods or spirits could create perfection. The flaws and asymmetry honored that belief.

Some believed that these flaws, called daus, would allow the weavers' spirits to come and go freely. Navajo weavers incorporated "spirit lines"—unwoven strands of yarn extending from one corner so their spirits could escape from the rugs and return to their souls.

One of the few lessons I remember clearly from my teens came from my high school art teacher. She said the hardest thing about watercolor was knowing when to stop.

You must learn to recognize when you've applied just enough color to the canvas to reveal a design or form and then have the discipline to stop. If you apply more paint, you'll introduce more moisture, and your painting will usually become "muddy."

$\mathcal{A}$ **poem is never finished, only abandoned.**

—French poet, essayist, and critic Paul Valéry (1871–1945)

This idea applies to other forms of art as well. Often, less is more. You must be willing to let go.

■ ESTIMATE COSTS AND SET A BUDGET

This tends to be a tough one. Where do you start when this is the first time you're doing a project of this sort? Or, where do you start if you've completed similar projects but can't recall how long they took or how much they cost? All you can do is a little research and make your best "guesstimate." But sometimes you'll run into situations that drastically affect your original estimates.

Before writing my first book, I'd researched self-publishing and attended a couple of workshops on the topic. In one, I got this great tip about shipping books by priority mail through the post office. At the time, you could send anything that fit into a priority mail envelope—up to two pounds—anywhere in the United States. And because the post office provides free cardboard envelopes for this purpose, you didn't have to pay for shipping supplies. All this for about $3.50 (though it's recently gone up to $4.05). Still, that's not a bad deal.

Knowing this, I told the printer I needed a paper stock that would limit my book's weight to no more than two pounds. Because the book contained lots of charts with heavy lines, the paper had to be opaque enough that the lines on the other side of the page wouldn't show through. The printer calculated what the book would weigh, based on the paper stock we chose and the total number of pages there'd be. Armed with this information, I set the cost of my book and the amount I'd advertise for shipping.

When I shipped the first copy, though, it weighed in at two pounds and *one lousy ounce.* I hadn't considered the weight of that free cardboard envelope. Not only that, but once you went beyond that two-pound limit, the cost of priority mail leapt up to more than $7.00. Ouch!

Given that the price of *anything* could change before you complete your project, be sure you build a cushion into your budget.

BUDGETING FOR PROJECTS

ONE OF THE most intimidating parts of project management for many of us is developing a project budget. The approach I use is to think of the budget's parts in terms of the following:

- "People" costs
- Project-specific costs
- Marketing costs

By "people" costs, I mean the cost of labor. This includes what you pay employees (if you have them), freelancers or contractors (if you need them), and yourself. Even if you don't yet pay yourself for creative projects, your time is valuable. It's wise to tie a dollar figure to the time you invest in a project because if you weren't doing the work, you'd have to pay someone else to do it. Including your own time helps you determine the true cost of a project.

The project-specific costs might include legal fees for reviewing a contract, writing a partnership agreement, filing trademark paperwork, and similar expenses. You might also pay for special supplies, studio or theatre rental, and transportation to an out-of-town site. If an agent or other professional gets a percentage of your income on a project, include that cost too. (Day-to-day business expenses, such as letterhead or file folders, are *not* project-specific costs.)

Finally, don't forget marketing! Marketing costs might include print or electronic ads, promotion materials, publicity services, postage and shipping for mailings, and long-distance calls to marketing outlets (magazines, newspapers, radio and TV stations, and specialty Web sites).

See the Creative Life Toolkit for a blank budget form. Here's a same budget for a singer whose "project" is to make and copy a demo CD to help her obtain work: She'll be hiring a three-person band she sings with to back up her performance and paying each band member fifteen dollars an hour. They'll be recording in a local professional studio. And she'll be paying for one hundred duplicate CDs and the cost of mailing them to potential agents and business managers.

SAMPLE DEMO CD BUDGET

"PEOPLE" COSTS	NOTES	COST
My time (practice & record)	24 hr @ $15/hr	[$360.00]
Band's time (practice & record)	8 hr @ $15/hr x 3	360.00
PROJECT-SPECIFIC COSTS		
Production costs (studio time & backup CD)	8 hr @ $100/hr	800.00
Duplication cost (100 CDs with color labels in slip sleeves for mail - provided by studio)	CDs $1, labels $.50 slip sleeves $.10 each x 100	160.00
MARKETING COSTS		
Promotional mailing (three-day 1st class mail)	(CD plus letter) $.63 each	63.00
TOTAL PROJECT COST:	(out-of-pocket)	$1,383.00
ACTUAL PROJECT COST:	(with my time)	$1,743.00

I always pad my budget some to allow for surprises. For instance, in our example, recording this demo CD might take twice as much studio time if the performers are nervous or having a bad day. Things rarely go exactly as planned.

■ ASSESS CHALLENGES AND RISKS

Virtually every project carries some challenges and risks. It may take longer or cost more than you anticipated. It may take more skill or people than you have. You may be less than thrilled with the results.

*P*roblems **worthy of attack prove their worth by fighting back.**

—Hungarian mathematician Paul Erdös (1913-96)

Personal and technical problems nearly *always* arise. For instance:

- You may have to change psychiatrists, psychologists, or meds.
- You may require unexpected surgery.
- An employer or client may not pay on time—or at all.
- That "great" new computer you bought may turn out to be a lemon.

- Someone unexpected might join and disrupt your household, like a new baby, an adult child who boomerangs back to your empty nest, or a friend in need of shelter.
- You may get so hypomanic or manic that you can't focus for weeks.
- You may have taken on so many commitments that you can't give them the degree of attention you'd like and still complete them on time .
- A parent may fall ill and need professional care or a nursing home.
- Your best friend or a beloved pet may die, throwing you into long-term grief.
- Your car may catch fire and have to be replaced.
- You may fall into a depression you can't shake for months.

Need I say such a list could go on and on? I don't mean to scare or discourage you, but stuff happens. *Every single one* of these things has happened to me since I first started freelancing! That *doesn't* mean they'll happen to you. But something will. I guarantee it.

Realize you'll run into a few surprises. Allow for them during your planning, deal with them, and then get back to work!

■ Track Your Expenses

Obviously, if you don't track your expenses, you may be in for an unpleasant surprise. This is especially crucial for people with bipolar disorder, as we tend to spend freely without considering consequences and then get shocked later on.

See chapter 14 for more about bookkeeping.

■ Consider Collaborators, Services, and Assistants

Creative projects frequently involve several people. You therefore must consider their roles and needs. Chapter 13 discusses how to effectively work with and communicate with others.

■ MONITOR YOUR PROGRESS

Professional project managers, some whose job consists entirely of project management use a variety of tools to plan and monitor projects.

Often you can get by with informal methods like simple checklists, calendar notations, and tickler files. At other times, you're better off with more formal methods. Thoroughly explore any bundled software that came with you computer, as well as programs you purchased separately. There may be features you're not using or aren't aware of that could help you tremendously. Many software bundles include calendar or datebook programs in which you can create reminders and request advance notification for important dates.

I used two types of checklists while writing this book, one for listing steps and substeps and the other for checking my progress.

■ STEP AND SUBSTEP CHECKLISTS

The first checklist I used was a step and substep checklist. I experience frequent memory problems, due to my disorder, the meds I take, my age—or possibly all three! I constantly forget where I've placed things and what work I've completed on a project—even if I did it the day before.

My checklist had two main steps: (1) checking paper files, and (2) checking electronic files for the following:

Paper files—
- An accordion file folder in which I kept paper copies of articles
- Books in which I'd marked information I wanted to incorporate
- Hanging folders in which I stored additional notes
- A red three-ring binder in which I kept drafts of chapters as I wrote them

Electronic files—
- Chapters and chapter segments I'd already written
- Downloaded articles and other resource information
- Profiles I wrote from interviews and survey responses

When working on a chapter, my list helped me remember each place I needed to look for information or what I'd already written. I kept my checklist on a clipboard so I would know how much I'd done.

You can use such a checklist for any project that requires cycling through the same steps for each part. For instance, when producing a video series, you might create a list for each show that includes checking costumes, makeup, props, sets, and lights, and then shooting several takes and viewing the results before editing.

Such a system works pretty well *as long as you use your checklist consistently and don't misplace it!* Keeping it on a clipboard increases the chance of finding it if papers and files get out of control.

■ PROGRESS CHECKLISTS

For the second checklist, I adapted a detailed list that my friend and fellow writer Steve Birch shared with me. It's based on an expanded outline and table of contents.

SAMPLE PROGRESS CHART

CHAPTER 1 (Goal: introduce main ideas)	WORDS: Est. 4,000	REFERENCES	DEFINITIONS
* Introduction		Wills & Cooper	creativity, talent & genius
* Creative/"Crazy" Connection	✔	Jamison–*Touched with Fire*	artists, creative artists, & fine artists
* Creative Mystique	✔	Mallin/Szasz	
* Reservations re: Connection		Csikszentmihalyi–*Creativity*	creative [noun] & creatives
* Who This Book is For	✔	Barron–*Creators on Creating*	madness, insanity, & mental illness
* How This Book is Organized (research questions)		Berman	
* Definitions	✔	Rothenberg	recovery & healing
* Committing to Creativity	✔	Barzun/ Young	
CHAPTER 2 and so on			

It's a challenge for many creatives to maintain a detailed checklist. It's even harder when you have depression or bipolar disorder.

If you're depressed, you may get overwhelmed and may decide it's not worth the effort, you probably won't complete the project anyway.

If you're manic or hypomanic, you may lack the patience or believe it isn't necessary. After all, you are invincible!

It's tempting to speed up your work when things start getting out of control and then to "clean up mistakes" later. But this is rarely wise. Sometimes you have to slow down and "regroup."

In fact, my friend Dennis Romig, an organizational psychologist and president of the international "think and do tank," PRI, once shared that Edward de Bono, the world's expert on creativity and thinking, wrote that "if he could give only one recommendation to people it would be 'Slow down your thinking.'"

■ OTHER PLANNING AND MONITORING TOOLS

PERT charts (project evaluation and review technique) and Gantt charts (named after management consultant, Henry Gantt) are two common types of project management tools. You can use either for single-person projects or for collaborative work.

During many projects, some steps come before others, some overlap, and some happen simultaneously. When this is the case, a PERT chart may be helpful.

PERT charts—These charts look like mind maps and display a sequence of steps in flowchart form. They can show where steps overlap and how they relate to one another.

For example, if you're involved in a full-length play, you might suggest using a PERT chart if the cast and crew are disorganized and overwhelmed. That way, you'll all get a sense of the major steps and which ones can be done simultaneously. Here's an example:

SAMPLE PERT CHART

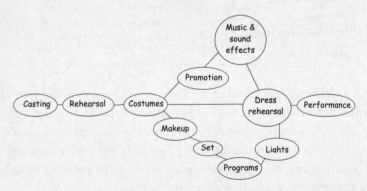

Because creatives tend to be visual, sometimes they prefer PERT charts. A PERT chart can provide most of the information you need to *plan* a project. However, when *monitoring progress* on a project, you'll probably need something more detailed.

Gantt Charts—Gantt charts are more linear and tend to be more specific. They're particularly useful for planning and monitoring steps and substeps that need to be done in a certain order, those that can overlap, and those people can do simultaneously.

Gantt charts are especially useful for collaborative efforts because each person can see how their role relates to others' roles and to the project's success. Here's a sample Gantt chart based on the previous PERT chart.

SAMPLE GANTT CHART

PROJECT: Our New Play	WEEK							
STEP/SUBSTEP	1	2	3	4	5	6	7	8
CASTING								
* Tryouts & callbacks	X							
* Announce cast & schedule	X							
REHEARSALS								
* Regular rehearsals		X	X	X	X	X		
* Dress rehearsal							X	
COSTUMES								
* Design costumes		X						
* Measure cast & order fabric			X					
* Make costumes				X	X	X		
MAKEUP								
* Order makeup		X						
SET								
* Design set & buy materials		X						
* Build & paint set			X	X				
PUBLICITY								
* Create posters & postcards				X				
* Contact media & mail postcards				X				
* Hang posters & do interviews					X	X		
PROGRAM								
* Line up advertisers		X	X					
* Design & create program				X	X			
* Print program						X		
MUSIC & SOUND EFFECTS								
* Select music/effects				X	X			
* Record music/effects						X		
LIGHTING								
* Design & set lights						X		
* Check lights on cast's skin tones							X	
PERFORMANCE!								X

Monitoring projects regularly can help people with depression see that they're making progress and that their goals are achievable. It can also help moderate the grandiose visions of mania and hypomania.

If you find yourself behind and think, "Well, I'll make up for being behind during the next few steps," watch out! You're probably fooling yourself. If you've underestimated how long one step will take, you may have underestimated them all.

In either case, careful project management will cut down the confusion and memory problems that mood disorders often bring.

■ DEBRIEF AND CELEBRATE

Last of all, remember to debrief and celebrate when your project's over. Talk about how things went and think about ways to make things easier or be more effective next time. And don't forget to celebrate the project's completion—whether that means celebrating great success or the relief it's over!

A good plan today is better than a perfect plan tomorrow.

—from the 1997 movie *Wag the Dog*,
written by David Mamet and Hilary Henkin

· 12 ·

Promoting Yourself and Your Creative Work

IF YOU INTEND to get anyone other than your family, friends, and colleagues to buy your products or services, or to attend your performances, you absolutely must know the basics of marketing and promotion.

You may be thinking, Well, I'm an artist. The venue/producer/publisher will promote me, so I don't have to think about that. Unfortunately, that's not the case.

A theatre or club will usually advertise your performance in some way, though quite likely not the way you envision. A store or gallery may announce that you're coming, but your ad might be only a small blurb in an in-house bulletin or a tiny listing in a community newspaper. Publishers will announce that your book's out and help get it into bookstores and libraries, but they may not do much more than that; nor can you assume that newspapers and magazines will review it. Crafts fairs and festivals usually list everyone who's coming, but your name may get lost in the mix.

Until you're really well known, that's about the extent of it. As a "professional creative," you need to market your performances, products, services, and yourself. You may require help from outside services or individuals to get the word out about your projects.

The majority of your promotion and its expense will fall directly on you. You'll need to use your imagination to make yourself stand out and use your dollars well.

This chapter explains the basics of marketing and promotion (which, incidentally, also includes advertising and publicity). Many creatives detest such activities; they'd rather be working directly on their art. Some actually thrive on doing them.

Marketing and promotion are particularly frightening when you're depressed and your self-esteem is down. And, when you're hypomanic or manic, you're likely to go overboard or even do something detrimental.

COMING TO TERMS WITH MARKETING

ALTHOUGH PEOPLE OFTEN use the terms *marketing*, *promotion*, *advertising*, and *publicity* interchangeably, there are some differences.

■ MARKETING

Marketing encompasses everything you do to sell your performances, products, and services, and to build your professional reputation. It takes a big-picture view and can make or break your success. It's something every business simply must do.

The "umbrella" of marketing includes the following:

- Informing everyone you know and meet about yourself and what you're doing
- Persuading others to book your performances, exhibit your work, carry your products, or fund your projects
- Getting others to attend your performances, purchase your products, use your services, and inform other potentially interested parties about your products or services

Some creatives enjoy promoting their work, while others detest it. When you have a mood disorder, that preference may change as your mood swings back and forth, as it does for this creative: "I have spurts of confidence, during which I get moving on plans around marketing my work. I will wake up some mornings with my head spinning with ideas of new things to make and sell—designs, materials, entire series of products."

▪ PROMOTION

Promotion is a branch of marketing that focuses on getting the word out about your performances, products, and services.

Promotion includes:

- Informing people about yourself and your art through your own printed and electronic materials, including Web sites
- Presenting yourself in a way that people remember you
- Informing people about yourself and your art through the media (newspapers, magazines, radio, TV, etc.)
- Providing a portfolio, audio or video demo, film clips, sample articles, and columns
- Providing résumés and lists of credits, head shots, and photos of performances
- Delivering presentations and giving public speeches
- Posting information in the form of posters and fliers (with the permission of places where you place them)
- Passing out such freebies as bookmarks, buttons, gadgets, pens and pencils, sample CDs or DVDs, and T-shirts

TEXAS ROCK SINGER/SONGWRITER/CARTOONIST *Daniel Johnston gained recognition on the Austin music scene in the mid-'80s—both for handing out free tapes of his work and for his "iconoclastic" performances. Some of Johnston's albums include* Fear Yourself, Rejected Unknown, *and* The Late Great Daniel Johnston. *He has appeared on MTV's* Cutting Edge *and has been profiled in the* New York Times, Rolling Stone, Spin, *and* Texas Monthly.

His illness surfaced as severe depression when he was twelve. Like many of us, he wasn't diagnosed as bipolar until his midtwenties. When his depression shifted to ecstatic mania, "It got out of control." Johnston found himself "head-to-head with the law." Five years in and out of psychiatric hospitals followed.

> *Since finding the right combination of medications, Johnston has been stable more than ten years. He sometimes misses mania, though. He thinks it inspired some of his best music. "When you hit the mania, it's better than any drug. But it's not worth suffering through the depression. Not worth it."*
>
> *Now forty-four, Johnston draws and sells cartoons and other products over the Internet and says he's doing very well. "I always wanted to be an artist. . . . I'm doing it more and more. I spend most of my day doing artwork, though I want to get back to music more."*
>
> *Johnston's efforts are paying off, and his star is rising once again. He and his band, Danny and the Nightmares, recently produced some four-track recordings and got "a real record deal." He's really happy about that.*
>
> *The New York Whitney Museum of American Art chose a selection of Johnston's cartoons for its biennial. And in March 2006, Sony Pictures Classic released* The Devil and Daniel Johnston, *a full-length award-winning documentary about Johnston's creativity and struggle with manic depression {bipolar disorder}.*

Advertising and publicity are two facets of promotion.

■ ADVERTISING

Advertising is paid promotion that helps sell products or services by delivering a message to many people simultaneously.

Advertising includes:

- Business listings in the telephone directory
- Newspaper or magazine display or classified ads
- Radio or TV commercials
- Direct-mail brochures, postcards, or fliers
- Ads and pop-up windows on Web sites
- Special placement of your product on a store's table, in a window, or any purchasable display exclusive to your item

Advertising is often extremely expensive, and a one-shot ad is rarely even noticed. On average, people must be exposed to the same information seven times before it sinks in! Publicity is much more cost effective.

▪ PUBLICITY

Publicity is essentially free promotion (other than the costs you pay to set it up, such as postage and long-distance). Publicity requires careful advance planning; each newspaper, magazine, TV/radio show, and venue has its own set of deadlines, sometimes months in advance.

Publicity includes:

- Articles that you or someone else writes
- Profiles of you that appear in newsletters, newspapers, or magazines
- Radio or TV interviews, performances, or public service announcements
- Classes that you teach to raise your visibility
- Benefits for special causes
- Readings, signings, or demonstrations that you do in a public or commercial space

The possibilities for marketing, promotion, advertising, and publicity are as wide as your imagination.

THREE KEYS TO MARKETING SUCCESS

BEFORE YOU INVEST time, energy, and money in marketing of any kind, it's a good idea to form a brief marketing plan—even if it's just one page. To do so, first carefully examine these three keys: (1) Your audience, customers, or clients, (2) your performances, products, or services, and (3) the location that offers the greatest chance for your success. You may find it helpful to return to the dream, goals/strategies/steps, and mind mapping exercises in chapter 5.

A simple marketing plan might address:

- A statement that communicates what you're about
- Your goals for a well-defined period (frequently the quarter or year)
- The performances or products you plan to develop during that time
- The services you plan to continue or add during that time
- The market or markets you plan to target during that time
- The results by which you'll measure your success

Remember, you also have to work the plan and do so regularly. It's tempting to concentrate only on rehearsing performances, developing products, or providing services to someone else. You may think, "I'll get around to marketing after that's done." To be successful, however, you must market during the time that you're creating. Set a regular time or day each week to concentrate on marketing tasks.

I must confess, I didn't have much of a marketing plan for my first two books. For the first, I had a kind of "build it and they will come" attitude. When I took a workshop to help prepare for TV interviews, the first question the interviewer asked was, "What makes your book different from all the other style books out there?"

I knew my book was unique, but the question still threw me for a loop. All I could do was stammer and blush! I clearly hadn't thought things through.

For the second, I got overwhelmed with too many opportunities and couldn't decide which ones to follow up on. The planning I had done wasn't *specific* enough.

Don't let the same thing happen to you!

YOUR AUDIENCE, CUSTOMERS, OR CLIENTS

SUCCESSFUL BUSINESSES KNOW who their customers or clients are. These businesses know what people buy and why, when, where, and how they buy it. They also know how much those people will pay.

Who are you pitching yourself or your work to? The more specifically you define your target audience, the easier it will be to reach them. You may think, "Well, they're the general public," but that's way too broad. Marketing to the general public is virtually impossible. You're much better off if you can narrow the field.

Who might your art most appeal to? Some questions are relatively easy to answer, like:

- Children? Teenagers? Middle-aged people? Senior citizens?
- Men or women? Married, attached, or single? Parents or not?
- Highly educated or not?
- People with a strong interest in the art, or those who might know very little about it yet?
- A particular social, political, or religious audience?

Other questions require an educated guess. For instance, Where do they live? What's their level of income? What lifestyle do they have? What activities do they participate in? How can you best reach them: newspapers, magazines, commercial radio or TV, public media, schools or community centers, or the Internet?

Even if you can't answer these questions—particularly at first, answering those you can helps form a clear picture of your "target market."

YOUR PERFORMANCES, PRODUCTS, OR SERVICES

IT'S OFTEN SAID that successful businesses find a need and fill it. But how does this advice apply to creative arts? Can people live without your artwork? Your book? Your film? Your photos? Your performance?

People must need or want your products, services, or performances if they're going to pay for them. This need or desire must be adequate to keep your business going. Sometimes the potential customers or clients already have that need or desire. Sometimes you must persuade them that they need what you're offering. Or you must create a desire to have it. When it comes to creative arts, you've got to be persuasive.

Next, check out the competition. Your competitors may be indirect competitors, direct competitors, or both.

Indirect competitors supply products, services, or performances that people might spend the same money on instead of yours. For instance, they might buy a purse or a pair of shoes rather than your jewelry. Or they might go to a play or a concert instead of your film.

Direct competitors supply the same or similar products, services, or types of performances as you do. For instance, if you make jewelry and sell it at crafts fairs, your direct competitors would be jewelry and department stores. And if you're screening an independent film, people might go to a Hollywood-produced movie instead.

Are other artists producing the same types of products as you are? Are they providing the same types of services or giving the same types of performances as you are? If so, it's particularly important that you find some way to stand out. Ask yourself these questions:

- What makes you or your product special and unique?
- What do you have that might attract customers or clients?
- How can you distinguish yourself from your competitors?

LOCATION, LOCATION, LOCATION

IF YOU SELL products out of a physical storefront or studio, or perform or provide services somewhere other than online, is the building conveniently located? Is it in a safe area? Is there adequate parking? Is the building clean and inviting? Does it have a pleasant ambiance? Are you renting space or paying an owner a commission on the pieces that are sold?

Do the store and adjacent businesses appear to be successful, with a good turnover of merchandise and the kind of clientele you wish to attract? Good business locations are close to their target markets and near compatible businesses as well.

 TEXAS ARTIST WR *has a pretty simple marketing plan. He decorates store windows for holidays and paints announcements about sales. He targets businesses with large windows in storefronts. WR's clients include fast-food locations and restaurants, dentists' and doctors' offices, car dealerships, and so on.*

He doesn't have to think much about his location because he comes directly to his clients. He targets only stores within ten miles of his home, approaching only the most visible so people see him as he paints. By limiting his commute, he gains more painting time— time he both enjoys and he can bill for.

WR leaves business cards at each location and gets more than enough referrals from his clients and the customers who see his work.

If you sell products or services online or through the mail, is it easy for the customer to order? Do you offer convenient payment options? Do you have a system set up for quick, reliable delivery? Have you thought about your returns policy, or how to handle a client's request to stop work on a project you've already begun? How will you deal with late payments or nonpayments for your work? What if something comes up that prevents your delivering as ordered?

Working out practical answers to these questions is hard work for anyone starting a business, and it gets even more complex when you have a mood disorder. If you are depressed, it might seem impossible. When you're hypomanic or manic, you might be tempted to blow it off. After all, you already have the answers to everything, right? You'll "just think of something as the need arises."

Questions about your audience, your product, service, or performance, and your location are all answerable. You'll just need a bit of market research. If such activities intimidate you, or you find yourself getting overwhelmed, ask other people for feedback. You don't have to go it alone!

MARKET RESEARCH

THE TERM MARKET RESEARCH may bring visions of expensive consultants, focus groups, and surveys, but your research doesn't have to be that expensive or involved. All you may need is a little footwork. Try talking with:

- Potential customers
- Colleagues and competitors
- Agents and representatives
- Retailers such as bookstore, gift shop, and gallery owners
- Your local chamber of commerce
- Even family members and friends, if they're able to be direct and honest

As an author, I do all I can to "wear the shoes" and "get into the brains" of my audience. If I'm writing in a new area, I attend conferences, meetings, and trainings for those in the field. I read books and articles about it. And I talk with people who are involved in that area.

You can use similar techniques to get feedback about your art. Prepare to clearly communicate why people should buy your products, use your services, or attend your performances!

SELF-PROMOTION

HAS ANYONE EVER warned you not to brag about yourself or your accomplishments? Has someone told you people don't like braggarts and that bragging isn't "nice" or that it's rude? Has anyone called you self-centered when you talk about yourself and your interests? If so, it's time to turn those thoughts around.

Peggy Klaus, author of *Brag! The Art of Tooting Your Own Horn Without Blowing It*, defines bragging this way: "To talk about your best self (interests, ideas, and accomplishments) with pride and passion in a conversational manner intended to excite admiration, interest, and wonder, without pretense or overstatement—in other words, without being obnoxious."

"Learning to brag," says Klaus, "is not about becoming something you aren't or trying to put something over on someone." It's just sharing yourself and telling your story in an enthusiastic, authentic, and unobtrusive way. When you brag in this way, you move yourself and your creativity toward greater success.

Klaus encourages us to drop brief "snippets of impressive information" into our conversations to ensure that people remember us. A "brag bite" should be brief but compelling. Klaus says some suitable topics include colorful details about your accomplishments, interests, and passions that reveal who you are both professionally and personally.

Many marketing and networking experts suggest you develop a thirty-second "elevator pitch." An effective elevator pitch describes what you're about and generates a person's interest. Keep your elevator pitch on the tip of your tongue. This may take a lot of practice, but it's worth it.

When you're depressed, having this information memorized can boost your self-confidence and help you get through it. When you're manic or hypomanic, remind yourself that you have thirty seconds to get your point across. Don't rush it. On the other hand, don't follow a person off the elevator and down the hall!

Now let's take a look at some basic marketing and promotion tools most all creatives need.

PAPER-BASED MARKETING MATERIALS

YOU'LL NEED OFFICE supplies such as business cards, letterhead and envelopes, and a fax cover sheet. Some people may also want customized shipping labels, memo sheets or adhesive notes, and pocket folders.

You'll also want performance-, product-, or service-specific materials like brochures, flyers, posters, news releases, and press kits.

Most likely, you won't need all of these or need them all at once. You can always add more over time. Just save the information that you'll need so you don't have to re-create it.

Avoid using a hodgepodge of unique materials. Maintain a consistent look. Creating a consistent image to communicate what you're about is part of "branding."

Match font names and point sizes, ink colors, colors, and weights of lines and of paper stock. Don't make your design so busy or loud, or so delicate or small, that the actual content is obscured. If your materials contain photos or artwork, keep both print and electronic master copies readily accessible.

■ BUSINESS CARDS

On business cards, you'll need some or all of the following elements:

Company Name—Many artists simply use their own name rather than a separate business name. There's no rule that you have to have a separate business name. (If you do, though, be sure you register that business name (often called a DBA—"doing business as") with your city, county, or state. Where you register varies from state to state. Also obtain any other legal registrations required in your area. An accountant or lawyer, or a state comptroller's office will tell you where to go.

Logo—If you have a logo, use it in all of your materials, whether print or electronic. Just as with a separate business name, you don't have to have a logo. It can however make you stand out from your competition and make your business more memorable. It doesn't have to be fancy or expensive to be effective. You can often get by with type alone and add a simple piece of clip art or a photo. Just be sure your card is attractive and, most of all, readable.

Your Name—If you don't use your own name as your business name, you may wish to add it. If you work with other artists in your business, your name may be optional.

Business address—If you work at home and wish to maintain your privacy, consider getting a post office box. If you have an online business, your Web site may be all you need.

Business phone number—This need not be a separate line but should be a number (or several) where people can usually reach you or leave a message. If you include more than one number, label them clearly, such as Office: 123-456-7890, Cell: 123-456-0987.

Fax number, e-mail address, and Web site: This assumes you have a stand-alone fax machine, or Internet-based fax service and Internet access. Although fewer people rely on fax machines these days, a stand-alone fax is useful for sending printed materials not easily sent online, such as writers' clips (published samples). If you wish to be perceived as a professional creative or an "up-and-going concern," you'll need an e-mail account and Web site. If you don't expect to use your e-mail on a large scale, a free account offered by such Internet sites as Gmail, Juno, or Yahoo! may be sufficient. They still require an Internet connection to access, of course.

Business slogan or tag line—Some people also add a slogan to their business materials.

At one point my business focused on editing and publication services. I also wrote question-and-answer columns about these topics under the pseudonym, "Style Meister." I therefore included the slogan "Home of the Style Meister" on my business cards, stationery, and fax cover sheets. I'll admit that the slogan itself wasn't particularly creative, but it was memorable because the name "Style Meister" was unique.

Your specialty or specialties: Information about what you do or who or what you do it for helps jog clients' or customers' memories about what you said when you gave them your card. For instance, a filmmaker might add "documentary films." A pianist might list the types of events he or she plays at, such as graduations, weddings, parties, and so forth, or simply "pianist."

An inspiration quote—I've even see some business cards that include an inspiration quote. For instance, "To succeed it is necessary to accept the world as it is and rise above it.— Michael Korda."

The trick with business cards is to make contact information readily accessible and easily readable and to have an aesthetically pleasing design.

■ STATIONERY

At a minimum, business stationery needs a company name (or your name), a logo (if you have one), a business address, and, on the letterhead, a primary business phone number (though not necessarily more than one). Other common elements include a fax number, an e-mail address, and a Web site. Make all print-based and electronic materials as consistent as you can.

Slogans, tag lines, specialties, and quotes are rarely used on stationery and tend to clutter the page.

■ Fax Cover Sheet

E-mail is rapidly outpacing faxes, but faxes still have their place. Some clients and customers may even prefer faxes to e-mail.

Your fax cover sheet should include your business name, your name, and your business phone number, in case the recipient needs to discuss the fax with you. In addition, fax cover sheets should include the business you are faxing to and the recipient's name and phone number, as well as the date and the total number of pages you're faxing (including the cover sheet). It may or may not include a logo.

You'll also need enough room to write your message or comments on the cover page. These can be handwritten (if your handwriting is legible) or typed. Some people also add boxes to check or words to circle such as Urgent, Reply ASAP, or For Your Information.

You can even use your fax cover sheet as a marketing device. For instance, when I publish a book, I include an image of its cover on my fax cover sheet.

■ E-mail Messages

Be as professional with your e-mail's appearance as with your printed materials. Set up your e-mail account with your business name or your name, or a creative phrase that won't confuse recipients about what you do. For example, if you are a caterer, goodcookin'@[server] might serve your purposes, whereas yummygirl@[server] may be treated as spam and never be opened.

Your e-mail software may allow you to add a "signature," to appear at the bottom of messages. This should include your name, your position in your company, its street mailing address or post office box, telephone number, fax number, your e-mail address (just to be complete), and Web site, if you have one. Some people include a very small logo. Once you've set up a signature, you don't have to retype the information on each message that goes out.

You might also add a brief tag line that sets you apart. Humorous tag lines can be especially effective. One of my writer friends, Linda Bingham, uses "Metaphors be with you" in with her signature.

Be careful, however, not to include too much. People hate scrolling through line after line to absorb a message. Also ensure that whatever you use is in good taste. If you have a mood disorder, run all of your materials by a friend to ensure that your message isn't morose or off the wall.

Some e-mail software let you control the font size, style, and color of your message. Coordinate these with what's on your printed letterhead.

For reasons of security, some e-mail recipients don't open attachments from unknown senders. Learn how to paste short documents, such as a flier or résumé, directly into the body of your message. Don't send large, *unsolicited* files, especially if they contain graphics that demand a lot of memory to download.

NEWS RELEASES AND PRESS KITS

NEWS RELEASES AND press kits are standard ways to contact the media. News releases are appropriate for announcing news and for announcing upcoming events. Press kits are more appropriate for introducing yourself and your work.

SAMPLE NEWS RELEASE

Main Street Galleries
456 South Main
Yourtown, ST 24680
123-456-7899

FOR IMMEDIATE RELEASE
CONTACT: Harry Hanger, 123-456-7899

NEWS RELEASE

MONTH-LONG EXHIBIT HIGHLIGHTS PLIGHT OF ELDERLY

(YOURTOWN, YOURSTATE) We owe our freedom to what Tom Brokaw calls "The Greatest Generation." Yet, we've left many of its members behind.

Nearbytown photographer/writer Anita Flash shares the stories of 80 elderly residents now living on the streets. Main Street Galleries will host this exhibit throughout May 2007 to highlight Older Americans Month.

Main Street Galleries owner Harry Hanger says, "Flash's poignant images and stories portray the heart-breaking poverty many older citizens face."

Photo exhibit for Older Americans Month
Donations go to Yourtown Meals on Wheels.

WHEN: Tuesdays–Sundays, May 1-30, 2007

WHERE: Main Street Galleries, 456 South Main

CONTACT: Main Street Galleries 123-456-7899

# # #

The media consists of newspapers, wire services, magazines, radio, TV, e-zines, and Internet sites. Remember that, besides your local newspaper, there are community, regional, and national general interest and specialty publications.

A good news release summarizes a story to help newspaper reporters and radio and TV producers understand it with a glance. Write your news release as if it will be a lead story on a newspaper's front page.

Make certain what you write is factual and well organized. Use one major idea per paragraph, and short, simple sentences.

Your release needs to answer Who, What, When, Where, and Why, and when appropriate, also How. Use one double-spaced page whenever possible. Print your releases on letterhead when you can. If you must use a second page, label it clearly.

Carefully check the grammar and spelling. Computers can't catch everything; they're not as bright as you! Proofread each page carefully, and when possible, run it by another person.

- Start your release either with a "hook"—an intriguing statement to draw a person's interest—or with the most important information.
- In the first or second paragraph, answer What, When, and Where.
- Include a brief quote from someone involved with the event, or write a quotable description. Frequently, newspapers and magazine print news releases verbatim.
- Be certain all details are clear and accurate! Double-check days of the week, dates, times, contacts, and phone numbers. Sending a second (or third) release to correct previous information will reduce your credibility. (But do so when it's necessary.)

Before sending a news release, contact the newspaper, magazine, radio, or TV station to ask which reporter, editor, or producer you need to contact. Frequently, the people who handle story ideas will be different than the people who handle announcements.

Ask whether to send a news release, a letter, or a press kit. Some organizations require you to use their own form in place of a news release. Be sure to ask what their deadlines are for date-sensitive material.

If you send photos or illustrations, ask what size and format is best. Many media outlets prefer electronic files. Include the number of minutes an announcement to be read aloud is likely to take (read it aloud several times, using your computer's lower-right-hand clock or a clock with a secondhand, to time it).

Find out if your contact prefers to be contacted by e-mail, fax, mail, or phone. Check the spelling of your contact's name, as well as the street or e-mail address, or fax number.

Whenever you speak to reporters, editors, or producers, first ask if they're "on deadline." Remember that even if they prefer phone calls, you might not be calling at a convenient time. They won't appreciate your call if it comes fifteen minutes before they must send an article they're writing or they're going on the air.

Instead, ask them to suggest a good time to call back. Show them you respect their time.

GETTING MATERIALS PRINTED

YOU CAN CHOOSE from several options for designing and reproducing paper-based materials. These include:

- Professional graphic designers or desktop publishers
- Friends or relatives with design skills or printers
- Full-service printers
- Copy shops
- Your personal printer

You don't necessarily need a designer if you have some basic design sense and a computer. You may, however, get something you're happier with if you work with a professional.

You also don't necessarily need an outside printer or copy shop to produce acceptable or even outstanding materials. And you can do so as you need them. You can print materials on a high-quality ink-jet or laser printer. If the printer can print at least 600 dpi (dots per inch), many people won't know you haven't used a commercial printer. Blank sheets of business card stock are readily available at most office supply stores.

For press kits, you can purchase sturdy paper folders with two pockets on the inside. Rather than get them custom printed, you can adhere a label or a business card on the cover.

When I first went into business as Castle Communications, I had a professional design my logo (a simple castle with a waving flag). I have both physical masters and electronic masters of my logo that I use on my paper-based business materials, on my self-published products, and on my Web site and electronic communications.

I began with very simple business cards and stationery. Then later—in a hypomanic state—I invested several thousand dollars in fancier materials. I paid a professional designer to create the masters and a full-service printer to have them produced. But to keep the cost down per item, I had to order such large quantities that nearly a decade later I still haven't used them up!

My fax number has changed since that printing, so I'm now crossing it out and using a rubber stamp to show the new one. It's a bit tacky, but easier on my budget. Even if you sense you're only marginally hypomanic, it's best to run big purchases by another person to verify that the costs are reasonable.

ELECTRONIC MARKETING ELEMENTS

TODAY LOTS OF business gets done electronically. I've dealt with several out-of-state editing clients exclusively over the Internet and phone. Electronic marketing elements include your e-mail signature and/or e-mail business card, and your Web site. And one of the most important and inexpensive ways to promote performances, products, and services is through a Web site.

Three things you need for a Web site are:

- A Web site host—A company or organization that stores Web site files on their server, keeps those sites, and offers other services.
- A domain name—This can be either a "subdomain name" following your host's name (like thehostname.com/yourname) or a domain name you obtain separately (like yourname.com).
- The Web site pages people will see on your site—which you or a friend or family member designs, or that you hire a professional to do.

■ WEB SITE HOSTS

Arts organizations often offer a small free site to members. Or you can shop for a free or low-cost host online. Some offer free sites in exchange for allowing them to display a banner or pop-up window ads on your site. For less than $10 a month, however, you can find great hosts that don't require that. I'm pleased with my current host, iPowerWeb, which charges less than one-sixth of what I used to pay a local Web site host.

If people you know have Web sites, ask who hosts theirs and how satisfied they are with the service. You can also find a wealth of options by searching the Internet for terms such as "free Web site" or "Web site hosting."

■ DOMAIN NAME

Having your own domain name provides more credibility. Some hosting companies offer free or low-cost domain names, along with or in addition to their hosting cost. Otherwise, you can purchase your own domain name from companies like www.godaddy.com, www.network-solutions.com, or www.register.com.

Your domain name must be unique. All the shorter domain names I had in mind for Castle Communications were already taken when I set up mine. That's why my Web site name (castlecommunications.com) is so long. Ideally, your e-mail address and domain name will be nearly identical, so that your clients can easily remember them.

■ MERCHANT ACCOUNTS

If you plan to sell anything from your site, you'll need an easy way for people to pay for it. Some hosts offer "merchant accounts" that allow you to collect payments by credit card, check, and/or debit cards from your online customers. If yours doesn't do this, you can obtain low-cost merchant services from such companies as www.paypal.com, www.merchant.com, or www.2checkout.com.

■ WEB SITE PAGES

If you're reasonably computer-literate, you can design and create your own Web site. Word-processing and page layout programs frequently provide Web site templates and/or allow you to save files as Web pages.

Most Web site hosts also offer free templates and/or software for designing and building your site. This is often a good option because whatever they provide should work well with the server that stores your Web site.

If you don't want to design your Web site, ask a computer-savvy friend or relative, barter with someone who's familiar with Web site design, or hire a professional Web designer. Ask around for referrals or search the Internet using the term Web site designers. Reputable designers have an appealing, easily used Web site and an online portfolio so you can get a sense of their work.

These are options even if you don't have a computer. You may be able to send e-mails from a friend or relative's home or you can usually use a computer at a public library. You may be able to get an individual or organization to host a small Web site to advertise what you have to offer. Even a one-page site may do.

Remember, both your print and electronic materials present an image of you as a creative artist. Do whatever you can to make it easy for customers or clients to reach you. And, above all, use your imagination and have fun!

*H*ide not your talents, they for use were made. What's a sun-dial in the shade?

—Inventor and statesman Benjamin Franklin (1706–90)

• 13 •

Communicating and
Collaborating Effectively

ALTHOUGH SOME CREATIVE specialties appear to be solitary endeavors, many bring more interaction with others than people typically realize. If you choose to use your creativity publicly, rather than for therapy or private self-expression, you'll communicate and interact with fellow creatives and/or professionals at some point.

Depending the type of art you choose, you might even get involved in frequent collaborations. These could be anything from one-on-one partnerships to collaborations involving hundreds of people.

If a craftsperson, artist or photographer, you may need to work with models, suppliers, printers, and people who frame your work. You might develop relationships with organizers and volunteers at crafts fairs. If you show your work at galleries, gift shops, and museums, you'll probably deal with artist representatives, store or gallery owners, and curators.

If an actor, dancer, or filmmaker, you'll rarely perform alone, because plays, films, and live shows nearly always require more than one individual. You'll team up from the time of auditions until the performance run or screening is over. Even if presenting one-person shows, you'll probably deal with booking agents, lighting and sound technicians, and venue owners.

If a musician or singer, you may work with bands, orchestras, conductors, accompanists, or choir members. You might join forces with event planners and religious community leaders.

If a writer, you might talk with open-mic organizers, bookstore owners, and librarians. You may collaborate with other writers and work with designers and printers, as well as an agent or members of a publisher's staff.

Some creatives also schmooze with "stakeholders"—funding agencies, community organizations, patrons, and those who commission their work. It's important to relate well with all of these people and to keep everybody well informed.

All of this interaction requires clear communication and good people skills. And, let's face it, mood disorders often challenge these skills.

Depression makes us reluctant to emerge from our protective shells, and sometimes even to stay in touch with or approach anyone.

When hypomanic or manic, we barely contain ourselves and wind up talking nonstop. Although others may feed off our enthusiasm for a while, they get uneasy if we prattle on too long. If our comments and behaviors soar too far above the norm, they won't understand us. We'll have pushed them out of their comfort zones. We may quickly lose patience and interrupt, insult, or anger everyone.

---

*J*ACO PASTORIUS (John Francis Pastorius III) (1951–87), was a jazz composer who began playing with his guitarist friend Pat Metheny in 1974. Two years later he recorded first album, *Jaco Pastorius*, which many consider one of the finest bass albums ever. He also played on Metheny's breakthrough album, *Bright Size Life*.

Soon after, Pastorius joined the band Weather Report, with whom he recorded *Heavy Weather*, one of the most popular jazz albums of all time. However, his flamboyant presence upstaged other band members and alienated some of their fans. He left in 1982, the same year he received his bipolar diagnosis. Afterward, he toured with his own band, Word of Mouth.

Pastorius's mental health deteriorated even further due to heavy alcohol and drug abuse. After several "uncontrolled and reckless incidences," his family had him admitted to a mental hospital and placed on lithium. Pastorius was hospitalized a number of other times, including at Bellevue Hospital, but he often refused medication because of its side effects.

His musical performances suffered, he became an outcast in the music business, and was even homeless for a time. In 1987, he snuck onstage at a Carlos Santana concert and, afterward, had a barroom altercation with a martial-arts-trained bouncer, who beat him into a coma. Pastorius died just ten weeks short of his thirty-sixth birthday.

Pastorius popularized the fretless electric bass. His unique technique and his "punk jazz" style influenced bassists in several genres. Some of his most notable albums featured singer/songwriter Joni Mitchell—*Hejira, Don Juan's Reckless Daughter, Mingus,* and *Shadows and Light*, which was recorded live.

Often, those of us with mood disorders must learn how to relate to others more appropriately. That's why interpersonal therapy exists.

This chapter provides tips to help you communicate and collaborate with others more effectively. We'll explore the communication process and what effective collaborations involve. When you look closely at your own communication patterns and work style, it becomes easier to partner with people whose communication patterns and work styles differ significantly from yours.

THE COMMUNICATION PROCESS

PEOPLE OFTEN THINK of communication as one person talking (the speaker), a second person listening (the receiver), and that receiver understanding—or not understanding—what the speaker meant.

The speaker must speak loudly and clearly enough for the receiver to hear the message. And the speaker must state the message using words the receiver knows. Then, of course, the receiver can't be distracted, disinterested, or extremely angry. Right?

But communication is more complicated than that. In fact, *it's one of the most challenging activities we undertake!* Our emotional filters and feelings, and preconceptions about the speaker tend to get in the way. Given how different our backgrounds and viewpoints often are, it's a *miracle* we get anyone's point—the first, second, or even tenth time around! Communicating effectively is not an easy task. But when we understand and work with the process, we learn and improve.

■ INACTIVE LISTENING

Ever have someone cut you off to "help" finish a sentence (or several) and supply a completely inaccurate conclusion? Or, ever have a person hear the *first* part of your message, start forming a response, and miss your major point? Especially when discussing emotional issues, the last part of the message is the most crucial part.

A conversation might also start in one room and then continue in another—with disastrous results. Ever have someone walk away before you've finished talking? Or talk without actually looking at a person who leaves the room, and you didn't even notice the person is gone? Some of us try to continue conversations by following or shouting at a person who wishes to end the discussion.

Obviously, these situations impede effective communication. Effective communication requires *active* listening. (And active listening requires staying in the room!)

■ ACTIVE LISTENING

When we listen actively, we acknowledge each other and demonstrate our interest in what each of us has to say. Active listening shows that we care about each other's thoughts and feelings. That we're in this together, and respect each other as human beings. We all deserve that.

Active listening works extremely well, but it's not the way most of us learned to communicate (or, more accurately, miscommunicate). Changing ineffective and deeply ingrained habits takes lots of practice. But it's amazing what a difference it makes.

Here's how the communication process goes when people practice active listening.

- Both parties make eye contact and give each other their full attention.
- The speaker sends a message with words, and transmits his or her feelings with tone of voice and body language.
- The receiver listens carefully to the speaker's words and tone of voice, and observes the speaker's body language.
- While listening, the receiver acknowledges the speaker and sends "I'm listening" feedback, such as "Um-hmm" and his or her own body language.
- The receiver also tries not to interrupt or correct the speaker, unless too confused to catch the rest of the message.
- Once the speaker's finished talking, the receiver paraphrases the speaker's words to verify his or her understanding. Or the receiver *calmly* asks for clarification.
- If the receiver hasn't heard what the speaker intended, the speaker can *calmly* clarify the message. The speaker needs to provide clarification without calling the receiver names or scolding for the misinterpretation.

When the speaker talks, the receiver must listen both for content and the speaker's intent. This requires setting aside emotional filters and preconceptions about the speaker and focusing on the here and now. The longer people know each other, the harder this process becomes—at least when they don't use an effective communications process.

When we have a mood disorder, setting aside preconceptions becomes particularly difficult. Often, we "just know" receivers can't understand because they've never experienced depression or hypomania/mania. In addition, those of us with mood disorders often must overcome more emotional filters, particularly if we've had a disorder for several years.

We who have mood disorders are more likely than many people to:

- Label ourselves or others ("I was such an *ass* when I got manic")
- Overgeneralize ("My pots *always* shatter in the kiln")
- Predict disaster ("I *know* I'll forget that verse")
- Think we can read other people's minds ("They think I'm incompetent")
- View messages in black-and-white terms ("I'm either a star or a failure")

We therefore need to become aware of our emotional fillers and be more careful about both our verbal and our nonverbal communications.

■ INEFFECTIVE RESPONSES

It takes practice to overcome poor listening skills and to learn how to better respond to others, and the majority of us have a long way to go. We have extensive repertoires of inappropriate responses to other's communications. Here are just a few:

Passive listening—Passive listening results when we're physically present but not truly listening to the speaker. We may pick up a few words here and there, but we don't catch the gist of the speaker's message.

During depression, we're absorbed in our own pain or too numb to look outside ourselves. During hypomania or mania, we have trouble accepting that our ideas may not be feasible. After all, we're superhuman. It becomes difficult to deal with authorities, as *we're* the authorities then.

Selective listening—When we hear only what we want to hear or our emotional filters distort the speaker's words, that's selective listening.

Unfortunately, selective listening frequently accompanies mood disorders. We have trouble concentrating. Our thinking may slow down. Or, our senses become overloaded with information, and we're compelled to share every thought. During mood episodes, it's hard for us not to misinterpret the speaker's message.

When depressed, we're oversensitive and easily hurt. Our pessimism leads us to conclude that others are rejecting us and that we'll never fit in. We may not stand up for our needs, hesitate to express our opinions, and turn our resulting anger within.

When hypomanic or manic, we think everyone should follow us, and anyone who doesn't shouldn't be involved. Or, we may believe others don't want us around or are out to get us.

Even when we're familiar with the concept of active listening, sometimes we respond inappropriately to the speaker's message. Some types of problematic responses include *derailing, discounting, parroting,* and *placating.*

Derailing—Derailing is changing the subject to indicate disinterest in the speaker's message and/or in the speaker him- or herself. Derailing says, "What you're saying isn't important. You're not important. So let's move on." For example:

Speaker: Shouldn't we discuss how we'll promote this CD?
Receiver: We can worry about promotion when we're done recording it.

Speaker: Why don't we play at this benefit?
Receiver: We need to concentrate on paying gigs instead.

Discounting—Discounting belittles the speaker and starts a one-upmanship game. We often use this ploy to prove our superiority. For example:

Speaker: It took at least a hundred shots for me to get this picture.
Receiver: That's nothing. It took me at least two hundred to get this one.

Speaker: I never get cast in lead roles.
Receiver: You're just exaggerating! You played the lead in that fourth-grade play.

Overidentifying—A close relative to discounting is overidentifying. This happens when we interrupt the speaker's message to add "me, too" statements in an attempt to steal the limelight. Overidentifying takes the focus off the speaker to place it on us. For example:

Speaker: I studied jazz in New York City.
Receiver: I studied there, too!

Speaker: I'm auditioning for summer stock this year.
Receiver: So am I!

Parroting—Parroting is mechanically repeating the speaker's exact words—a technique many of us used to annoy siblings or parents during childhood. For example:

> Speaker: You never listen.
> Receiver: *You* never listen.

> Speaker: You don't understand.
> Receiver: *You* don't understand.

Placating—Placating is the "walking on eggshells" response. Placaters fear saying *anything* negative, either to prevent rocking the boat or because they want to be "nice" or because they secretly hope that the other person will somehow guess what they really want. Placaters who disagree with a speaker often share their true opinions or disappointments with others behind the scenes. If such secret conversations are negative, speakers who learn about them often interpret them as backstabbing. This destroys trust and does nothing to help the person grow. Placating is particularly detrimental to collaborations. For example:

> Speaker: Would this look better with a different color of glaze?
> Receiver: Not unless you have a different color in mind.

> Speaker: Think we should cut this shot?
> Receiver: Do whatever you think is best.

By stating opinions honestly *and diplomatically*, both people get better support. This is crucial for successful collaboration. Another important skill is to openly share thoughts and feelings with others.

SHARING THOUGHTS AND FEELINGS OPENLY

ONE OF THE most effective ways I've found to respond to other's statements or behaviors is the "When you/I feel" format. It's particularly effective in situations where people disagree. Here's how it goes:

When you _____, I feel
_____.

For example:
Speaker: When you say my makeup is too extreme, I feel like you're rejecting me.

This format works well because the "When you" part factually describes a troubling statement or behavior. It lessens the likelihood of name-calling and judging, and simply presents the facts. The "I feel" part relays one person's feelings, which the other can rarely dispute.

In *The Success Principles*, Jack Canfield suggests some other phrases to use when starting difficult conversations:

"I'm wondering if . . . ?"
"Would it be okay if . . . ?"
"Are you feeling . . . ?"
"Is there a possibility of getting . . . ?"
"What would have to happen for you to be able to . . . ?"

People often think the most important part of communicating is our words. Nearly everyone is aware that tone of voice and body language matter, but they frequently underestimate how much.

Body language accounts for 55 percent of what we communicate, and tone of voice accounts for 35 percent. Assuming my calculations are accurate, that leaves just 10 percent for words.

Since body language plays such a large role, let's examine that first.

BODY LANGUAGE

BODY LANGUAGE IS so important that human beings use it to communicate with those who speak a different language—often quite successfully. Whether we recognize it or not, we send messages with our facial expressions and eyes, arms and hands, legs and feet, and the position of our torsos.

Merely by using our bodies, we can communicate:

- Agreement or disagreement
- Belief or skepticism
- Cooperation or stubbornness
- Enthusiasm or boredom
- Understanding or confusion
- And much, much more

However, sometimes we read body language incorrectly. Although body language provides some pretty good clues, it's best not to make assumptions. Whenever possible, check out those assumptions rather than proceed as if they were facts.

Once, when I was speaking about mood disorders at a Texas PTA convention, a woman in the front row kept nodding off. Being somewhat insecure and oversensitive, I assumed I was boring and doing a poor job. I became so concerned about my performance that I "awfulized" the situation. I was *certain* I was a flop.

Afterward, though, many people came up to thank me and express their gratitude for my sharing my experience of bipolar disorder. They were genuinely appreciative, but I doubted their sincerity. I was still obsessing about the woman in the front row.

Later, the woman saw me in the hall and came over to apologize. She said she'd been quite interested in my talk but had had so little sleep the night before that she couldn't keep her eyes open. I was both surprised and relieved. Sometimes, even knowledgeable communicators misread body language.

Because depression and hypomania/mania affect our self-confidence so strongly, we need to verify our assumptions whenever possible.

This is especially important if you're speaking to or collaborating with people from another culture. What one culture considers polite or appropriate may differ in another. How physically or emotionally demonstrative a person is, how close to one another people stand, and even what looking directly into another's eyes and other facial expressions signify. For example, if you are presenting a workshop to inner-city kids, they may be threatened by your sincere attempts to establish eye contact. They may look away from you and appear to not be paying attention when they actually are.

TONE OF VOICE

WE MIGHT BELIEVE it's less possible to misinterpret tone of voice. After all, animals usually understand it. But, just as with body language, we sometimes draw erroneous conclusions from a person's tone of voice.

For instance, although raised voices commonly indicate anger, sometimes people raise their voices merely to be heard. A stage whisper might indicate shyness or, conversely, barely controlled anger. It might be just a way to get people's attention. Because most people shout when they want others to listen, the contrast between shouting and a deliberate stage whisper works well.

We who have mood disorders tend to be especially sensitive and more prone to draw inaccurate conclusions. So, remembering to verify how someone thinks or feels is extremely helpful. When we practice open communications, we can resolve conflicts and problems more easily and get on to the good stuff—using our creativity through successful collaborations. Let's see what collaboration typically involves.

CREATIVE COLLABORATIONS

COLLABORATION INVOLVES WORKING cooperatively with one or more people several to accomplish a mutual goal. Collaboration can involve anything from one-on-one partnerships to projects involving huge numbers of people. Most of my projects as an editor and writer involve one-on-one interactions or small collaborations with a handful of people.

When editing, I usually work with an individual writer or with a small group of co-writers. When writing articles or columns for magazines, I'm usually in contact with only one editor. When writing books, I interact with my literary agent, editor, and publisher, and sometimes with an illustrator, printer, and distributor. In these cases, I talk with conference and meeting organizers, event planners, bookstore employees, librarians, and readers.

When working contract jobs, I often work with people who have fewer artist talents. For a series of videos, I wrote scripts and manuals to train technicians to repair laptop computers. I relied on electrical engineers for input and feedback and then interacted with studio technicians to produce polished master tapes.

For a multimedia CD, I supplied the script and storyboard, and my fellow collaborators consisted of the project manager (an educator) and the programmer who integrated everything.

All of these people had backgrounds, mind-sets, and vocabularies that differed significantly from mine. All of us had to communicate and negotiate our visions, project goals, needs and priorities, and many other things.

Actor, musician, and writer RP of London says, "I start to lack people skills and become aggressive in dealing with people who lack the same commitment to a project as I do. I do not accept that things cannot be completed and will shout at those who have worked hard, but, in my eyes, have not put in the level of intense commitment that I have." RP's shouting antagonizes people, and she loses control over the group.

Creative visions frequently differ. Goals are frequently incompatible or misunderstood. Priorities may conflict or go unstated. Individual needs often get discounted or ignored. Yet, some collaborations work extremely well.

---

*I*RISH WRITER AND comic, Terence "Spike" Milligan (1918–2002) first experienced bipolar symptoms after being wounded and suffering from shell shock during World War II. He once said, "If people want to know where down is, tell them Spike Milligan knows."

But, despite these challenges, he and another comic began to entertain the troops and, later, Milligan moved on to radio, stage, and film. Milligan also wrote memoirs, poetry, plays, and TV series. In the 1950s, he wrote for and led the comics who appeared in *The Goon Show*—a BBC radio hit that preceded Monty Python. In 1999, Britons voted his "Ning Nang Nong" comic poem of the year. In 2000, the British awarded him an honorary knighthood.

To collaborate successfully, we need not only be aware of the communication process but of hurdles that often appear when working in groups. One of these hurdles is differing work styles.

■ WORK STYLES

Understanding different work styles is especially important for those of us with mood disorders. We often have unrealistic views about our abilities and schedules, extremely high or extremely low self-esteem, and tend to be oversensitive. Quite frankly, sometimes working with us is pretty "difficult."

A test called the Myers-Briggs Type Indicator has helped me better understand and interact with others in group and collaborative situations.

MYERS-BRIGGS TYPE INDICATOR

THE MOTHER-DAUGHTER team of Isabel Briggs Myers and Katharine Cook Briggs developed the Myers-Briggs Type Indicator in the early 1940s. The Myers-Briggs uses four categories of "preferences" to identify sixteen personality types and work styles. Note that in this context, "preference" describes your natural tendency rather than the tendency you might consider most acceptable.

Each preference category has a code:

- Introversion (I) vs. Extraversion (E)
- Intuition (N) vs. Sensing (S)
- Feeling (F) vs. Thinking (T)
- Judging (J) vs. Perceiving (P)

Although any of these preferences can vary with the situation or over a lifetime, one pattern usually dominates.

Energy flows—Introversion and Extraversion, in the Myers-Briggs, describe a person's inward or outward energy flow—the way that person relates to the environment and to others.

Introversion (I) relates to inward orientation and solitude. Introverts often prefer to work alone. They relate best to others one-on-one or in small, intimate groups. They find concepts, ideas, images, memories, and reactions energizing and appealing. Introverts tend to spend more time planning, thinking, and reflecting before committing to a project than extraverts do.

Extraversion (E) relates to outward orientation and action. Extraverts are "people persons" who prefer to work with others. They are change-seekers who find people and things outside themselves stimulating. Extraverts tend to plunge right into projects with little planning, thought, or reflection.

Information gathering—Intuition and Sensing, in the Myers-Briggs, describe the way in which a person gathers information.

Intuition (N), as defined in the Myers-Briggs, relates to a sixth sense of the future and to being in tune with other people. Intuitives rely on impressions, insights, and reading between the lines. They're usually interested in abstract ideas, metaphors, symbols, and theories. They focus on newness, the big picture, and possibilities, sometimes overlooking practicalities and details.

Sensing (S) is not the same as emotional sensitivity. It relates to factual orientation and gathering information by hearing, seeing, smelling, tasting, and touching. Sensing people are observant, precise, and interested in detail and description. They're concerned with practicalities and the bottom line. They tend to value the customary way of doing things. Sensors focus so much on the past or present that they tend to miss new possibilities.

Decision-making—Thinking and Feeling, in the Myers-Briggs, describe the ways in which a person processes information and makes decisions.

Thinking (T) relates to task orientation and objectivity. Thinkers tend to be logical, analytical people who often value technology. They focus on tasks before focusing on people and tend to make decisions without taking others' concerns into account. This tough-minded approach may make them seem uncaring or indifferent.

Feeling (F) relates to warmth and subjectivity, not to emotionality. Feelers want what's best for all involved and tend to weigh other people's points of view before making decisions. Valuing relationships and harmony, feelers are compassionate and tactful. They may miss the "hard truth" of a situation, and others may consider them too idealistic.

Lifestyle—Judging (J) and Perceiving (P), in the Myers-Briggs, describe a person's dominant lifestyle and approach to time.

Judging (J) does not mean being judgmental or negative. It relates to being structure-oriented and organized. Judgers value order and control and tend to make lots of lists. They schedule time carefully so they don't have to rush. Although open to new information, judgers crave closure. They may make a decision before gathering enough information or be so focused on the goal that they overlook a need to change direction.

Perceiving (P) is not the same as comprehending or knowing. It relates to flexibility and spontaneity. Perceivers keep planning to the minimum so they can remain open to whatever captures their attention. Rather than work steadily and consistently, Perceivers tend to work in spurts and may seem impulsive. Being so adaptable sometimes makes it difficult to focus on one direction and to meet a deadline.

According to the director of talent development education at Ashland [Ohio] University, Jane Piirto, two preferences most common to artistic people are Feeling and Intuition. However, no preference or work style is inherently "better" than another. As in the Medicine Wheel Native Americans used, each type has its own purpose and plays off the others. The Medicine Wheel is a circle in which "all things are connected and equal." It incorporates many parts, including:

- North, south, east, west
- Mother Earth, Father Sky, Grandmother Moon, Grandfather Sun
- Childhood, youth, adult, elder
- Earth, fire, air, water
- Spring, summer, fall, winter
- Mental, emotional, physical, spiritual

DISCLOSURE

WHEN YOU HAVE a mood disorder, your personality traits, behaviors, and work-style preferences tend to vary with your mood. Therefore, if you disclose your illness to fellow collaborators, they can better understand why you work in inconsistent ways.

If you work one-on-one with a collaborative partner or a small group of collaborators regularly, disclosing your illness can solidify your relationship. Your fellow collaborators might help you avoid an episode if you tell them what to expect. If you collaborate with larger groups, especially on one-time projects, disclosure isn't as important.

In any case, whether to disclose your illness to others, and if so to which people, is entirely up to you.

Because we creatives pour lots of emotion into our work, the more people involved, the more complex and perhaps even messy collaboration gets.

TWENTY-SEVEN-YEAR-OLD *British filmmaker and artist Craig*

Whyte believes that "the best work of art comes from someone with strong emotions and moods, because that is what real art is." His creative urges make him feel "like a saucepan boiling with energy."

Whyte channels that energy into works of art or film. Using his creative talents keeps him from getting bored. "Otherwise, it goes the other way and becomes destructive."

Numerous dancers, musicians, filmmakers, and other creatives have contributed to Whyte's current project—The Human Clock. He says the BBC Big Screen executives are interested in using The Human Clock as part of their programming.

Whyte finds interactions with other creative people helpful, though he says he sometimes feels isolated because he hasn't met another creative with bipolar disorder. "I'm trying to lay foundations right now to support a creative career in the arts or film; otherwise, I see no other possible future."

Whyte's always looking for new inspirations. He visits different environments "whether it be a city, forest, or wheat field," and says he finds that helpful. "I like to be in a place that evokes a mood, a place where my thoughts can float freely and not be distracted."

He believes that when people with mood disorders have troubling symptoms, "it is probably because they are having difficulties channeling their creative energy." Whyte encourages others to find ways to discharge that energy imaginatively. "Doing something creative," he says, "is like doing exercise, and that helps me combat my mental health problems."

During mood episodes, we tend to get involved or committed to a project at a different level than we do when stable. If we're depressed, we may be reluctant to interact with others. We might hold back and keep thoughts and feelings to ourselves. We may be less committed to collaborative goals.

When manic or hypomanic, we may become overinvolved and over-enthusiastic, and volunteer to take on more than we should. When I was involved in theatre, I'd find myself painting sets or altering costumes until three in the morning, even when cast in major roles. I should have been studying my lines or getting some sleep, but I wanted to do *everything* and do it all at once. I became much too invested in each play. This not only endangered my health, but it kept fellow collaborators from "owning" the show. Collaboration works best when everyone's invested in the results.

COLLABORATIVE LEADERSHIP

EFFECTIVE COLLABORATION NOT only requires good people skills and clear communication but strong leadership. When you're the leader, you may have to motivate those you're working with, but you must refrain from coming on too strong. Rather than being the boss, become a cheerleader. Remember, you're still a member of the team.

Collaborators must also work toward a common goal, rather than compete. Doing this is particularly important in dance, filmmaking, and theatre, where cooperation and trust are larger issues.

Some important responsibilities for leading collaborative teams include effectively launching projects, managing meetings, delegating, resolving problems, settling conflicts, and acknowledging and rewarding the team. The following sections address each of these responsibilities.

■ LAUNCHING PROJECTS

Whether leading a collaborative group or making an individual contribution, you can improve its chances of success by helping with the following:

- Create a positive, nonthreatening atmosphere.
- Clarify project goals and priorities, each person's role in the project, and how it relates to the overall picture.
- Identify crucial deadlines and milestones, and set the schedule.
- Discuss procedures for things like purchasing project supplies and recording expenses.
- Keep everyone informed and encourage them to do the same.

■ MANAGING MEETINGS

- Encourage meetings only when absolutely necessary and only with the people who really need to be there.
- Communicate the purpose of any meeting and notify everyone involved as soon as possible.
- Stay focused on the purpose of the meeting.

- Ensure that one individual is accountable for each "action item."
- Get meeting notes, including action items and who's accountable for them, to all fellow collaborators.

■ LISTENING ACTIVELY

- Build a supportive climate where fellow collaborators can concentrate on the discussion by eliminating distractions.
- Give everyone a chance to talk without interruption.
- Listen actively to each collaborator's opinion.
- Don't allow inappropriate or destructive behaviors like name-calling, threats, and personal attacks.

Whether you're leading the collaboration or you're just a member of the team, you need the following skills:

■ DELEGATING

- Communicate what needs to be done and why, then ask the person you're delegating a task to to restate your message to verify his or her understanding.
- Ensure the person has the resources needed to do the work.
- Clarify how much leeway the person has regarding how to do the work versus following exact specifications.
- Give the person the authority needed to do the job and communicate that person's authority to fellow collaborators.
- Follow up regularly to ensure that the work is being done in a way that will fulfill project goals.

■ RESOLVING PROBLEMS

- Get the facts and check out everyone's assumptions.
- Review project goals and people's expectations.
- Brainstorm solutions and make decisions by consensus.
- Ensure that responsibilities are adjusted when necessary.
- Reach resolutions that all parties can accept.

■ SETTLING CONFLICTS

- Don't publicly confront people who are causing problems. Meet privately, instead.
- When someone isn't doing what's expected, find out why.
- Focus on problem behaviors rather than on the person.
- When two or more people disagree, get all sides of the story.
- Always show respect for fellow collaborators and encourage others to do the same.

■ ACKNOWLEDGING AND REWARDING

- Take an interest in fellow collaborators as individual human beings.
- Recognize each individual's good work and, when necessary, suggest improvements sensitively.
- Express appreciation for everyone's accomplishments in front of the entire group.
- When the project is complete, celebrate as a group.
- Try to learn from what went right as well as what went wrong.

Knowing that different people have contrasting perspectives helps you better understand and work with each other. It's helped me better work with people who see situations differently. We've been able to appreciate each other's strengths and weaknesses and apply what we've learned for the project's success.

Collaborating and leading collaborative teams successfully comes with practice. The preceding tips will speed the process, but don't expect outstanding results immediately. That's not realistic. Instead, aim for continuous improvement.

This chapter lays the foundation for communicating, working with others who have different personalities and work styles, collaborating, and leading a collaborative team. Your actual relationship will evolve over time.

Praise does wonders for the sense of hearing.
—Anonymous

· 14 ·

Starting and Running
Your Own Creative Business

MANY CREATIVES START their own business out of frustration with their day jobs. When you devote all of your working time to a day job, when do you make time for your art? It's a vicious trade-off between having too little time or too little money.

Having too little time frustrates your creative spirit, as you'll tend to be consumed with ideas you never have time to develop.

Having too little money will mean you may have trouble meeting basic needs—like food and shelter—needs that may be already compromised by your mood disorder. Or you won't have funds to buy supplies and equipment for your creative work. Or you'll live off unpredictable payments for the creative work you do get paid for. Or you'll have to live on the kindness of family members, friends, or someone else—any one of whom could withdraw that support with little warning.

I'm living so far beyond my income that we may almost be said to be living apart.

—Poet, writer, artist E. E. Cummings (1894–1962), known for *The Enormous Room* and *Tulips and Chimneys*

The lack of money can certainly block your creative spirit. I get extremely anxious and obsessed by my dwindling money when I can't predict where the next project will come from, let alone when I'll get paid.

I beat myself up for deciding to freelance. I scold myself for being so stupid. I lose my faith that anything will turn out okay. Yes, running your own business brings freedom and flexibility, but it also brings potentially crippling fear. Yet, I continue because I know that most full-time day jobs aren't a good option for me. They compromise my health, to say nothing of my happiness.

Julia Cameron, author of *The Artist's Way*, says, "Most of us harbor a secret belief that work has to be work and not play, and that anything we really want to do—like write, act, dance—must be considered frivolous and be placed a distant second. . . . We are operating out of the toxic old idea that God's will for us and our will for us are at opposite ends of the table. 'I want to be an actress, but God wants me to wait tables in hash joints,' the scenario goes. 'So if I try to be an actress, I will end up slinging hash.'"

We deserve to enjoy our work. What if creative work is our "calling"? Perhaps we're meant to use our talents—no matter what it takes. But we who have mood disorders need to be especially careful.

We must look before we leap. Even if you're *sure* you'll be in high demand within a couple of months (which may pop into your mind when you're manic or hypomanic), don't ignore this advice. The arts aren't the sort of business to jump into without first taking a very careful look.

When we prepare for what we're getting into and have some idea about how to handle the challenges that may come up, however, we can make things work. Challenges accompany every type of career and business, but that doesn't make them insurmountable. Creative businesses are different in some ways but not that different.

This chapter introduces you to some basic facts about starting and running a small business. This doesn't mean that business has to be full-time. Even those who freelance but sell only part of their work have a "business."

THE BASICS OF BUSINESS

MOST CREATIVES FACE tremendous challenges to make a decent living, and for creatives who have a mood disorder, those challenges may seem insurmountable. But they're not.

NEW JERSEY WRITER *and Web designer John McManamy, a former financial journalist, began treatment for bipolar disorder when he was forty-nine. He now publishes an authoritative mental health newsletter and Web site. McManamy enjoys working for himself from home. "I can work at my own pace, knowing my periods of super productivity make up for my periods of no productivity."*

Starting the business, he says, "required a grand vision, and keeping it going involves outside-the-box thinking."

McManamy credits his bipolar disorder for his steady supply of inspirations. "I never suffer from want of brilliant ideas. My mind can often subconsciously solve problems and connect disparate thoughts into an inspired vision. . . . I can literally prime my brain with a thought." Although it may take days to follow through, he says, "The result always amazes me, as if a higher power put the idea in my head."

McManamy recently finished a manuscript for a book about depression and bipolar disorder. He also has three unpublished novels that he's written for pleasure. "Your creativity is your best means to your healing," asserts McManamy. "Doing what you love doing is life-affirming and gives you a reason to get out of bed."

I believe that much of the difficulty creatives face in generating income is a lack of knowledge about the sort of information in this book. They frequently don't know what's involved in project management, marketing and promotion, effective communication, business plans, and bookkeeping.

But many creatives with mood disorders have faced those "insurmountable" challenges—and thrived. Using our talents has helped turn around our lives. That's the major reason I wrote this book.

■ STARTING UP

If you're considering going into business, it's wise to write a business plan. Business plans guide your business activities to help you achieve your goals. They also help you obtain business financing (at least theoretically). Most describe the business, its purpose, how you'll market and manage it, and your financial "guesstimates."

Writing a business plan isn't nearly as difficult as it sounds, and even a one-page plan can help.

When I decided to start a small publishing business, I learned I needed a business plan only after my husband and I approached my credit union for a loan. The only costs I thought I'd need the money for were printing and production costs for books and CDs. I'd been banking there for decades, had good credit, a great idea, and I felt certain I could get a loan.

The loan officer thought otherwise. Wrinkling her nose, she said that, without a business plan, she couldn't give me a loan. Publishers, she sneered, often lose money. I'd have trouble paying it back.

$\mathscr{A}$ bank is a place that will lend you money if you can prove you don't need it.

—English-born American comedian and vaudeville performer
Bob Hope (1903–2003)

I left somewhat defeated, but not enough to abandon my idea. Writing a business plan seemed not only unnecessary, but impossible. How could I possibly know many books and CDs I'd sell? How could I know what customers would buy?

Rather than waste time on a stupid business plan, I opted for my standard bipolar solution: charge it all to Visa! Surely I'd recoup my costs and pay the full balance in no time. Wrong, wrong, wrong, wrong, wrong!

After mulling the situation over, my husband Ralph began obsessing about business plans. With no such plan in place, he decided he'd have to keep me on track.

Ralph started harassing me constantly (as I saw it). Almost daily, he'd pop into my office, wave his arms and exclaim, "You need a business plan!" or "Did you work on your business plan today?" or "If you had a business plan, you'd know these expenses would be coming."

I completely resisted his "help." To me, "business plan" became the B-word. Did Hemingway have a business plan? Did O'Neill or Dickinson? I just wanted to write books, get them printed, produce interactive CDs to accompany them, and start raking in the bucks. The rest would take care of itself.

I made some costly decisions, based on hunches and grandiose ideas. I changed what plans I did have midstream and ordered more materials I could afford. I spent way too much to ever produce the CDs.

I've come to see the value of business plans and strongly suggest you write one. It might help keep your credit card balance down!

> $\mathscr{T}$he difficult we do immediately. The impossible takes a little longer.
>
> —Anonymous

Many resources exist to teach you how to write a business plan, and some are surprisingly simple.

If you need financing but can't obtain it, in spite of your brilliant business plan, you can pay for start-up costs other ways. The government offers a number of resources to help small business owners, including grants and loans. One woman and her partner financed their pottery business by selling shares of "stock." Within five years, they were able to buy back all the shares. It may take more—or less—time for you to do the same, and there are no guarantees this approach will work. But it is an option.

If you decide to start your own business, see the Resources section for more about business plans, grants and loans, and other means of getting off the ground. And, by all means, don't forget you'll need health insurance! (As if you hadn't thought of that.)

THE THREE "HATS" OF BUSINESS

ONE DIFFICULTY CREATIVE businesses often face is an imbalance of certain skills. Michael Gerber, author of *The E-Myth* and *The E-Myth Revisited*, describes these skills in terms of three basic roles: *entrepreneur*, *manager*, or *technician*—essentially three different "hats." Different individuals may wear each hat, or the same individual may wear two or three hats at different times.

The entrepreneur is the "dreamer and visionary"—the innovator with the bright ideas. Entrepreneurs are good at finding or creating new opportunities.

The manager is the "detail person"—the one who plans and oversees most business activities. Managers tend to be systematic, orderly, and organized.

The technician is the "doer"—the nuts-and-bolts person with the skills required to create or deliver what the customer or client buys. Technicians are more concerned with the task at hand than with day-to-day business matters.

Ideally, you and your collaborators must ensure that at least one of you can wear whatever hat needs wearing or that you find someone to wear the hat or hats you can't or don't wish to wear.

If you're uncertain try this exercise. The Creative Life Toolkit contains a blank copy. In this sample, the strongest hat is technician and the weakest is manager.

SAMPLE STRONGEST "HAT"

☑ 1. I'm deadline oriented.

☑ 2. I'm a risk taker.

☐ 3. I'm task oriented.

☒ 4. I'm a problem solver.

☑ 5. I'm an inspiring leader.

☒ 6. I don't like interruptions that distract me from my work.

☐ 7. I'm good at determining the steps necessary to complete a job.

☒ 8. I function extremely well on my own.

☐ 9. I love to think up better ways to do things.

☒ 10. I'm an expert in my field.

☑ 11. I have a great imagination.

☐ 12. I'm very good at delegating and then following up.

ENTREPRENEUR	**MANAGER**	**TECHNICIAN**
2. I'm a risk taker.	1. I'm deadline oriented.	3. I'm task oriented.
5. I'm an inspiring leader.	4. I'm a problem solver.	6. I don't like interruptions that distract me from my work.
9. I love to think up better ways to do things.	7. I'm good at determining the steps necessary to complete a job.	8. I function extremely well on my own.
11. I have a great imagination.	12. I'm very good at delegating and then following up.	10. I'm an expert in my field.

My strongest "hat": __technician__   My weakest "hat": __manager__

As you begin a creative business, seriously consider getting help for the hat or hats that least describe you.

Frequently, creatives will be either technicians or entrepreneurs, but less often managers. To some extent this explains why creatives need agents, choreographers, directors, editors, producers, publishers, and business managers.

London musician and writer AT, age forty-one, says, "I am utterly useless at managing myself. I find that the hardest thing . . . is simply turning up to appointments. . . ." His advice to other creatives with mood disorders is, "Get a good manager, which you know you can trust. . . . If you are unreliable . . . , you are doomed." AT adds that managers working with creatives who have mood disorders "have to be very, very patient."

For many creative businesses—or creative projects—you need some kind of assistance. Before seeking any type of help, determine exactly what tasks or services you need and how often.

Understanding your strengths and weaknesses—and acting on that knowledge—will improve your chances of success. If you're not interested or skilled in any particular area, it's time to seek outside help. And, often, it's wise to get help, even for areas you're strong in. It's very difficult to do it all yourself.

FINDING A SERVICE AND VENDOR

CREATIVES OFTEN DO the bulk of the work on a project but need someone else to help wrap it up. Some examples of services or vendors creatives might need include:

- Art and photo framers
- Sound, TV, or film recording studios
- Designers, illustrators, or graphic artists
- Desktop publishers and printers
- Advertising and publicity firms

It's best to locate these services or vendors before you start a creative project. Talking with them in advance often reveals crucial information you'll need for the success of your project. Knowing what they need to best meet your needs will prevent having to revise your work or to start over from scratch. It can also save you lots of money.

For instance, suppose you're mailing promotional postcards. Knowing what sizes best fit each printer's press and learning what "house" papers the printer usually keeps in stock will save money. Or, knowing the specific size and type of master a newspaper or magazine you're advertising in wants photos or electronic files produced on will ensure the ad prints at a higher quality.

When first talking with new services and vendors, ask to see samples and similar projects they've worked on. Also ask for several references. Nearly every type of service or vendor will provide a fee estimate for your project. It may not be the exact price they'll wind up charging, but it should be in the ballpark. Expect to pay for revisions or for rush charges if you require them.

■ CHOOSING A SERVICE OR VENDOR

When choosing a service or a vendor, you'll need to consider priorities in terms of cost, quality, and speed of turnaround. You can rarely get all three at once.

It's usually not a good idea to use the first service or vendor you find. Unless they can provide exactly what you need—without question— it pays to check around.

At one point, I dipped into a money market account to hire a publicity service. I chose one based on the owner's talk at a meeting and without considering any other. I didn't ask much about what I'd get for my investment. I didn't ask for references. I just put the job in their hands.

What I got was a news release I had to rewrite myself, calls to about thirty publications to seek reviews, a handful of reviews in publications I'd suggested myself, and some interviews on radio stations with very small markets in remote locations. I will admit that the media kits the service put together for me looked okay—not great.

For this, I spent several thousand dollars. Publicity services aren't cheap! When I complained, the publicist explained the amount of time it takes for follow-up calls to land a review or interview. She said I'd actually received a great response. Needless to say, I was less than thrilled. I could have accomplished just as much, I believe, with a bit of imaginative brainstorming and an enthusiastic intern.

I should have first clarified my expectations, asked the publicist if they seemed reasonable, and spoken to other publicity firms. I should have asked other authors who worked with a publicist whom they used or at least asked the service for references. But I didn't.

When choosing between services and vendors, try to compare at least three. By putting expectations in writing, you can ensure that the facts you use for comparison are more accurate.

For instance, suppose you need a studio to record and duplicate demo CDs or DVDs. You'll need to provide the same information to each studio you approach. How much studio time you expect to need, what type of master you want, how many copies you need, and what type of case you want to put them in. You might also ask what type of backup they provide for the master. Whether they design inserts and get them printed.

Get all bids, agreements and expectations, and renegotiations in writing. Discuss details like schedules and delivery or shipping arrangements and costs. Get those in writing, too.

FINDING HELPERS

SOMETIMES YOU'LL NEED help on a project from an individual—or from several. The following questions will help you determine exactly what you need. Write everything down to keep it clear in your mind and to help you communicate it to others.

- Do you need someone to perform a one-time service or to provide the same or a similar service sporadically?
- Should you give this vendor your entire job or split the work between several companies?
- Do you need a freelancer for a specific project or for occasional work, or do you need ongoing help?
- If you need ongoing help, do you need someone part-time or full-time?
- What is the going rate for such services, and can you afford it? Will you face any additional costs, such as paying for help-wanted ads?
- What kinds of tax, insurance, and other issues may be involved if someone works for you?

Once you decide what assistance you need, you should also write down what you expect the end result to be. Putting the end results you want in writing helps clarify your expectations as well as prepare you to locate appropriate services and people, bid out jobs, and conduct interviews. Make certain any service or individual you bring on board knows your goals, what you want from them, and where their role fits into the overall project or organization.

If you're part of collaboration, make certain fellow collaborators buy into your decision that it's time to obtain outside help.

When considering a new person, ask for a résumé or credit list and, when applicable, samples or a portfolio. As with a service, ask the person for several references.

One mistake people tend to make is assuming they'll need full-time help if they hire someone. Hiring an employee means making a big commitment, and other options are worth exploring first. These include *freelancers* or *contractors*, *interns* or *apprentices*, and *temporary employees*.

■ FREELANCERS OR INDEPENDENT CONTRACTORS

Freelancers and contractors are in business for themselves but work for others "on loan." They usually work on a project-by-project basis. Such people may be fellow creatives or individuals who provide a special creative or business service.

You can usually find a freelancers or contractors by asking fellow creatives, an arts organization, or an organization or university to recommend someone. You can sometimes find them online, in a phonebook, or through business cards posted in other creative businesses.

When you obtain services from freelancers or contractors, they control when, where, and how they do the work. You merely decide if the final result is acceptable. If you need to discuss a project, you arrange a mutually acceptable time and place to do so.

If you plan on hiring freelancers or contractors, verify that the IRS won't consider them "employees." And if you hire employees, be sure you understand the tax implications.

Here are some of the questions the IRS may ask to determine whether someone is an employee or a freelancer or contractor:

- Does the person work for you exclusively rather than also working for others?
- Do you set the person's schedule?
- Does the person work onsite or at specific places that you designate?

- Do you require the person to comply with instructions about when, where, and how work is done?
- Do you direct the sequence in which work must be done?
- Are the person's services integral to your business operations?
- Do you provide training so the person will perform the job using a particular method or in a certain manner?
- Do you hire, supervise, or pay assistants to help the person on this job?
- Do you require the person to submit regular oral or written reports?
- Do you pay the person hourly, weekly, or monthly as opposed to by the job?
- Do you reimburse business and/or traveling expenses?
- Do you furnish equipment, tools, and materials for the person?

You don't have to withhold money for federal income tax or Social Security when you pay a freelancer or contractor. As a self-employed person, the freelancer or contractor is responsible for that. However, if you pay an individual more than $600 during a tax year, you must complete a 1099-MISC, Miscellaneous Income Form for them. You then provide a copy to the individual and to the IRS. Completing a 1099-MISC is pretty straightforward and nothing to be scared of.

Likewise, if anybody pays you more than $600 during the tax year, they should provide a 1099-MISC form for you.

■ EMPLOYEES

Employees provide services under your control. You determine when, where, and how employees perform their work. When you pay an employee's wages, you must withhold federal income tax and Social Security, as well as the employer's contribution. You deposit this withholding for each pay period throughout the year.

Then, at the year's end, you provide a Form W-2, Wage and Tax Statement, to each employee and to the IRS.

I've worked both with employees and with freelance/independent contractors. The paperwork and long-term commitments are much simpler when you go the freelance/ contractor route.

■ Interns or Apprentices

One short-term option is to hire an intern or apprentice. College students often do great work for reduced pay or class credit alone. They may take their jobs more seriously, however, if you pay them what you can afford. You get inexpensive help, and the student gains valuable experience.

I've had very good luck with interns from the local community college and university. Some of my interns continued working with me as freelancers beyond their internships.

Interns are usually students working short-term who receive class credits, whether or not they're being paid for their work. Sometimes, organizations hire recent graduates as interns for a limited time. When that time is over, the intern usually either gets a job offer or moves on. Apprentices are more likely to work with you long-term.

■ Temporary Workers

In my experience, temporary agencies don't place workers in home offices. However, if you have an office or storefront, you can sometimes hire workers from an agency. Hiring temps allows you to get employees without making a long-term commitment because the agency handles the worker's benefits. The "temp" gains flexibility and gets exposed to different businesses.

■ Interviewing and Hiring

Before advertising for help or meeting with anyone, clarify your expectations in writing. Consider what you want to or must do yourself and what you wish to keep control of. Consider how much time you'll devote to training and to getting the person up to speed, or who can do so if you can't. Determine what skills the person absolutely must have versus the skills that would be nice but not essential.

Compile a list of open-ended questions (those that can't be answered with a yes or no). Asking about marital status, sexual orientation, age, and health is illegal if it has no bearing on the job. Your questions should not be personal but relate directly to the job.

During the interview or meeting, ask the questions, and then let the person do most of the talking. Be sure you ask what the person wants or expects from the job as well.

After interviewing several candidates (I suggest at least three), choose the best qualified, check his or her references, and agree on the schedule and price. Always put your agreement in writing. And, for heaven's sake, notify everyone you've interviewed about your decision! Sometimes, you may need to go back to your second or third choice if the first person leaves or doesn't work out.

If you're hiring an employee, though, especially your first time, start small. A mood disorder can complicate this process.

If you're depressed, you might hesitate to turn anyone you interview away because you're afraid they'll think less of you. You might hire someone who doesn't fit your needs to relieve your anxiety about having to interview more candidates. Or, you might not hire a better candidate because you fear the person is superior.

If you're in a hypomanic or manic phase, you may believe no one can do as good a job as you. You might convince yourself that it's pointless to get help and that you don't really need to hire someone. Or, you might think you can manage more employees than you can.

Don't attempt to hire more people than you planned to, or to hire everyone you've interviewed!

Lastly, whether or not you disclose your illness to people working for you is entirely your decision.

THE NUTS-AND-BOLTS OF BOOKKEEPING

AS A FREELANCER or business owner, you need to track business income and expenses—both to see where you stand financially and for tax purposes. Your business records could be as simple as keeping expense receipts in an envelope or shoebox, and recording income on a single page. Often, though, they're more complex.

Basic bookkeeping isn't all that hard if you use a computer and simple accounting software. You do, however, need to set up your records carefully. The simplest way to track them is to match the categories in your records to those on the IRS Schedule C: Profit or Loss from Business (assuming you live in the U.S.).

If you sell books, CDs, T-shirts, or similar goods, you'll need to learn about inventory control. Recording what goes in and out is simple enough (provided you're not in a depressive or manic/hypomanic episode), but figuring "cost of goods" and "overhead" can get a bit complex.

Whatever you earn from commissions, performances, products, or anything you do as a freelancer or self-employed individual (sole proprietor) must be reported as gross income. Rather than list that income on your 1040 (the regular tax form), you report it on a Schedule C.

■ DEDUCTING EXPENSES

You can deduct from your taxable income expenses such as advertising (head shots, event postcards, a Web site), legal and professional fees (what you pay to lawyers and accountants), office supplies, and rent on a studio. But only when the IRS considers your work a business. If they say it's a hobby, you must still include the income you make from it on your tax return. However, you can't deduct your expenses to reduce the tax you owe.

*D*on't be seduced into thinking that that which does not make a profit is without value.
—American playwright Arthur Miller (1915–2005)

If you wish for the IRS to consider your freelance work as a business, you must convince them that your work is not a hobby. You must demonstrate that the primary purpose of your creative work is to produce an income. The IRS expects freelancers and the self-employed to produce a profit during at least three consecutive years out of five.

*I*f your outgo exceeds your income, your upkeep will be your downfall.
—Anonymous

To deduct expenses for a home office, you must use that space "exclusively" and "regularly." It must be the principal place where you do business and meet with customers or clients. This means you use the space for business 100 percent of the time. You can't use it sporadically, or also use it for another purpose.

Even if your home business qualifies for the deduction, you may not wish to take it. Doing so affects what happens when you sell your house. And it's also a red flag for a potential audit. The IRS is pretty picky about business meals and travel, and car or truck expenses as well.

■ DEPRECIATING ASSETS

Another area that gets a bit tricky is depreciation. Property (or assets) lose value over time. The IRS requires you to deduct the cost of many assets over a span of several tax years, deducting a predetermined percentage each year.

However, you can deduct the entire cost of some assets—up to a certain amount—during the same year that you purchase them. If an item loses value quickly, like a computer, which may be obsolete within about five years, you can deduct it using Section 179.

Section 179 depreciations are easy to do and provide an advantage when your income is higher than normal that year. If you have more complex depreciation issues, you may wish to talk to an accountant or tax specialist.

■ PAYING SELF-EMPLOYMENT (ESTIMATED) TAXES

Self-employment tax takes the place of the Social Security and Medicare taxes that conventional employers and their employees pay. As a self-employed person, you calculate the self-employment tax you expect to owe at the end of the year and pay estimated tax each quarter. Predicting the amount you'll owe is often guesswork. You just have to do the best you can, and if you realize during the year that you've under- or overestimated, adjust your quarterly payments. In addition to federal taxes, you may also need to pay local taxes. Check with your accountant, chamber of commerce, or tax advisor.

One straightforward resource for business, bookkeeping, and tax information is Bernard Kamoroff's book *Small Time Operator*.

Software programs, tax workshops, accounting books and IRS publications also provide advice on bookkeeping and tax matters.

> *Tax Tip*
>
> $\int$AVE 25–30 PERCENT of your income in a separate (preferably interest-bearing) account. Then put it out of your mind until your tax payments are due.

*T*o me, money is alive. It is almost human. If you treat it with real sympathy and kindness and consideration, it will be a good servant and work hard for you, and stay with you and take care of you.

—British writer Katharine Butler Hathaway (1890–1942), best known for *The Little Locksmith*

Some Final Words

PLEASE DON'T ALLOW your illness to prevent you from using your creative gifts! You have them for a reason. Embrace them. Explore them. Enhance them.

Whether you tap your talents privately, form a company, or aim for the stars, using your creativity will speed your recovery. Creative endeavors are great for building self-esteem, generating income, and reclaiming your life.

Move forward deliberately and carefully, attending to your mood disorder as well as your creativity. Believe in yourself and your worth, don't let your mood swings define you. Keep your dreams alive, and never give up hope!

Thank you for reading this book. I hope you've found it valuable. I wish you the greatest success.

May your creative dreams bloom like daisies in the sun!

Creative Life Toolkit

MY CREATIVE DREAM (Chapter 4)

- Describe your dream as clearly as you can.
- Are you working alone or with others? Place a check mark to the left of your answer.
- If working with someone, who is it? Write your answer to the right of Who?
- Are you creating something for yourself? Your family and/or friends? The public? Place a check mark to the left of your answer, then add any details below.
- Where will you be creating your work? Describe that place(s) on the line to the right.

MY CREATIVE DREAM: _____

_____

☐ WORKING ALONE?   ☐ WITH OTHERS?   WHO? _____

☐ FOR MYSELF?   ☐ FOR FAMILY/FRIENDS?   ☐ FOR THE PUBLIC?

WHO? _____

_____

WHERE? _____

_____

LOSE YOUR BUTS (Chapter 4)

- In the I'd Like To column, write the creative activity/activities you'd like to do.
- In the But column, write the reasons you tell yourself you can't.

I'D LIKE TO . . .   BUT . . .

_____   _____

_____   _____

_____   _____

_____   _____

MY TERRIBLE TOO'S (Chapter 4)

- Check-mark the boxes by every "Terrible Too" that applies to you. Add more if needed.
- In the Source column, write where each "Terrible Too" came from. Guess if you have to.
- In the Supporting and Rejecting Facts columns, write *indisputable facts* that *prove* or *disprove* each "Terrible Too."

✔ TERRIBLE TOO	SOURCE	SUPPORTING FACTS	REJECTING FACTS
☐ Too ill			
☐ Too medicated			
☐ Too few ideas			
☐ Too little time			
☐ Too little energy			
☐ Too little money			
☐ Too many demands			
☐ Too old or too young			
☐ Too unachievable			
☐ Too unfocused			
☐ Too little knowledge			
☐ Too little talent			
☐ Too shy/intimidated			
☐ Too much criticism			
☐ Too little support			
☐ Too little space			
☐ Too little equipment			
☐ Too financially risky			

MY EXPECTATIONS & INVESTMENTS (Chapter 5)

- List up to five of your creative interests in the left-hand column. Don't worry about their order.

- In the Expectations columns, prioritize what you expect to gain from each creative interest. Place a 1 in the column that motivates you most and a 3 in the column that motivates you least.

- In the Investments columns, prioritize what you believe it will take to meet your expectations. Place a 1 in the column indicating the highest investment and a 3 in the column indicating the lowest.

⭐ = Fame   💚 = Satisfaction $ = Money   🕐 = Time   ⚡ = Energy

Creative Interest(s)	Expectations			Investments		
	⭐	💚	$	🕐	⚡	$

MY OPTIONS & PRIORITIES (Chapter 5)

- In the Options column, list up to five different options you want to prioritize. Don't worry about their order.
- Compare the first option to the second and circle the "winning" number on line 2 under Winners & Losers.
- Compare the winning option to the option on line 3 and circle that winning number.
- Continue through the list, comparing options and circling winners. The final winner is your top priority.
- You can use this form to prioritize most anything. That's why two appear below.

	Options		Winners & Losers			
1						
2		1	2			
3		1	2	3		
4		1	2	3	4	
5		1	2	3	4	5

	Options		Winners & Losers			
1						
2		1	2			
3		1	2	3		
4		1	2	3	4	
5		1	2	3	4	5

MY GOAL, STRATEGIES, & THEIR STEPS (Chapter 5)

- Describe your goal—what you want to do and how you want to do it.
- Set a date by which you want to complete your goal.
- Describe how you'll know when you've achieved your goal—how many and/or how much.
- Write down three different strategies you might use to reach your goal.
- Next, list the major steps you might follow for each strategy.
- Start with what seems to be the best strategy.

GOAL: _____

_____

DEADLINE: _____

MEASURE: _____

STRATEGY #1: _____

STEP #1: _____

STEP #2: _____

STEP #3: _____

STEP #4: _____

STEP #5: _____

STRATEGY #2: _____

STEP #1: _____

STEP #2: _____

STEP #3: _____

STEP #4: _____

STEP #5: _____

STRATEGY #3: _____

STEP #1: _____

STEP #2: _____

STEP #3: _____

STEP #4: _____

STEP #5: _____

MY CREATIVITY CONTRACT   (Chapter 5)

When you feel ready, complete the Creativity Contract below. If you wish, also have a witness sign it, but remember your contract is a commitment to *yourself*.

I, _____ , commit to spend _____
         [Print Your Name]   [Time/Frequency]

on my creative project(s) while carefully fulfilling my basic needs, managing my mood

disorder, and balancing the rest of my life.

_____   _____
[Sign Your Name]   [Day/Date]

_____   _____
[Witness's Name]   [Day/Date]

CONGRATULATIONS!

MY EARLY WARNING SIGNS (Chapter 6)

Write what feelings and symptoms you often have just before a mood episode starts.

BEFORE DEPRESSION   BEFORE MANIA/HYPOMANIA

_____   _____

_____   _____

_____   _____

_____   _____

_____   _____

_____   _____

_____   _____

_____   _____

_____   _____

WHOLE LIFE GRID (Chapter 7)

- Label each box below for a part of your life. Use whatever labels you find meaningful. Feel free to leave one or more boxes empty, but *don't add any additional boxes.*

- Some suggested parts include Home, Financial, Leisure, Relationships, Self-Growth, Social Contribution, and Spirituality. Remember to include all of your physical needs!

- If you wish, add more details to the boxes. For instance: your job, budgeting, and bill paying in a Financial box; your friends and family members' names in a Relationships box.

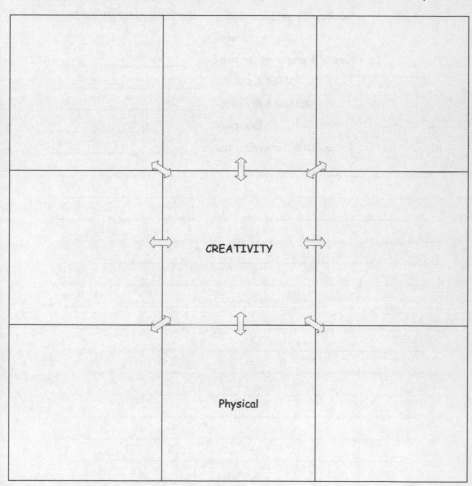

MY WEEKLY TIME ALLOTMENTS (Chapter 7)

- Estimate how many hours you will spend each week on each activity in your Whole Life Grid. To give you more room to write, there are two blank lines per box.

- Avoid making your schedule too tight. Leave some flexibility for taking breaks and dealing with surprises.

HOURS PER WEEK = 168   MY TIME ALLOTMENTS

Sleep: _____

De-stressing & preparing for bed: _____

Meals & snacks: _____

Bathing & dressing: _____

Exercise: _____

Commuting, errands, etc.: _____

_____
[Top left box]
_____   _____

[Top center box]
_____   _____

[Top right box]
_____   _____

[Middle left box]
_____   _____

[Middle right box]
_____   _____

[Bottom left box]
_____   _____

[Bottom right box]
_____   _____

Subtotal: _____

BALANCE FOR CREATIVE ACTIVITIES: _____

MY TIME & SCHEDULE FORM (Chapter 7)

Block out time for basic physical needs. Treat monthly or semimonthly appointments as if they occurred every week. Then plug in creative time and time for other responsibilities.

TIME	MON	TUES	WED	THURS	FRI	SAT	SUN
MIDNIGHT							
1-2 AM							
2-3 AM							
3-4 AM							
4-5 AM							
5-6 AM							
6-7 AM							
7-8 AM							
8-9 AM							
9-10 AM							
10-11 AM							
11 AM– NOON							
Noon							
1-2 PM							
2-3 PM							
3-4 PM							
4-5 PM							
5-6 PM							
6-7 PM							
7-8 PM							
8-9 PM							
9-10 PM							
10-11 PM							
11 PM – MIDNIGHT							

MY TIME & SCHEDULE FORM (Chapter 7)

When you've finished working with the preceding form, record your new schedule below.

TIME	MON	TUES	WED	THURS	FRI	SAT	SUN
MIDNIGHT							
1-2 AM							
2-3 AM							
3-4 AM							
4-5 AM							
5-6 AM							
6-7 AM							
7-8 AM							
8-9 AM							
9-10 AM							
10-11 AM							
11 AM- NOON							
Noon							
1-2 PM							
2-3 PM							
3-4 PM							
4-5 PM							
5-6 PM							
6-7 PM							
7-8 PM							
8-9 PM							
9-10 PM							
10-11 PM							
11 PM - MIDNIGHT							

MY LEARNING OPTIONS & INVESTMENTS (Chapter 8)

- Check into at least three options for learning or strengthening your creative skills.
- Obtain information about each option, including the time and money you'll need to invest.

LEARNING OPTIONS   INVESTMENTS

Name, Place, & Teacher	Phone & Address	Day, Time, & Dates	Cost (include Books, Tools, & Supplies)

MY CREATIVE SPACE NEEDS (Chapter 9)

- List the furniture, equipment, and tools you expect to use in your creative space.
- Carefully consider *why* you need each item. Is that item truly necessary, or is it just something that would be nice to have? Write your answer under Why/Why not?
- When do you need that item? Write your answer under When?
- About how much will the item cost? Write your estimate in the *Cost* column.
- If the cost exceeds your budget, consider borrowing, trading, buying secondhand, or substituting something else.

WHAT?	WHY/WHY NOT?	WHEN?	COST
Furniture			
Equipment			
Tools			

MY PROJECT BUDGET (Chapter 11)

- In the "People Costs" column, list the names of those you'll depend on to complete the project and the total amount you expect to pay them.
- List project-specific and marketing cost estimates next. Later, total the actual costs.
- Record whatever details you need in the Notes column.

"PEOPLE" COSTS	NOTES	COST
PROJECT-SPECIFIC COSTS		
MARKETING COSTS		
TOTAL ESTIMATED PROJECT COST:		
TOTAL ACTUAL PROJECT COST:		

MY STRONGEST & WEAKEST "HATS" (Chapter 14)

- Cover the chart with the hats on the bottom half of the page.
- Place a star by the four statements—but *only* four statements—that best describe you.
- Cross out the four statements—but *only* four statements—that least describe you.
- Place a check mark by those remaining statements you agree with.
- Cross out those statements you don't agree with.

☐ 1. I'm deadline oriented.

☐ 2. I'm a risk taker.

☐ 3. I'm task oriented.

☐ 4. I'm a problem solver.

☐ 5. I'm an inspiring leader.

☐ 6. I don't like interruptions that distract me from my work.

☐ 7. I'm good at determining the steps necessary to complete a job.

☐ 8. I function extremely well on my own.

☐ 9. I love to think up better ways to do things.

☐ 10. I'm an expert in my field.

☐ 11. I have a great imagination.

☐ 12. I'm very good at delegating and then following up.

- Your strongest "hats" will be those with most stars and check marks. Your weakest "hat" will relate to the most crossed-out statements. Compare your results to the key below.
- Get help for the "hat" or "hats" you're weakest in.

ENTREPRENEUR	MANAGER	TECHNICIAN
2. I'm a risk taker.	1. I'm deadline oriented.	3. I'm task oriented.
5. I'm an inspiring leader.	4. I'm a problem solver.	6. I don't like interruptions that distract me from my work.
9. I love to think up better ways to do things.	7. I'm good at determining the steps necessary to complete a job.	8. I function extremely well on my own.
11. I have a great imagination.	12. I'm very good at delegating and then following up.	10. I'm an expert in my field.

My strongest "hat":_____ My weakest "hat":_____

Resources

Many of the listings in this section are organizations or professionals' Web sites. Some are publications you may find quite helpful that are not listed in the bibliography. Where an author name appears after a title, please turn to the bibliography for full details.

CHAPTER 4: CLEARING CREATIVE CLOGS

Esteemable Acts: 10 Actions for Building Real Self-Esteem by Francine Ward. New York: Random House, 2003—*An inspiring book about moving ahead with your dreams despite tremendous challenges.*

Manage Your Muse—Professional Coactive Coach Lynn Cutts's Web site: www.manageyourmuse.com *The Musing section contains free articles to help you manage both your creativity and other areas of your life. The site's "First Muse Bank" and Weekly Challenger e-mail messages help you make small positive changes.*

CHAPTER 5: CHOOSING YOUR FOCUS AND SETTING YOUR GOALS

The New Drawing on the Right Side of the Brain: A Course in Enhancing Creativity and Artistic Confidence by Betty Edwards. New York: Tarcher/Putnam, 1999.

The Power of Focus: How to Hit Your Business, Personal and Financial Targets with Absolute Certainty by Jack Canfield, Mark Victor Hansen, and Les Hewitt. Deerfield Beach, FL: Health Communications, 2000.

Trust the Process: An Artist's Guide to Letting Go by Shaun McNiff. Boston: Shambhala, 1998.

CHAPTER 6: SUPPORTING CREATIVITY BY HANDLING THE BASICS

SUPPORT GROUPS—

A.R.T.S. Anonymous, PO Box 230175, New York, NY 10023, Hotline: 212 873-7075, www.artsanonymous.org—*A twelve-step program developed to honor and use creative talents. Has both chapters throughout the United States and internationally.*

Depression and Bipolar Support Alliance—Depression and Bipolar Support Alliance (DBSA), 730 N. Franklin Street, Suite 501, Chicago, IL 60610-7224, Toll-free: 800-826-3632, Fax: 312-642-7243, www.dbsalliance.org.—*The nation's leading patient-directed organization focusing on depression and bipolar disorder; has more than 1,000 patient-run support groups across the country; excellent educational materials and conferences, and advocates in Washington, DC, providing testimony about mood disorders before Congress.*

Recovery Inc., 802 N Dearborn Street, Chicago, IL 60610, Office: 312-337-5661, Fax: 312-337-5756, inquiries@recovery-inc.com, www.recovery-inc.com—*Uses a self-help approach similar to cognitive-behavioral therapy; Teaches simple, yet practical, coping techniques that help members change their reactions to people and situations they can't control; Sponsors over 700 active groups in the U.S., Canada, England, Ireland, Israel, Puerto Rico, Spain, and Wales.*

MOOD-TRACKING CHARTS

Available from both of the following sources:

Depression and Bipolar Support Alliance—See www.dbsalliance.org/bookstore/brochures.html for a free downloadable brochure or call 1-800-826-3632 to have a copy mailed to you.

My Web site—See www.bipolar-tightrope.com for a free downloadable two-page 8½ × 11-inch Daily Tracking Form. Or, request a free copy by mailing a self-addressed envelope with a single first-class stamp to: Free Tracking Form, Castle Communications, PMB 358, PO Box 200255, Austin, TX 78720.

CHAPTER 8: SHORING UP YOUR SKILLS

About.com University: http://u.about.com

Adobe Systems: Adobe Systems Incorporated, 345 Park Avenue, San Jose, CA 95110-2704, 408-536-6000, www.adobe.com

American Creativity Association: www.amcreativityassoc.org—A resource for exploring and actualizing your creativity.

Arts and Healing Network, PO Box 276, Stinson Beach, CA 94970: www.artheals.org.

Arts Resource Network: Office of Arts & Cultural Affairs, 700 Fifth Ave., Suite 1766, PO Box 94748, Seattle, WA 98124-4748, 206-684-7171, www.artsresourcenetwork.org/resources_issues/arts_resources_outside_seattle/service_organizations.asp.

Barnes & Noble University: http://university.barnesandnoble.com/index.asp

The College Board: The College Board Headquarters, 45 Columbus Avenue, New York, NY 10023, 212-713-8000, www.collegeboard.com/pay.

FastWeb, LLC: 444 North Michigan Avenue, Suite 3100, Chicago, IL 60611, 800-327-8932, www.fastweb.com.

The Foundation Center: 79 Fifth Avenue/16th Street, New York, NY 10003-3076, 212-620-4230 or 800-424-9836, http://fdncenter.org

Putting Creativity to Work, Scribner: www.vsarts.org/x630.xml—*An extraordinary collection of sometimes hard-to-find resources for training, financial support, and careers and businesses in creative fields. Also contains information about associations and publications for creatives. Extremely well-organized and easy to use. Download it free at www.vsarts.org/x630.xml.*

Sallie Mae/College Answer: Corporate Communications, 12061 Bluemont Way, Reston, VA 20190: www.collegeanswer.com.

Social Security Administration, 800-772-1213, PASS program: www.socialsecurity.gov/pubs/11017.html.

Writer's Digest Book Club: PO Box 9274, Central Islip, NY 11722-9274, 386-447-6354, www.WritersDigestBookClub.com.

CHAPTER 9: FINDING AND ORGANIZING YOUR CREATIVE SPACE

Clutterless Recovery Groups Inc., 5413 N. 32nd Street #764, McAllen, TX 78504, 512-351-4058, www.clutterless.org—*A 501(c)3 organization run by clutterers for clutterers.*

CHAPTER 10: STAYING AFLOAT FINANCIALLY

Americans with Disabilities Act: www.usdoj.gov/crt/ada—*Includes information about employers' responsibilities to disabled workers.*

FabJob.com: http://fabjob.com—*An informative site with advice and tips about a variety of both creative and "backup" jobs. Also sells books specific to creative interests.*

Putting Creativity to Work. [See chapter 8 above.]

Ticket to Work: www.ssa.gov/work/Ticket/ticket_info.html; www.yourtickettowork.com—*Government information about the Ticket to Work program.*

United Cerebral Palsy, 1660 L Street, NW, Suite 700, Washington, DC 20036, 800-872-5827, www.ucp.org—*Additional resource for information about the Ticket to Work program.*

VSA Arts, 818 Connecticut Avenue, NW, Suite 600, Washington, D.C. 2006, Phone: 202-628-2800, Fax: 202-429-0868, www.vsarts.org—

Provides career development resources, technical assistance, and promotion opportunities for creatives with disabilities.

CHAPTER 11: MANAGING CREATIVE PROJECTS PRODUCTIVELY

The Foundation Center: 79 Fifth Avenue/16th Street, New York, NY 10003, Phone: 800-424-9836 or 212-620-4230, Fax: 212-807-3677, http://fdncenter.org—*A good starting place for information about grants.*

National Endowment for the Arts: www.arts.gov/federal.html—*Funds some individual creatives but more nonprofit organizations for projects in all areas of fine arts.*

The Project Manager's Partner: A Step-by-Step Guide to Project Management by Michael Greer. Amherst, MA: HRD Press, 1996—*A practical guide with worksheets. Somewhat "businessy," but helpful.*

CHAPTER 12: PROMOTING YOURSELF AND YOUR CREATIVE WORK

Chase's Calendar of Events, by the Editors of Chase's. New York: McGraw-Hill, 2005—*An annually updated resource directory listing special days, weeks, and months sponsored by various (mainly nonprofit) organizations. A potential way to participate in or create events to publicize your work (mid-March: Arts Advocacy Day; September Is National Piano Month; and so on).*

Jay Conrad Levinson's Guerrilla Marketing books and Web site: swww.gmarketing.com—*Levinson' books suggest free or inexpensive marketing methods. The Web site offers articles on all sorts of marketing issues.*

Toastmasters International PO Box 9052, Mission Viejo, CA 92690, Automated phone: 949-835-1300 (24/7), Office: 949-858-8255 (Mon.–Fri., 8 a.m.–5 p.m., PST), www.toastmasters.org—*This wonderful organization helps you learn and practice speaking skills—a tremendously valuable skill for promoting creative work. The supportive environment of Toastmasters clubs can help you boost self-confidence, become more outgoing, and develop contacts and friends. Toastmaster clubs are nearly everywhere, and I highly recommend them.*

CHAPTER 13: COMMUNICATING AND COLLABORATING EFFECTIVELY

Myers-Briggs: www.knowyourtype.com/google.html

CHAPTER 14: STARTING AND RUNNING YOUR OWN CREATIVE BUSINESS

The Business Start-Up Kit by Steve D. Strauss. Chicago: Dearborn, 2003.

Center for Business Planning, www.businessplans.org/businessplans.html—*Offers several sample business plans and sells business-plan software.*

Home Business Magazine: www.homebusinessmag.com.

SCORE (Service Corps of Retired Executives), 800-634-0245,

www.score.org—*A volunteer organization sponsored by the U.S. Small Business Administration. SCORE consists of business people who donate their time and talent to help U.S. entrepreneurs. SCORE volunteers provide confidential one-to-one and team business counseling and low-cost workshops and seminars.*

Small Business Administration (SBA), 800-827-5722, www.sba.gov/index.html—*Another great source of business information.*

Small Business Development Centers, *http://sbdcnet.utsa.edu—A national clearinghouse for all sorts of business information.*

Turn Your Talents Into Profits: 100+ Terrific Ideas for Starting Your Own Home-Based Microbusiness by Darcie Sanders and Martha M. Bullen. New York: Pocket Books, 1998—*A handbook containing brief suggestions for setting started in various low-cost businesses, including some in arts and crafts.*

Working from Home: Everything You Need to Know About Living and Working Under the Same Roof by Paul and Sarah Edwards. New York: Tarcher/Putnam, 1999—*Extraordinary resource packed with useful information for all types of home businesses. Includes checklists and worksheets.*

Notes

CHAPTER 1: THE CREATIVE/"CRAZY" CONNECTION

p. 5: . . . the very real stressors: Wills and Cooper in Wills.

p. 5: Another argument set forth: Jamison, *Touched with Fire*, 90.

p. 5: . . . poverty and rejection accompanied by: Mallin citing Szasz, 112.

p. 6: Freud's observations about Edgar Allan Poe: Mallin, 111–12.

p. 6: Creativity is a systemic phenomenon: Csikszentmihalyi, *Creativity*, 23.

p. 6: . . . tap their heightened sensitivity: Barron in Barron, et al., 16.

p. 6: Is it simply that pathological personalities: Berman, 61.

pp. 10–11: Definitions: Creativity, genius, talent, insanity: *American Heritage Dictionary of the English Language*; *Merriam-Webster's Collegiate Dictionary*; Morehead; *The Oxford American Dictionary of Current English*; *The Random House College Dictionary*; Rodale; Rothenberg, *Creativity & Madness*.

p. 10: . . . the production of: Rothenberg, 5.

p. 11: . . . the power of accomplishing great things: Barzun, 147, quoting Edward Young in Dacey and Lennon, 29.

p. 12: . . . a gift from the gods, Barron, 16

p. 12: Any attempt to arbitrarily polarize: Jamison, *Touched with Fire* 95, in Dacey and Lennon 141–42.

CHAPTER 2: THE FAUCET OF CREATIVITY

pp. 23–24: . . . depressions may have an important cognitive: Jamison, *Touched with Fire*, in Neihart.

CHAPTER 3: RESEARCH ON THE CONNECTION

p. 25: Plato, Aristotle, Ficino, Lombroso: Dacey and Lennon, 15–19, 32; Neihart.

pp. 26–27: . . . three general types of creativity/"crazy" research: Simonton, *Psychiatric Times*.

p. 26: . . . prominent eighteenth- and nineteenth-century: *Touched with Fire*.

p. 27: . . . psychometric tests measure creativity by: Plucker and Renzulli in Sternberg, 38

p. 27: Iowa Writers' Workshop study: Andreasen, "Creativity and Mental Illness: Prevalence Rates in Writers and Their First-Degree Relatives," in Waddell.

p. 28: After an IQ of 115: Barron, et al., 13.

p. 28: . . . most IQ test items: Barron, et al., 13.

p. 28: . . . an extraordinarily high IQ: Csikszentmihalyi; de Bono; Gardner; Gardner and Wolf in Feldman, et al. in Dacey and Lennon, 7–8.

p. 28: . . . personality traits, brain function, Dacey and Lennon, 8.

p. 28: . . . when creativity tests are untimed: Wallach and Kogan in Davis, 53.

p. 29: . . . assess music . . . motor activities: Davis, 159–60.

p. 29: Many. . . changes: Jamison in Neihart, 105.

p. 30: Creative Traits/Behaviors Chart: Dacey and Lennon, 137, Domino in Davis, 189; Weiss, 38, 60.

p. 30: . . . intense concentration and focus: Andreasen, *The Creating Brain*, 37.

p. 30: . . . unrealistically pessimistic: Nettle, 211.

p. 31: Stanford University study (Strong, Ketter): McCook.

pp. 31–32: As we understand more: Andreasen, *The Creating Brain*, 38.

p. 32: . . . fantasize more: Flaherty, 62.

p. 32: Psychotic thinking rarely turns: Rothenberg, *Creativity & Madness*, 6 in Neihart.

p. 32: . . . translogical thinking: Rothenberg, *Creativity and Madness*, 11.

p. 32: . . . conceptual over-inclusiveness: Powers, Stavens, and Andreasen in Neihart.

p. 32: . . . strong egos and self-sufficiency: Cattell and Butcher in Simonton, "Are Genius and Madness Related?"

pp. 33–34: Virginia's great-grandfather: Bond, "Virginia Woolf, Manic-Depressive Psychosis and Genius," in Panter, et al., 224.

p. 34: . . . patterns in other artistic families: Jamison, *Touched with Fire*: Schumann 202, James 208–13, van Gogh 233–34.

p. 34: Even though there is some evidence: Shaller; Ludwig in Simonton.

p. 34: Children of bipolar parents study, Simeonova et.al, 623–31; Stanford School of Medicine.

p. 35: . . . a mix of genes and environments: Barron, et al., 15.

p. 35: William James: James in Dacey and Lennon, 89.

pp. 35–36: . . . the nurturing parent: Dacey and Packer, in Dacey and Lennon, 117.

p. 36: . . . only one percent: Simonton, "Creativity: Cognitive, Personal, Developmental, and Social Aspects" in Dacey and Lennon, 47.

p. 36: . . . willingness to take risks, Albert cited in Runco in Dacey and Lennon, 56.

p. 36: . . . many artists report: Neihart.

p. 37: Moses Hadas in Dacey and Lennon, 18–19

pp. 37–38: If to survive as an artist: Csikszentmihalyi, *Flow*, 266.

p. 38: Having low latent inhibition, Carson, et al.

p. 38: Creative people are more prone: Andreasen, *The Creating Brain*, 38.

p. 39: . . . brain's frontal lobes: Heilman, Nadeau, and Beversdorf.

p. 39: . . . the role of dopamine: Jamison, *Exuberance*, 114.

p. 40: . . . creativity and cerebral blood flow: Carlsson, Wendt, and Risberg.

p. 40: The myopic focus on just one factor: Dacey in Dacey and Lennon; Dacey and Lennon 15.

p. 40: . . . outright psychopathology: Simonton, "Are Genius and Madness Related?"

CHAPTER 4: CLEARING CREATIVE CLOGS

p. 50: I saw, time and time again: Virshup in Panter, et al., 260.

pp. 50–51: . . . varying degrees of mental illness: Cook in Jackson.

p. 51: . . . music can reduce anxiety: Balch and Balch, 720.

p. 51: Music and dance: Jamison, *Exuberance*, 156.

p. 52: Muses: Dacey and Lennon, 16; *Encyclopaedia Britannica*; Hershman and Lieb, 8: Piirto, 49–50.

p. 54: . . . ten-year investigation: Ludwig, v, 25.

p. 54: . . . a large number of his subjects: Ludwig, 219–29.

p. 55 . . . her grief was all-consuming: Epstein in Panter, et al., 244.

p. 55: Mendelssohn, Moss; Wikipedia.

p. 56: Suzuki, *Encyclopaedia Britannica*.

p. 58: . . . must we require: Andreasen, *The Creating Brain*, 14.

p. 60: Emily Dickinson, *Encyclopaedia Britannica;* Johnson 21; Lowell in Johnson, 45–46.

CHAPTER 5: CHOOSING YOUR FOCUS AND SETTING YOUR GOALS

p. 73: Use this decision matrix: Crystal and Bolles, Appendix E.

p. 74: . . . the inevitable consequence: Csikszentmihalyi, *Flow*, 224.

p. 76: . . . saturation bombing: James-Enger.

pp. 77–82 The Creative process: DeSalvo, 134; Wallas cited in Dacey and Lennon, 35–36; Zhou and George.

p. 78: Root-Bernstein, *Sparks of Genius*, 11.

pp. 79–80: . . . no words came (advice from Gertrude Stein), Preston in Ghiselin, 160.

p. 81: . . . moodling: Ueland, 32–33.

CHAPTER 6: SUPPORTING CREATIVITY BY HANDLING THE BASICS

p. 87: People become so involved: Csikszentmihalyi, *Flow*, 53, 74.

p. 88 lithium study: Shou in Waddell.

p. 88: Because of the high risk: Andreasen, *The Creating Brain*, 105, 107.

p. 89: . . . send a thank-you note: Fisher, 76.

p. 90: . . . artistically paralyzed [photographer Sheryl]: Friedman.

p. 91: I've found that my creativity: Duke, 289.

p. 92: Creators should have no fear: Simonton

pp. 96–100: Nutrition information: Balch and Balch; Somer and Snyderman

p. 101: People who stick with an exercise program: Somer and Snyderman, 164–65.

p. 102: A team of researchers at Middlesex: Steinberg, et al.

p. 102: Torrance test: Davis, 162–65.

p. 106 . . . choose our surroundings: Nettle, 205.

pp. 107–108: . . . balance high energy with calming: Mountain, 61.

p. 110: For successful creative performance: Nettle, 210.

CHAPTER 7: SCHEDULING CREATIVE TIME

p. 112 Whole Life Grid, Jeffers, 140.

p. 124: reticular activating system: Castle, 106; *Encyclopaedia Britannica*.

p. 127: creativity workout: Andreasen, *The Creating Brain*, 161–68.

p. 128: . . . to write the worst junk: Goldberg, 11.

p. 128: Lamott, back cover.

pp. 128–129: morning pages and artist dates, Cameron.

p. 129: "[Write] every day: Lamott, xxii.

CHAPTER 8: SHORING UP YOUR SKILLS

p. 133: abnormally, almost irrationally, buoyant: Nettle, 153.

p. 133: what distinguishes: Simonton in Nettle, 153.

pp. 135–136: Georgia O'Keeffe's formal art education: Robinson, 78–110.

p. 136: If the society we live in: Barron, et al., 18.

CHAPTER 9: FINDING AND ORGANIZING YOUR CREATIVE SPACE

p. 153: surroundings for creative work: Csikszentmihalyi, Creativity, 140–146.

p. 159: When you experience this feature: Mountain, 59.

p. 165: Color Your World: Balch and Balch, 145–46.

p. 168: Too much 'organization': Nelson, 123.

p. 168: . . . filing methods: Dorff, Fine, and Josephson, 33.

p. 170: . . . cross-reference folders, Nelson, 122.

p. 170: Stephen King, *On Writing*, 155.

CHAPTER 10: STAYING AFLOAT FINANCIALLY

p. 173: . . . so incapacitated and so frightened: Solomon, 53.

p. 175: . . . creatives with disabilities: Scribner.

pp. 178–179: "Backup skills" for creatives: Nagrin, 228–29.

pp. 179–180: . . . how to decide exactly: Bolles.

p. 183: Advice on disclosure to employers: Fitter and Gulas, 67–73, 82–85.

p. 186: Creative individuals usually are forced: Csikszentmihalyi, *Creativity*, 193.

p. 186: Diane Arbus, Wikipedia.

CHAPTER 11: MANAGING CREATIVE PROJECTS PRODUCTIVELY

p. 194: When you experience grandiosity: Mountain, 57.

p. 194: What I don't do well: Pauley, 210.

p. 195: . . . deliberate weaving flaws: Armstrong; Tapestry Institute. www.tapestryweb.org/navajorug.html.

p. 202: . . . slow down your thinking: de Bono in Romig.

CHAPTER 12: PROMOTING YOURSELF AND YOUR CREATIVE WORK

pp. 213–214: Klaus, xxiv, 18–19.

CHAPTER 13: COMMUNICATING AND COLLABORATING EFFECTIVELY

pp. 226–227: Jaco Pastorius, Wikipedia; www.musicbizadvice.com/ jaco_pastorious_rediscovered_talent.htm

pp. 232–233: . . . format for sharing thoughts and feelings: Faber and Mazlish, 64.

p. 233: . . . other phrases to use when starting: Canfield, 349.

p. 236: Spike (Terence) Milligan: www.namiscc.org/newsletters/ February02/McMan4-10.htm.

pp. 236–239: Myers-Briggs Type Indicator: Emerson; Luzader.

p. 239: two preference most common to artistic people: Piirto, 400 .

p. 239: Medicine Wheel: www.shannonthunderbird.com/medicine_wheel_teachings.htm.

pp. 241–243: Collaborative leadership tips: Baker, et al., 216–17, 223, 275–76.

CHAPTER 14: STARTING AND RUNNING YOUR OWN CREATIVE BUSINESS

p. 246: Most of us harbor a secret belief: Cameron, 106.

p. 249: . . . financed their pottery business: Hopper, 85–89.

pp. 249–250: The three "hats" of business: Gerber, *The E-Myth*.

pp. 254–255: Questions the IRS may ask: U.S. Department of the Treasury, Internal Revenue Service. Employer's Supplemental Tax Guide, Publication 15-A (Rev. January 2006).

p. 260: One straightforward resource: Kamoroff.

Annotated Bibliography

Albert, Robert. "Some Reasons Why Childhood Creativity Often Fails to Make It Past Puberty into the Real World," in Runco.

Aleinikov, Andrei G. *Mega Creativity, Five Steps to Thinking like a Genius.* Cincinnati: Walking Stick Press, 2002. *Provides exercises and puzzles to break through conventional thinking to innovation.*

American Heritage Dictionary of the English Language: http://education.yahoo.com/reference/dictionary.

American Psychiatric Association. *Diagnostic and Statistical Manual of Mental Disorders,* 4th ed., Text Revision. Washington, DC: American Psychiatric Association, 2000. *The psychiatrists' "bible" for diagnosing mental illness, detailing how psychiatrists identify and classify them.*

Andreasen, Nancy. *The Creating Brain: The Neuroscience of Genius.* New York: Dana Press, 2005. *Psychiatrist, researcher Andreasen describes how our brains create as well as the importance of exterior factors (culture, environment).*

____. "Creativity and Mental Illness: Prevalence Rates in Writers and Their First-Degree Relatives." *American Journal of Psychiatry* 144, no. 10 (October 1987): 1288–92.

Arieti, Silvano. *Creativity: The Magic Synthesis.* New York: Basic Books, 1976.

Armstrong, Heather. "Weaving Changed through the Times." *Gallup Independent,* June 8, 2001.

Baker, Sunny, Kim Baker, and G. Michael Campbell. *The Complete Idiot's Guide to Project Management,* 3rd ed. New York: Alpha (Penguin Group-USA), 2003. *Despite the insulting title, offers straightforward advice, practical information about budgeting, project management, scheduling, leadership, and staffing.*

Balch, Phyllis A., and James F. Balch. *Prescription for Nutritional Healing,* 3rd ed. New York: Avery/Penguin Putnam Inc., 2000. *Detailed nutritional information and advice geared to specific illnesses.*

Barron, Frank, Alfonso Montuori, and Anthea Barron, eds. *Creators on Creating*. New York: G. P. Putnam's Sons, 1997. *From actor Laurence Olivier and illustrator Maurice Sendak to musician Frank Zappa and writer Maya Angelou, thirty-nine creatives describe their own work.*

Barzun, Jacques. *Science: the Glorious Entertainment*. New York: Basic Books, 1964.

Basco, Monica Ramirez, and A. John Rush. *Cognitive-Behavioral Therapy for Bipolar Disorder*. New York, London: The Guilford Press, 1996. *Written for mental health professionals, but also useful for patients and families. Contains detailed guidance on managing bipolar disorder with both medication and therapy; includes many worksheets to help you work through problems and plan changes.*

Bentley, Toni. "Reaching for Perfection: The Life and Death of a Dancer." *The New York Times*, April 27, 1986.

Berman, Leon, "An Artist Destroys His Work: Comments on Creativity and Destructiveness," in Panter, et al.

Biography.com (A&E Television Networks).

Bolles, Richard N. *What Color is Your Parachute: A Practical Manual for Job-hunters and Career-Changers*. Berkeley, CA: Ten Speed Press (updated annually). *The information-packed "Bible" to find the career of your dreams.*

Burns, David D. *Feeling Good: The New Mood Therapy*. New York: New American Library,1980.

Cameron, Julia with Mark Bryan. *The Artist's Way: A Spiritual Path to Higher Creativity*. New York: G. P. Putnam's Sons, 1992. *A practical spiritually based creativity program, offering many helpful exercises. Organized to guide the reader through a twelve-week "course."*

Canfield, Jack. *The Success Principles: How to Get from Where You Are to Where You Want to Be*. New York: HarperCollins, 2005. *An excellent book with many helpful suggestions for addressing both personal and business goals and earning more money.*

Carey, Benedict. "Who's Mentally Ill? Deciding Is Often All in the Mind." *The New York Times*, June 12, 2005.

Carlsson, Ingemar, Peter E. Wendt, and Jarl Risberg. "On the Neurobiology of Creativity: Differences in Frontal Activity between High and Low Creative Subjects." *Neuropsychologia* 38, no. 6 (2000): 873–85.

Carson, Shelley, Jordan Peterson, and Daniel Higgins. "Decreased Latent Inhibition is Associated with Increased Creative Achievement in High-Functioning Individuals." *Journal of Personality and Social Psychology* 85 no. 3 (September 2003): 499–506.

Castle, Lana. *Bipolar Disorder Demystified, Mastering the Tightrope of Manic Depression*. New York: Marlowe & Company, 2003. *"Owner's manual" for those with bipolar disorder, and their families and friends.* Library Journal *calls it a "winning combination of Castle's lifelong experience with the disorder and her professional yet accessible writing."*

Cattell, Raymond B., and Harold J. Butcher. *The Prediction of Achievement and Creativity*. Indianapolis, IN: Bobbs-Merrill, 1968.

Crystal, John, and Richard Bolles. *Where Do I Go from Here With My Life?* Berkeley, CA: Ten Speed Press, 1974.

Csikszentmihalyi, Mihaly. *Creativity: Flow and the Psychology of Discovery and Invention*. New York: HarperCollins, 1996. *A classic but accessible study of what's known about creativity, with many examples from the lives of famous creatives.*

____. *Flow: The Psychology of Optimal Experience*. New York: Harper & Row, 1990. *A groundbreaking study of flow (complete absorption in an activity) and how to increase your own flow experiences, with many personal stories from artists and athletes.*

Dacey, John S. *Fundamentals of Creative Thinking*. San Francisco: Jossey-Bass, 1989. Cited in John S. Dacey and Kathleen H. Lennon, *Understanding Creativity*.

Dacey, John S., and Kathleen H. Lennon. *Understanding Creativity*. San Francisco: Jossey-Bass (John Wiley & Sons), 1998. *A thorough but succinct tour through both historical and current research, examining creativity from every angle.*

Dacey, John S., and Alex J. Packer. *The Nurturing Parent*. New York: Fireside (Simon & Schuster), 1992.

Davis, Gary A. *Creativity is Forever*, 2nd ed. Dubuque, IA: Kendall/Hunt, 1983, 1986. *Written by a psychologist for the lay reader. An engaging, humorous presentation of creativity research and suggestions for expanding your creative thinking.*

de Bono, Edward. *Serious Creativity: Using the Power of Lateral Thinking to Create New Ideas*. New York: HarperCollins, 1992.

DeSalvo, Louise. *Writing as a Way of Healing: How Telling Our Stories Transforms Our Lives*. San Francisco: HarperCollins, 1999. *Writing teacher DeSalvo shares a wealth of exercises for accessing your writing ability and understanding the writing process. Provides many personal examples from writers' lives.*

deWolfe, Adrienne (author and speaker). Stress reduction workshop, October 19, 1995.

Domino, George. "Identification of Potentially Creative Persons from the Adjective Check List." *Journal of Consulting and Clinical Psychology* 35:48–51.

____. Adjective Check List. Palo Alto, CA: Consulting Psychologists Press.

Dorff, Pat, Edith Fine, and Judith Josephson. *File . . . Don't Pile! For People Who Write*. New York: St. Martin's Press, 1994.

Duke, Patty, and Kenneth Turan. *Call Me Anna: The Autobiography of Patty Duke*. New York: Bantam/Bantam Doubleday Dell, 1987. *Autobiography sharing award-winning actor Patty Duke's career and the effect that her manic-depression had on her life.*

Encyclopaedia Britannica Premium Service. *Encyclopaedia Britannica*, 2006.

Faber, Adele, and Elaine Mazlish. *How to Talk So Kids Will Listen & Listen So Kids Will Talk*. New York: Avon Books, 1982. *Straightforward book on communicating with both children and adults.*

Feldman, David Henry, Mihaly Csikszentmihalyi, and Howard Gardner, eds. *Changing the World: A Framework for the Study of Creativity*. New York: Praeger, 1994.

Fisher, Carrie. *The Best Awful*. New York: Simon & Schuster, 2003. *Novel describing Hollywood actor's wild experiences with bipolar disorder.*

Fitter, Fawn, and Beth Gulas. *Working in the Dark, Keeping Your Job While Dealing With Depression*. Center City, MN: Hazelden, 2002. *Step-by-step guidance about employment, including your legal rights and what to expect when you're struggling with depression on the job. Contains examples drawn from experiences of people who've "worked in the dark."*

Flaherty, Alice W. *The Midnight Disease: The Drive to Write, Writer's Block, and the Creative Brain*. New York: Houghton Mifflin, 2004. *Fascinating book by a neurologist who describes hypergraphia and her overwhelming desire to write. Addresses creative writing and connections between the brain and creativity.*

Friedman, Richard. "Connecting Depression and Artistry." *The New York Times*, June 3, 2002, www.nytimes.com/2002/06/04/health/psychology/04CASE.html?tnte-mail0.

Gardner, Howard. "Creativity: An Interdisciplinary Perspective." *Creativity Research Journal*, 1, 8–26.

Gardner, Howard, and Constance Wolf. "The Fruits of Asynchrony: A Psychological Examination of Creativity." in *Changing the World: A Framework for the Study of Creativity,* David Henry Feldman, Mihaly Csikszentmihalyi, and Howard Gardner, eds.. New York: Praeger, 1994.

Gerber, Michael. *The E-Myth: Why Most Small Businesses Don't Work and What to Do About It*. Cambridge, MA: Ballinger, 1985.

____. *The E-Myth Revisited: Why Most Small Businesses Don't Work and What to Do about It.* New York: HarperCollins, 1995, 2001.

Ghiselin, Brewster, ed. *The Creative Process*. New York: Mentor (New American Library), 1952. *Thirty-eight artists describe their experiences of the creative process with fascinating accounts.*

Goldberg, Natalie. *Writing Down the Bones*. Boston: Shambala Publications, 1986. *Well-known writing teacher, novelist, and poet shares her methods for tapping creativity daily. Well written, practical, and encouraging. Goldberg's suggestions also apply to other creative fields.*

Greer, Michael. *The Project Manager's Partner: A Step-by-Step Guide to Project Management*. HRD Press. 1996, 2001.

____. "Ten Guaranteed Ways to Screw Up Any Project." www.michaelgree.com/screw_up.htm.

Heilman Kenneth M., Stephen E. Nadeau, and David Q. Beversdorf. "Creative Innovation: Possible Brain Mechanisms." *Neurocase* 9, no. 5 (October 2003): 369–79.

Hershman, D. Jablow, and Julian Lieb. *Manic-Depression and Creativity*. New York: Prometheus Books, 1998. *Hershman and Lieb explain their belief that creatives need not always suffer for their art. These authors investigate the creative/"crazy" connection through the ages, paying special attention to bipolar disorder and the lives of famous creatives like Charles Dickens and Vincent van Gogh.*

Hopper, Robin. *Stayin' Alive: Survival Tactics for the Visual Artist*. Iola, WI: Krause Publications, 2003. *Beautifully illustrated with ceramic art by the artists who share their stories here. Offers practical advice on how to make ends meet, market your work, make a living, and persist in your art.*

Jackson, Melissa, "Dance Therapy for Mental Patients." BBC News Online, March 4, 2004, www.news.bbc.co.uk.

James-Enger, Kelly. "Narrow Your Focus: Why Writers Should Specialize." *Writing for Dollars* (Web site by Dan Case), March 3, 2003, www.writingfordollars.com/WFD_DisplayNewsletter.cfm?file=03103.

Jamison, Kay Redfield. *Exuberance: The Passion for Life*. New York: Alfred A. Knopf, 2004. *An intriguing look at the historical, cultural, and personal importance of exuberance, and its connection to hypomania and mania.*

____. *Touched with Fire: Manic-Depressive Illness and the Artistic Temperament*. New York: Free Press (Simon & Schuster), 1993. *Insightful landmark study of the creativity/"crazy" link. Psychologist, author Jamison examines lives of famous creatives from the past, their illnesses and symptoms, and signs of mental illness in their families.*

Jeffers, Susan. *Feel the Fear and Do It Anyway*. New York: Random House, 1987. *An excellent guide for facing your fears, changing negative self-talk to positive, expanding your comfort zone, and pursuing your passion.*

Johnson, Tamara, "Emily Dickinson: A Biography," in *Readings on Emily Dickinson*, Tamara Johnson, ed. San Diego, CA: Greenhaven Press, 1997.

Kamoroff, Bernard. *Small Time Operator: How to Start Yor Own Business, Keep Your Books, Pay Your Taxes and Stay Out of Trouble!* 29th ed. Willits, CA: Bell Springs Publishing, 2004. *Great straightforward guide to answer basic questions about starting a small business and setting up and maintaining financial records.*

King, Stephen. *On Writing: A Memoir of the Craft*. New York: Scribner, 2000. *Master storyteller shares his trials and triumphs in pursuit of a stellar writing career. King offers lots of hard-won, sensible wisdom that applies to writers as well other creatives.*

Klaus, Peggy. *Brag! The Art of Tooting Your Own Horn without Blowing It*. New York: Warner Books, 2003. *A great informal and humorous guide on how to market yourself politely, but memorably.*

Lamott, Anne. *Bird by Bird: Some Instructions on Writing and Life*. New York: Pantheon, 1994. *A funny, sometimes irreverent, but masterful writing guide.*

Lowell, Amy. "Dickinson Was Misunderstood by Those Closest to Her," in *Readings on Emily Dickinson*, Tamara Johnson, ed.. San Diego, CA: Greenhaven Press, 1997.

Ludwig, Arnold M. *The Price of Greatness: Resolving the Creativity and Madness Controversy.* New York: The Guilford Press, 1995. *Psychiatry professor shares his own extensive research on more 1,000 creative individuals, examining the creative/"crazy" link. Besides creatives in the arts, participants in Ludwig's study included architects, athletes, businesspeople, military leaders, politicians, scientists, social activists, and other high achievers.*

Mallin, Dea Adria. "Edgar Allan Poe: Descent into Madness," in Panter et. al.

McCook, Alison. "Creative Mind Shares Traits with Mentally Ill," *Reuters Health*, May 29, 2002. Reprinted at: www.namiscc.org/Research/2002/Creativity.htm.

Merriam-Webster's Collegiate Dictionary (10th ed.). Springfield, MA: Merriam-Webster, 1998.

Morehead, Albert H. *The New American Roget's College Thesaurus.* New York: World Publishing Company, 1962.

Moss, Charles K. "Felix Mendelsshohn (1809–1847)," www.carolinaclassical.com/mendelsohn.

Mountain, Jane. *Bipolar Disorder, Insights for Recovery.* Denver: Chapter One Press, 2003. *Valuable guidance and understanding from a psychiatrist who writes also from her own experience of bipolar disorder.*

Nagrin, Daniel. *How to Dance Forever: Surviving Against the Odds.* New York: William Morrow and Company, 1988. *Conversational, practical, step-by-step advice from this celebrated modern dancer on how to make a living while making art, for dancers as well as other creatives.*

Neihart, Maureen. "Creativity, the Arts, and Madness." *Roeper Review* 21, no. 1 (1998): 47–50.

Nelson, Mike. *Clutter-Proof Your Business.* Franklin Lakes, NJ: Career Press, 2002. *Detailed, practical tips on smoothing your way to success. Explains how to clear out what you don't need in your space and how to streamline your work process. Although targeted to small businesses, this guide applies to personal organization as well.*

Nettle, Daniel. *Strong Imagination: Madness, Creativity and Human Nature.* New York: Oxford University Press, 2001. *From a biological psychologist, an insightful, in-depth exploration of the biological processes involved in mental illness, its connections to heredity, and its links to creativity.*

The Oxford American Dictionary of Current English. New American Edition. Oxford University Press, 2002.

Panter, Barry M., Mary Lou Panter, Evelyn Virshup, and Bernard Virshup, eds. *Creativity & Madness: Psychological Studies of Art and Artists.* Burbank, CA: AIMED Press, 1995, 1996. *In-depth studies of the lives of many deceased artists, including Sylvia Plath, Elizabeth Layton, Jackson Pollock and Edvard Munch, and accounts of the healing power of artistic creativity.*

Pauley, Jane. *Skywriting: A Life out of the Blue.* New York: Random House, 2004. *The personal story of this well-known former news anchor and current talk show host. Pauley candidly discusses her insecurities about her career and her struggles with medically induced bipolar disorder.*

Piirto, Jane. *Understanding Creativity*. Scottsdale, AZ: Great Potential Press, 2004. A thorough and highly readable review of creativity research, with special attention to education and creativity training in schools. This educator specializes in talent development.

Powers, Pauline, Chris Stavens, and Nancy C. J. Andreasen. "The Ontogenesis of Intelligence: Evaluating the Piaget Theory." *Comprehensive Psychiatry* 16, no. 290 (1975): 149–54.

Prentky, Robert A. *Creativity and Psychopathology: A Neurocognitive Perspective*. New York: Praeger, 1980.

Preston, John Hyde. "A Conversation with Gertrude Stein," in Ghiselin, 159–68.

The Random House College Dictionary, rev. ed. New York: Random House, 1988.

Robinson, Roxana. *Georgia O'Keeffe: A Life*. New York: Harper & Row, 1989. *An intriguing, detailed, illuminating biography of the artist. Illustrated.*

Rodale, J. I. *The Synonym Finder*. New York: Warner Books, Inc., 1978, 1986.

Root-Bernstein, Robert, and Michele Root-Bernstein. *Sparks of Genius: The Thirteen Thinking Tools of the World's Most Creative People*. New York: Mariner Books (Houghton Mifflin), 2001. *Keys off of the creative process and explains how to shift your thinking for more creativity. Contains extensive and excellent examples of creative puzzles and concepts. Illustrated.*

Rothenberg, Albert. *Creativity & Madness: New Findings and Old Stereotypes*. Baltimore: The Johns Hopkins University Press, 1990. *Psychiatrist and researcher Rothenberg explains how untreated mental illness hinders rather than promotes creativity, and explores inspiration and the creative process in artists and scientists. Also addresses the creative potential in all of us.*

Rothenberg, Albert, and P. E. Burkhardt. "Difference in Response Time of Creative Persons and Patients with Depressive and Schizophrenic Disorders." *Psychological Reports* 54 (1984): 711–17.

Runco, Mark, ed. *Creativity from Childhood through Adulthood: The Developmental Issues*. San Francisco: Jossey-Bass, 1996.

Science Daily. "Biological Basis for Creativity Linked to Mental Illness." October 1, 2003, www.sciencedaily.com/releases/2003/10/031001061055.htm.

Scribner, Paul, ed. *Putting Creativity to Work, Careers in the Arts for People with Disabilities*. Washington, DC: VSA Arts, 2000.

Schaller, Mark. "The Psychological Consequences of Fame: Three Tests of the Self-Consciousness Hypothesis." *Journal of Personality* 65 (1997): 291–309.

Schou, Mogens. "Artistic Productivity and Lithium Prophylaxis in Manic-Depressive Illness." *British Journal of Psychiatry* 135 (1979): 97–103.

Shelley, Carson, Jordan Peterson, and Daniel Higgins. "Decreased Latent Inhibition Is Associated with Increased Creative Achievement in High-Functioning Individuals." *Journal of Personality and Social Psychology* 85, no. 3 (September 2003): 499–506.

Silber, Lee. *Self-Promotion for the Creative Person: Get the Word Out about Who You Are and What You Do*. New York: Three Rivers Press, 2001.

Simeonova, Diana I., Kiki D. Chang, Connie Strong, and Terence A. Ketter. "Creativity in Familial Bipolar Disorder." *Journal of Psychiatric Research* 39, no. 6 (November 2005): 623–31.

Simonton, Dean Keith. "Are Genius and Madness Related? Contemporary Answers to an Ancient Question." *Psychiatric Times* 22, no. 7 (June 2005).

____. "Creativity. Cognitive, Personal, Developmental, and Social Aspects." *American Psychology* 55, no.1 (January 2000): 151–58.

Solomon, Andrew. *The Noonday Demon: An Atlas of Depression*. New York: Scribner, 2001. *An extraordinary exploration of depression based on extensive research by a talented author who struggled through severe depression and found his way back. Due to its length and breadth of information, readers struggling with concentration may find it a difficult read.*

Somer, Elizabeth, and Nancy Snyderman. *Food & Mood: The Complete Guide to Eating Well and Feeling Your Best*, 2nd ed. New York: Henry Holt and Company LLC, 1999. *A detailed explanation of foods and their effects on thinking, sleeping, moods, and weight management. Discussions of food cravings, energy (and lack of energy), and the role of supplements. Contains recipes and cooking tips.*

Stanford School of Medicine, Office of Communication & Public Affairs: http://mednews.Stanford.edu.

Steinberg, Hannah, Elizabeth A. Sykes, Tim Moss, Sandra Lowery, Nick LeBoutillier, and Alison Dewey. "Exercise Enhances Creativity Independently of Mood" *British Journal of Sports Medicine* 31 (1997):240–45.

Sternberg, Robert J., ed. *Handbook of Creativity*. Cambridge, United Kingdom: Cambridge University Press, 1999. *Sternberg gathered the writings of outstanding creativity experts to compile this excellent review of creativity research. Primarily targeted to academics and researchers, this book also offers insights for lay people.*

Tapestry Institute, "Navajo Weaving." Harrison, NE: Tapestry: The Institute for Philosophy, Religion, and the Life Sciences, 1999, 2000. www.tapestryinstitute.org (current), www.tapestryweb.org/navajorug.html.

Ueland, Brenda. *If You Want To Write: A Book About Art, Independence and Spirit*. St. Paul, MN: Greywolf Press, 1987. *A classic work of advice to writers (and other creatives). Conversational, practical, and encouraging.*

U.S. Department of the Treasury, Internal Revenue Service. Employer's Supplemental Tax Guide, Publication 15-A (Rev. January 2006).

____. Independent Contractor or Employee, Publication 1779 (Rev. January 2005).

Waddell, Charlotte. "Creativity and Mental Illness: Is There a Link?" *Canadian Journal of Psychiatry* 43 (1998):166–72. *An extensive review of creativity research. A good starting place for scholarly research.*

Wallas, Graham. *The Art of Thought*. Orlando, FL: Harcourt Brace, 1926.

Wallach, M. A., and Kogan, N. *Modes of Thinking in Young Children*. New York: Holt, 1965.

Wills, Geoffrey I. "Forty Lives in the Bebop Business: Mental Health in a Group of Eminent Jazz Musicians." *The British Journal of Psychiatry* 183 (2003): 255–259.

Wills, Geoffrey, and Cary Cooper. *Pressure Sensitive: Popular Musicians Under Stress*. Long: Sage, 1988.

Zhou, J., and J. M. George. "Awakening Employee Creativity: The Role of Leader Emotional Intelligence." *Leadership Quarterly* 14, nos. 4–5 (August–October 2003): 545–68.

Acknowledgments

AUTHORS HAVE SAID it time and again because, time and again, it's true: Few books are the product of just one person. I'm ever so grateful to the following people who supported me in writing this book—

The many, many individuals who shared their stories through my creativity surveys, Web site, and interviews. Particularly, the many not-yet-famous creatives profiled along with Daniel Johnston, John McManamy, Jane Mountain, MD, Rick Reynolds, Frances Sherwood, Andrew Solomon, and Craig Whyte.

Laura Hoofnagle, Publications Manager at the Depression and Bipolar Support Alliance, for arranging the posting and reporting of my survey of DBSA members.

The insightful Old Quarry writers' group members, for "midwifing" my third book: Diane Barnet, Steve Birch, Dyanne Fry Cortez, Molly Dougherty, Marge Harrington, Jane Manaster, Audrey Mitchell, Terri Rector Fann, Elizabeth White, and Judy Woodard.

My editor, Renée Sedliar, the incredible, patient lady who inspired me to massage my disjointed draft into a much more valuable book. Copyeditor Iris Bass, who added several insights. My dear friend Lori Kadosh, who pitched in for an eleventh-hour proofing of the final pages.

My ever-gracious and supportive agent, Carole Bidnick, who continues to cast such a positive light on my career.

My publisher, Matthew Lore, who put his faith in me once again—even when my original vision shattered and I doubted I could provide much useful advice. The rest of the folks at Marlowe & Company and their associates, particularly Vincent Kunkemueller, Jamie McNeely, Pauline Neuwirth, and Karen Auerbach.

My parents, who supported my creative interests and drove me to endless dance and piano lessons, play rehearsals, and choir practices. My mother, in particular, for nurturing my interest in reading and writing—two of the greatest joys of my life.

My amazing, patient, loving husband Ralph, and talented stepchildren, Tom and Joy, for their continuing interest in and support of me and my work.

Most of all, my "right arm," fact checker, researcher, and cheerleader Suzanne Batchelor, for her undying enthusiasm for this book.

Index